THE KAISER'S DAUGHTER

THE KAISER'S DAUGHTER

Memoirs of
H.R.H. Viktoria Luise,
Duchess of Brunswick and Lüneburg,
Princess of Prussia

Translated and edited by Robert Vacha

Prentice-Hall, Inc., Englewood Cliffs, N.J.

The Kaiser's Daughter, Memoirs of H.R.H. Viktoria Luise, Duchess of Brunswick and Lüneburg, Princess of Prussia, has been translated, compiled, and edited by Robert Vacha from the three volumes of the German original :

Ein Leben als Tochter des Kaisers, © *1965, Göttinger Verlagsanstalt, Hanover;*

Im Glanz der Krone, © *1967, Göttinger Verlagsanstalt, Hanover;*

Im Strom der Zeit, © *1974, Göttinger Verlagsanstalt, Hanover.*

10 9 8 7 6 5 4 3 2 1
Library of Congress Catalog Card No.: 77-79339
ISBN 0-13-514653-4

In Memory of My Father

Contents

List of Illustrations

Foreword

It never really entered my mind to publish my memoirs. I thought, however, that later, different opinions might be formed, perhaps from posthumous accounts or from official documents which may or may not eventually be released.

Competent opinions of personalities intimately concerned with various events, which I could not obtain at first hand, were made available to me during the last few years, as were all comprehensive notes concerning my own lifetime.

Many generations have come and gone since the days of the German Emperors. The statements made today of those times come at second or even third hand and there are few who, from their own observations, can give a faithful picture of the last Kaiser. In the public interest, therefore, I feel it my duty to set down my own experiences.

I have taken up the challenge, but I must emphasise that I have written only what I personally have seen and experienced. I have added my own opinions, for I have never conformed to stereotyped patterns. I have neither literary nor scholarly ambitions, but I will render a report on my life, nothing else. My wish is that this book may serve to bring back memories to the older ones among us and to give the young generation a true picture of the chequered destiny of our people.

The documents I have managed to preserve have given me truer and more reliable interpretations of their times than those written subsequent to the events, and I have found expert collaborators who helped me sift a great deal of material. To them, I owe a special debt of gratitude.

Now that I have decided to publish, I would, at the same time, like to thank the many faithful friends in all quarters of our divided Fatherland, in Europe, and overseas, who have taken such sympathetic interest in my affairs.

1 *Childhood*

The thunder of the cannons of the Guards Field Artillery reverberated over Potsdam as they fired a 21-gun salute, signifying the birth of a Princess. For a boy, a Prince, a 101-gun salute would have marked the occasion. In those days there was still no sex equality.

It was the 13th of September, 1892. The Empress, who kept a special diary of their daily lives for each of her children, began a brand new one. Her first entry read: 'After six sons, God has given us as our seventh child, a small but very strong little daughter. She was born at half past three in our much beloved Marmor Palace during the night of Monday/Tuesday.' She continued: 'The pleasure over this little ray of sunshine was great, not just for us parents and the nearest relatives, but indeed the whole nation rejoiced at the birth of the little girl. May she some day become a joy and a blessing for many and —as she has created happiness by her appearance—let her have happiness in life. Her father, who up to now had always wanted sons, was very happy and is marvelling still. Although a particularly healthy child,' the Kaiserin remarked further, 'she was very delicately formed.'

That child was I.

On the 22nd of October, my mother's birthday, I was christened Viktoria Luise by my parents. Viktoria after my grandmother, Empress Friedrich, and my great-grandmother, Victoria, Queen of England; Luise, after Queen Luise of Prussia.

Viktoria Luise, just two words. But my registered names were altogether a little longer. In full, they were Viktoria Luise Adelheid

Mathilde Charlotte, Princess of Prussia, Margravin of Brandenburg, Burggravin of Nuremberg, Princess of Hohenzollern, Duchess of Schleswig and Glatz, Duchess of Niederrhein and Posen, Duchess of Saxony, Westphalia and Engern, Pomerania, Lüneburg, Holstein and Schleswig, Magdeburg, Bremen, Geldern, Cleve, Jülich and Berg as well as Wenden and Cassuben, Crossen, Lauenburg, Mecklenburg, Landgravin of Hesse and Thuringia, Margravin of Upper and Lower Lausitz, Princess of Orange, Princess of Rügen, Ostfriesland, Paderborn and Pyrmont, of Halberstadt, Münster, Minden, Osnabrück, Hildesheim, Verden, Cammin, Fulda, Nassau and Mörs, Princess of Henneberg, Countess of the Mark of Ravensburg, Hohenstein, Tecklenburg and Lingen, of Mansfeld, Sigmaringen and Veringen, and Mistress of Frankfurt.

I grew up in a family circle which could never have been more harmonious. My father and mother were both at pains to be with us children whenever they could. It was reported that my father had said that he loved family life above all else and was never happier than when he, like every other Berlin citizen, could be among his own. I know that he thought so: we continually heard his eternal complaint that he had too little time for us at his disposal.

My earliest childhood recollection of my mother evokes the picture of her never-ending writing. I can still hear the continuous scratch of her pen on her diary as I went into her sitting-room. Then, I had to keep very quiet—which was not easy for me to do—and busy myself cutting out pictures from my picture book, or engage in some similar activity. I also remember I had to appear either before or after every family meal, since I was too small to attend, to bid them all good day. I was always nicely dressed, but though I didn't have curly hair, the laborious, painstaking efforts of my English nurse made it appear as if I did. These curls were the bane of my life. Owing to my unruly temperament, they barely lasted until I reached the threshold of my parents' drawing-room. Even worse, if any of my brothers pulled my hair, my elaborate coiffure would then resemble a set of corkscrews.

The jolliest time was breakfast, which I always had to attend, and in summer the table was set in the open air. Usually, my parents had already been out for their ride and dismounted close to us. Even while still on his horse my father would shout down to me: 'Now then, little Madam,' or, 'Well now, little Miss, what are we up to?' Then he would embrace me and let me hold his horse's reins while he fed it carrots. This was a task I enjoyed. My love of horses, of all animals in fact, began very early; I took after my parents in this respect. At that time my father owned some Russian greyhounds, presents, I believe, from relatives, but they were bad tempered and often snapped at us children. So we got rid of them and kept dachshunds instead.

After breakfast my father usually went to work at a table under a great big sunshade, and the dachshunds made themselves comfortable under his chair, while he sat right on the edge so as not to disturb them.

The children's education was scrupulously thought out by my parents. Their duties made it impossible for them to look after us as they would have wished, so they instituted an education and development plan whose execution they entrusted to worthy persons who would undertake the strictest programme for our education and moral upbringing. Naturally, I only learned much later what excellent teachers and governesses had been assigned to me. As a child one sees these things only very subjectively. That is what happened to me regarding Miss Topham, an English governess. When I first set eyes on her, I found her detestable. They had told me so much about this new one, and now I felt deceived. I had imagined her as young and fresh, and when I saw her she seemed old and pale. That made me despondent and I wept. My father, however, tried to console me and said: 'One should never judge too much by external appearances, so you cannot make any judgement on Miss Topham. First you must get to know her better, and see how she strikes you then.'

Our nursery was supervised by the greatly loved Nana, whose real name was Miss Matcham—but I never realised it until years later and the name meant nothing to me. She was always Nana to us and she lived only for us, *her* children. I cannot recollect her ever going on holiday: she was ever there. She always celebrated the birthday of her Queen, Queen Victoria, in her own fashion. On her table she had a glass of water placed in front of her wineglass, then, when she reached for the wine for the royal toast, she would take it by stretching over the water glass, indicating that while she was on the Continent, her Queen was over there, across the water, on the other side of the Channel.

When my brothers got older, they went 'up there', my interpretation of an upper floor, where they were educated by their tutors in masculine pursuits. Everything 'up there' was spartan in the extreme —no carpets, the simplest furniture, and every single thing was washable. I remember how unhappy I was when my brother Oskar, to whom I was particularly attached, had to go 'up there'. I remember standing on the stairs watching him disappear to those upper regions and fighting back my tears. But I did not cry. Only girls did that. However, Nana consoled me by saying that he would soon come down again to play with me in his free time. And she was right. Soon enough, Oskar would appear again, as he used to do every evening before he went 'up there', but it was only to come down to eat Nana's lovely crusty brown bread, of which he was inordinately fond. It was wonderful to see him again, even though he had to go back again. It was heartbreaking just the same when we had to part.

In later years it was my brother Joachim who became closer to me. He was a very delicate child and a continual source of anxiety to my mother. As I was a strong and sturdy child, I did not understand this at the time and it drew me even closer to Oskar. He ruled the nursery and sometimes helped Nana when she hadn't finished with us and when Joachim and I were quarrelling. Joachim often got the short shrift. It irritated me, too, when he couldn't run as fast as I and cried as a result. Once, when he had fallen, he cried out in English, 'I'm dying, I'm dying', and I told him indignantly: 'Well, if you're really going to die, then do find out for me what Frederick the Great's horse's name is up in heaven.'

My brother Oskar always had a great influence over the younger ones, and I obeyed him more than I did the governesses and teachers. He was also our protector and invariably felt it his duty to guard the smaller ones. We would at all times go to him for advice. Truly he was an upright, straightforward character, modest and devoted to duty, and so he remained all his life.

On Saturdays and Sundays I was allowed to go upstairs to see my brothers and for me those were my best times. In the gymnasium Oskar was in full command and he made me march about carrying a small wooden rifle, though he sometimes let me beat the drums.

I was particularly in my element when I was allowed to wear Highland dress and, outwardly at least, looked just like my brothers wearing theirs. It was dreadful when I was not allowed to wear it any more. I was ashamed to have to dress as a girl, not wanting, of course, to look like one. It was especially annoying when I first had to be photographed in girl's clothes. I was so indignant I turned my backside to the photographer. My scarf was crumpled, my hair all over the place, and the upshot was a picture which was frequently shown me afterwards. 'That's what a naughty Sissy looked like!'—I was called 'Sissy' by the family. My brother Oskar called me 'Mouse', and my eldest brother, Wilhelm, 'my little sister'. However, when I was bidden to come and have a group photograph taken with my parents, I was transformed. Without resistance, I allowed myself to be dressed and thus attired permitted to sit on Papa's lap. I was well behaved, proud and happy to appear together with my father in a picture. My brothers considered, however, that I had become very conceited, having eyes for no one else.

My two oldest brothers were the first to leave us to go to school in Plön. There they lived with their teachers at a beautiful country seat built in baroque style, and comrades of theirs from the Cadet School often went there for instruction as well. Here, my brothers were also given an insight into agriculture, and a special farm was set up for them where they could learn husbandry—manuring, sowing, ploughing, digging and planting, as well as cattle and poultry farming. This special use of their free time was an idea of the Princes' long established tutor, General von Gontard. It was wonderful for me to go down there with my mother and eat cream and black bread, and I was amazed at what my brothers had built, planted and reaped. My father thought it worth while that they should learn to appreciate manual labour. Each one, according to the tradition of our house, had to learn some handiwork. My brother Wilhelm, for instance, was apprenticed to a turner in Plön, my second eldest brother, Eitel-Fritz, proved to be best at farming, Wilhelm, the Crown Prince, was the sporting type. From early on he led his class, whether at hockey, tennis, or riding. He was young and often foolhardy, looked brilliant, and because of his natural, unaffected manner, won a lot of sympathy. However, he often kicked over the traces, but what energetic young man doesn't? As a result there were occasional differences with my father who, under his tutor, Hinzpeter, had been brought up in his younger days with harsh Lutheran discipline. The Kaiser expected that like himself his eldest son, even as a young man, had to have the utmost regard for the duties and responsibilities of his high station. The Crown Prince, on the other hand, was more modern in his outlook. Tensions between a monarch and his heir are not, after all, merely a problem of generations. In the course of the years my father found he could always rely on the loyalty of the Crown Prince, even in the most severe crisis.

For me life was beginning in earnest: I had to go to school. My first teacher was Fräulein Hellfritz, and she understood brilliantly the feelings of children and how to hold their attention. My tutor, Herr Fechner, who also instructed my brother Joachim, was a typical, good old village schoolmaster type who, in his own way, was touchingly patient with us. On the other hand, he could be very strict—which was essential, considering my liveliness and inability to sit still. I was happy when the bell rang and I could go out to play with Joachim. Time passed too quickly and then I bravely had to try and sit still again.

If I had done my lessons well, I was allowed to go out on my pony and ride in the park with my brother and an equerry. At that time there were only side-saddles for ladies, so I had two different ones, one for left and one for right. I was so completely at home on my little pony, and later also on horses, that it made no difference on which side I sat. I was quite secure. It was nice, too, to go out riding with my mother. She was a superb horsewoman and it was from her that I inherited the passion for riding. But she had to put up with a lot of anxiety, particularly when I galloped away and jumped over obstacles she considered dangerous and which I did not. When I sat on a horse I was aware of nothing else and it was only with difficulty that I was brought back home. Then I went into the stables so as to be present when my horse was unsaddled. I would really have liked to stay there all day to help with the grooming, but that was forbidden as it was considered dangerous for children. Now and then I did help, though, when Miss Topham, who also had a passion for horses, turned a blind eye.

For many years the nursery, with my old, beloved Nana, was my kingdom, but there came a dreadful day when they came to the conclusion that I had outgrown it, and I was placed in the care of a senior governess, whose task it was to educate me in ladylike deportment and all the things which went with it. She was a fabulous woman, very clever and highly cultivated, but no longer young. I believe it would have been better if she had come to me when I was older. She was decidedly frail and often sickly, but very strict and she took everything in deadly earnest. For a young girl such as I who had grown up with six brothers, she wasn't quite right. The worst of it was that she did not get on with my dear Nana, a fact I noticed very quickly. Then came the day when Nana had to go back to England. No grounds were given for her return and I was puzzled. I will never forget our farewell and my storm of tears. As I stood at the window and watched the carriage taking her away to the station, I thought my heart would break in two. I regret to say that at that moment I had no good thoughts about my governess, Fräulein von Thadden. Only very much later, when she had become Provost of the Altenburg Foundation and I had grown up, did I recognise what a fine, clever person she was. But within me, I never forgave her for having had my Nana taken away from me.

Every summer we went away on holiday. My recollections of the first trip we made are vague, but I do remember we went to Sassnitz— on the Baltic—where I had to climb down steep steps to reach the sea. We stayed there with my mother, who had acquired a sailing yacht called the *Iduna*, and it really was a joy to be on board, though I was scared at first when she skimmed through the water on her side. As I invariably wanted to run all over the boat and often fell, they put a restraining rope around me—and that was the first time I met our skipper, Captain von Karpf, who later took command of the Kaiser's yacht, the *Hohenzollern*. When he eventually took her over, I was already a grown-up young lady and laughingly he always used to tell me: 'I had you in my power in those days, and once you realised you could not have it all your own way you started to behave.'

The trips on the *Iduna* became more and more the highlight of the year. The cruise took us as far as Denmark, and then along the Schleswig-Holstein coast through some of the beautiful inlets where, when night fell, we would drop anchor. Small boats would sail out from the harbour and swarm all around us, while one of our sailors would play the ship's piano and we would sit on deck and listen in the moonlight, completely entranced. I have never forgotten those evenings. Then came the dinner gong, but we could already smell the delicious fragrances wafting up from the pantry, and we would hurry down to eat the superb fish dishes being prepared by the cook.

I was never so happy as when I was allowed to steer. It was a wonderful feeling to hold the rudder and to know she was under my sole control. 'Kärpfchen' (little Karpf) as we called Captain Karpf, had already instructed me how to manipulate the rudder, how to cruise against the wind and then, at the right moment, how to swing the ship around so that the sails remained with the wind and did not flap around anyhow.

Our walks along the Holstein coast were a pleasure, particularly as my mother loved the woods and lakes which proliferated there. The villagers used to come out of their thatched houses to greet her, their Empress, and talk to her because she had been good enough to visit their homeland. On our trips, we also visited my mother's brother, our Uncle Günther, in Gravenstein Castle, and met her sister, Aunt Calma, the wife of Duke Ferdinand of Schleswig-Holstein-Glücksburg. They lived on the other side of the Flensburg Ford in the old and venerable Glücksburg Castle, or sometimes in their other home in Grünholz. For us children it was a wonderful change. The two sisters were vastly different personalities, though they clung together with a deep, inner love which was later strengthened by the marriage of Calma's daughter, Alexandra, to my brother Auwi. This marriage, which was greeted with such joy by the two mothers, alas, did not live up to their expectations.

Our cruises finished either in Flensburg or at Kiel, and it was always sad when our lovely holidays were over, my little cabin had to be left behind, and I knew it was the end of our times of privacy. We went frequently to Wilhelmshöhe, where Auwi and Oskar stayed if they hadn't come sailing with us. One of the disadvantages of being at Wilhelmshöhe was that we were perpetually in the public eye, and there were always sightseers who wanted to see the Kaiser's family. I suppose that was our destiny, to remain exposed to the continuous glare of the spotlight. As a child, though, I was often tormented and angry at never having a moment to myself, always having to be on show. Wherever I went, whoever I visited, it was the same, as this report from a newspaper of the period shows:

'. . . the Princess was given a hearty reception and, as usual, long speeches were made, little girls recited poetry and, from all sides, bouquets were presented.'

Please do not misunderstand me. From my earliest years I had been brought up to appreciate such demonstrations of loyalty and affection, but I would have so much liked to have been as free and unhampered as other ordinary children. It was perhaps something other than a youthful snobbery which made me write thus to my father, regarding a trip I had made and thoroughly enjoyed:

'The day before yesterday I went to Rheinsberg, a journey that took two and a half hours. All the children from the surrounding neighbourhood as well as the Mayor were gathered there. It was all rather painful as he promised to deliver me a long speech. Only when that was over could I go and visit the castle. . . .'

In Wilhelmshöhe we were rejoined for a little time by my father, looking very brown and relaxed after his northern cruise, prior to going on manoeuvres. Here, we saw him more frequently than usual, which pleased us enormously, and the highlights of his stay were the picnics on which he took us. At them, he was free and easy and most entertaining. We would build a great fire and put potatoes in the ashes afterwards. I must say they tasted far better than any of the meals we had at home. My father mixed the salad himself, while mother cooked omelettes. I had to learn to toss pancakes expertly so as not to have them fall into the fire—which they often did when I was clumsy. We all gathered round on the ground, including the gentlemen of my father's entourage, though, some of them being rather fat, they found difficulty in sitting down. I rather feel that they had never been to a picnic before.

My father could laugh like a great big boy, and every now and then would slap his knees in mirth. He had a great sense of humour and could tell some wonderful stories. At such gatherings as this he was at his best. I think I must have inherited his zest for laughter. My husband, who also had a fine sense of humour but could nevertheless restrain himself, invariably gave me a little dig in the ribs if I guffawed too loudly on festive occasions. I would try to hold myself back, of course, but my heredity was not to be denied. That was my excuse. It is wonderful to be able to go through life with a sense of humour and be able to shrug off the worst vagaries of Fate with a laugh.

Even in Wilhelmshöhe my father had to carry on the affairs of State. Members of the Civil and Military Cabinets as well as a representative of the Foreign Office were always in his entourage. If there were events of outstanding importance, officers of the so-called 'mounted couriers' would bring him dispatch boxes from the Reich Chancellor himself. Fortunately it did not happen too often that parties or family gatherings had to be broken up because of my father having to be called away for urgent conferences.

Of all the numerous personalities who came to visit us in Wilhelmshöhe, two who were devoted to my father interested me most. One was John W. Burgess, a well-known political scientist from Columbia University—an exchange professor who taught American constitutional history at Berlin, Bonn, and Leipzig Universities. He used to come and see us with his wife, and my father spent long evenings and went on extended walks in deep discussion with Professor Burgess.

The other guest was Albert Ballin, the General Manager of the Hamburg-America Line. He had free access to the Kaiser and used the opportunities when my father was at Wilhelmshöhe to hold long conversations with him, and my father gladly obtained the advice of this clever man on political and economic questions. There were some people among the Kaiser's entourage—as elsewhere—who could not countenance this advice, especially from a man of Ballin's

Jewish parentage. My father shrugged these criticisms aside, and continued to discuss with him the State's critical and ticklish problems. He knew Ballin as a man with a deep love of his country, and whose life work was to uphold its esteem abroad. Ballin's ships carried our colours all over the world, in peaceful competition with other nations.

2   The Big Family

The Kaiser's routine was pretty well regulated throughout the year, but it so happened that 18 August fell during our sojourn in Wilhelmshöhe. That was the birthday of Emperor Franz Josef I of Austria. My father always laid on a celebration banquet in his honour, and for us children it was a real occasion to see him dressed up in full Austrian General's uniform early in the morning ready to greet his guests.

I remember the Austro-Hungarian Ambassador, Count von Szögyény-Marich, particularly well. He was a Hungarian like many in his Embassy, and these men would come to dinner dressed in their colourful Magyar uniforms. All were very charming and amusing and nothing like as stiff and formal as at our Court. My favourite banquets were the ones held at the Austro-Hungarian Embassy, where Viennese waltzes were never so hauntingly played and so beautifully danced as here, and since then I have always had a soft spot for Austria, its people and its countryside and also for its great history and culture.

My father felt a deep affection for the old Emperor, considered him as a most gallant Monarch with a tremendous sense of duty, and revered him as an old and fatherly friend. With the heir to the throne, Archduke Franz Ferdinand, too, he established a marked friendship and formed a high regard for his cleverness—a fact which seemed singularly ignored by his own country. Franz Ferdinand was only too well aware of the highly explosive situation which was developing in his multi-national State and planned wide-ranging reforms which were at least intended to meet the various nationalities half way. My father had long, candid discussions with him on the subject, and I can truthfully say that the Kaiser had great hopes of Franz Ferdinand.

The Archduke and his wife, the Duchess of Hohenberg, were guests of ours in Potsdam, too, but tremendous complications arose after the invitations had been issued and accepted, as the Duchess, born Countess Chotek, was not his equal in rank by birth. This had created great difficulties, too, at the Court in Vienna, and caused us a lot of headaches. Where could she be placed during official cere- monies, and where could she be seated at banquets? Here we had an heir to the Throne on a visit, and his wife not even of equal social rank! What a problem! However, my father found the solution. In order to avoid having the Countess Chotek set far down the banquet- ing table in her proper order of precedence, he arranged lots of little tables where the guests were seated. It was a delightful banquet and one could see how thankful the Archduke was at the way in which his wife had been received and honoured at the Kaiser's Court. When the Habsburg heir finally bade us farewell, he said to my father: 'I'll never forget you and these past few days.' And my father was happy that the Royal visit had gone off so well.

I paid my first visit to Vienna in May 1908, when Emperor Franz Josef was celebrating the sixtieth year of his reign, and all the German Princes were gathered there to offer him their good wishes. The official ceremony was held in the Marie Antoinette Room at Schön- brunn Palace, where my father the German Kaiser and King of Prussia offered the old Emperor his official congratulations. Surround- ing him were the other Princes—Prince Regent Luitpold of Bavaria, King Friedrich August of Saxony, King Wilhelm of Württemberg, the Grand Dukes of Saxony, Mecklenburg and Oldenburg, as well as the Mayor of the Free Hanseatic town of Hamburg. Certainly it was an imposing tableau, this gathering of German Regents.

'Your Majesty,' said my father as he paid homage, 'gathered here around you, you see three generations of German Princes, to all of whom you have shown yourself as an outstanding model even before they were called upon to perform the duties of their high office.'

I had to leave Vienna without my parents as they had other functions to attend. Besides, I had to return to school. I bade them goodbye on the platform, since my own train left from another station, then curtsied courteously in farewell to Emperor Franz Josef, who had accompanied my parents to the station. He asked me where I wanted to go and I told him I was just saying goodbye before having to leave for Potsdam from another station. The old gentleman then took me by the arm and escorted me past the assembled members of the Diplomatic Corps, who had also come to say goodbye to the Kaiser, right to my waiting carriage. I was not really aware of what was happening to me, but above all I knew that I was truly proud that, although I was not yet grown up, I had been allowed to leave on the arm of the benevolent old Emperor who, in his chivalrous manner, had not wanted to let me depart from the station alone and unescorted.

I met Emperor Franz Josef several times in the following years, both in Vienna and in Ischl where he went hunting. We travelled there from Gmunden, the Austrian seat of the Guelph family, and were always invited to his table. Everything was homely and simple and redolent of the modest way in which the Monarch lived. He was always very gracious to me, perhaps because I was called Sissy, and it brought him back memories of his beloved wife, the Empress Elizabeth, who had been assassinated in 1898.

It was on a journey to Corfu that I first got to know King Victor Emmanuel III of Italy. He had met my father in Venice when the Kaiser had befriended the King's mother, Margherita. Relations between Victor Emmanuel and the Kaiser were good, but not particularly friendly. The King was extraordinarily small, and he was perhaps somewhat suspicious. It was also possible that there had been some clumsiness on our part, since we had been inept enough to send some particularly big men to the Italian Court. I heard that this had embarrassed the King more than somewhat. The Kaiser himself at all events took great pains to take into consideration the feelings of his allies which, of course, included Victor Emmanuel III. He also had to balance adroitly the various latent tensions which existed between the other two of Germany's allies, Italy and Austro-Hungary. The Emperor Franz Josef's reluctance towards a State visit to Rome, for instance, was well known. However, my father considered it essential to improve relations with Italy, and he seized the opportunity to meet both monarchs, Franz Josef and Victor Emmanuel on this journey. That was in 1908, when I was allowed to accompany my father there. Next year, too, my father met the Italian King in Brindisi before he travelled to Vienna. Later, both Emperors telegraphed the following message in French to Victor Emmanuel: 'Our meeting has offered us a further opportunity of greeting our august ally and friend and to express our feelings of the warm and unalterable friendship which exists between us.'

The Italian attitude, however, was not particularly friendly towards Germany, and not only because of their Francophile leanings. Bismarck had already made it abundantly clear to Italy that the way to Berlin lay through Vienna, and that edict weighed heavily on the feelings of all classes of Italian society. My father made great efforts to achieve greater unity but was not overly successful. Nevertheless, he managed to arouse occasional feelings of warmth amongst the Italians by a gesture such as the spontaneous visit to the grave of King Humbert, murdered in 1900. It was gratifying, as a German to hear in Italy phrases like *'Come è gentile, il vostro Imperatore'*—'How kindly your Kaiser is.'

During my childhood, the closest family connection between us and a foreign ruling House was with England, with the House of Hanover-Saxony-Coburg. My father's mother was an English Princess and the daughter of Queen Victoria. When my father was born, an additional verse was added and sung to the British national anthem and it went:

> *'Hail the auspicious morn,*
> *To Prussia's throne is born*
> *A Royal heir!*
> *May he defend its laws,*
> *Joined with Old England's cause,*
> *This wins all men's applause!'*

The earliest memories of his childhood that my father could recall were of England, and they concerned his grandfather, Prince Albert the Prince Consort, Queen Victoria's husband. 'He spent much time with me,' my father was fond of telling me, 'and delighted in putting me in a napkin and rocking me backwards and forwards endlessly.' In his youth my father very often stayed with our English relatives, and he and my grandfather were a familiar sight in the Scottish Highlands. Regarding his relations with Queen Victoria herself, my father used to say: 'From the very beginning the Queen was kindness itself to me, a proper grandmother, and, until her death, no cloud darkened this close relationship between us.' Even after my father had ascended the Throne the close personal affinity between them never altered. The old Queen always referred to him as 'my boy' or 'my dear boy' and that, for the Kaiser, was an immeasurable pleasure. It is no exaggeration to say that she had drawn her grandson very close to her; she always referred important political questions to him and sought his advice. In the last few years of her life, for one reason or another, ill-feeling arose between Berlin and London. The Kaiser, however, endeavoured, as one biographer correctly remarked, to keep the Queen's trust by his manifest awe and respect of her.

Queen Victoria never made any secret of her German parentage, and through her marriage to a Prince of the House of Saxe-Coburg wove for herself personally another close bond to a princely German family. She bore the title of Duchess of Saxony, and had the Saxon arms included in her Royal Standard.

The Queen was revered by all of us. She was my godmother, although I personally never met her, but my brothers, Wilhelm, August Wilhelm and Oskar went to visit her. Naturally, they told me all about her when they returned, and each one was very impressed by her. She was a little woman and at that time already eighty years old, but her age was completely forgotten, my brothers enthused, when one met her. Escorted by two tall Indians, she was a truly regal sight. This impression of their visit to the Queen influenced my brothers' behaviour back home, and their arrogance aroused my childish anger. Over there they had played with English Princes and Princesses as well as with their cousins, and the Battenbergs had been very ill-behaved, doing just what they had wanted.

In January 1901 we received the news that the old Queen was dying while Berlin was celebrating the 200th anniversary of the Prussian Crown. The Queen's third son, the Duke of Connaught, was over here enjoying the festivities. He had married a daughter of Prince Friedrich Karl of Prussia, the famous army leader. Like his father-in-law, the Duke was a dedicated soldier and had been created chief of a Hussar regiment by Kaiser Wilhelm I. Immediately my father and the Duke heard the disquieting news they hurried back to London and as they left the station to behold the great mass of people waiting there in deep silence to greet them, a man came up to my father and said simply: 'Thank you, Kaiser.' The Queen was still conscious as my father arrived, but very soon after entered her last death throes. The Queen of England died in the arms of the German Emperor.

When Edward VII ascended the English Throne, my father firmly believed he had to strengthen the ties between the two Royal Houses even further, but his reasoning was at fault, for Edward was already over sixty and had waited for more than a generation to become King. Now, when the Crown was finally upon his head, there were few reigning years left to him. Where the old Queen had waited patiently and weighed things up carefully, Edward forced matters. This had already become most noticeable in England's European policy, and particularly in her attitude towards Germany.

My father was of the opinion that in the final analysis the basis of German-English policy lay in the relationship between the two ruling Houses, and held the close affinity he had had with Queen Victoria as the example. However, Edward was not susceptible to such sentiments. He was dispassionately calculating and, besides, as uncle looked upon his nephew in Berlin in a different light to that in which Queen Victoria had seen her grandson. The manner in which my father handled Edward was considered gushing, too extravagant in his use of words, and it was impossible to find the right atmosphere wherein he could talk to Edward or discuss anything with him. Between the familiarly extrovert nephew and his older, reserved relative there was an unbridgeable generation gap which excluded the possibility of reaching any understanding. I personally remember King Edward both in appearance and in manner as a cavalier, a *grand seigneur,* but imprinted in my memory is the feeling of tension that always hung over his visits to us.

He came to see us in Wilhelmshöhe in August 1907, and a toast my father offered on that occasion reflected his fundamental attitude towards England. He told the King: 'I perceive in this visit the expression of friendly and familial feelings that Your Majesty cherishes for the Empress, for me and my House, feelings which are founded in the long-standing connections between our two Houses, and which in the present day have found expression in our common grief at the coffins of my dear parents and at the bier of the great Queen, my grandmother.'

King Edward afterwards travelled from Kassel to Ischl to see the Austrian Emperor, and tried to convince him to give up his alliance with Germany. Now known in History as the man who isolated the German Reich, the King also sought to separate the Austro-Hungarian Empire from us, and, had he done so, would have achieved his purpose of completely isolating Germany. My father discovered that this critical move on Edward's part had taken place during a car ride with Emperor Franz Josef, but that the old Emperor had flatly rejected Edward's proposals.

Accompanied by Queen Alexandra, the King made his first official visit to Germany in 1909, only a year before his death. He looked dreadfully old, was suffering from acute bronchitis, and had been strongly advised by his doctors not to undertake the visit. But he came, nevertheless. In view of the underlying tensions he felt that a refusal would have been taken as an affront. At the Berliner Hof, the anxiety concerning his health caused great agitation and in the 1st Dragoon Guards Regiment's Mess he actually started a fearful fit of coughing, which would have done him even further harm due to the tightness of his high uniform collar. The Regimental Commander reacted swiftly and automatically. 'Your Majesty,' he said, turning to the King, 'it is our custom here to loosen our uniforms after dinner.' And to his officers: 'Gentlemen, please!' Every single one immediately unbuttoned his collar, so the King was helped to some extent to alleviate his discomfort.

It would be worthwhile at this point to say something about King Edward's sister, Princess Victoria the Princess Royal, daughter of Queen Victoria, my grandmother, who married Kaiser Friedrich III.

From Bad Homburg, where we often spent the summer, we went

to visit Grandmother, travelling to Friedrichshof in my father's coach drawn by a team of four small quick-running horses and followed by a light dogcart. Although it was a sort of family outing, it was always a worrying time preparing for it. It applied not only to our wardrobe, but we were continually warned to be on our best behaviour. We were told that Grandmama was sickly, and we had therefore to conduct ourselves properly in every way.

My brothers and I were very soon to learn that there were special reasons for all these preparations. Thus we joined my grandmother together with our Greek and Hessian cousins and the Empress's other grandchildren. But we were always astonished when we saw what our cousins—whom we generally liked—presumed to do in front of Grandmama. To our intense shock they used her best silver tea trays as sleighs to slide all the way down the stairs. And when we played with them in the park and we found ourselves in the stables, my cousin Georgie—as we called the eldest son of the then Greek Crown Prince, later King George II—found some cowbells. These we hung up and created a fearful din. My brothers and I knew we had done something we shouldn't, and that we would later be punished for it, but, wonderful to relate, nothing happened. It seems Georgie had told Grandmama that he had been the cause of it all. Another time my brothers and I were in a room in one of the towers of the castle having tea. We had a dreadful thirst after playing, and as the tea was still too hot, I took my spoon and stirred it noisily in my cup. At that very moment Grandmama chose to come in and very sternly admonished me: 'We are not in a zoological garden!' I was shattered. To make matters worse for me, I received meaningful looks from my brothers who, though they saw I had made no *faux pas*, considered such a rebuke uncalled for.

In short, my brothers and I recognised that our grandmother was far stricter with us than she was with her other grandchildren. The reason, we were eventually to learn, stemmed from the tension which existed between our father and his mother.

In our youth my father told us nothing of his relations with his mother; in fact he seldom mentioned her, though my mother occasionally talked to us about her, telling us only the best things about her, never criticising at all. What is certain is that there was

no loving relationship between mother and son. My father said later:
'In the first decade of her marriage my mother, as I know from
Hinzpeter [Georg Hinzpeter, Kaiser Wilhelm II's tutor, Ed.], was
more an adoring wife to her beloved husband than a doting mother,
and she left her first three children to be brought up with conscious
severity. The later children, however, recognised her as more than
a mere provider and idolised her. Perhaps the death of my brother,
Sigismund, which broke her heart, brought about the change in her
which occurred after 1870. She never got over this loss nor that of
my brother Waldemar thirteen years later.

'Empress Vicky's principal characteristics,' my father went on,
'were her unbounding energy, great vehemence and impulsiveness,
as well as an inclination to argument and contradiction. There was
no denying she had an intense love of power.' There is no doubt that
this latter led to even further estrangement between mother and son.
In the field of power politics, both took up different attitudes, and
to complicate matters there were advisers who took her side so that
there could be no compromise.

Much can be read in the phrase my grandmother Vicky wrote after
her husband's death to her mother, Queen Victoria. 'Now everything has been in vain.' Much more can be read about her actual
efforts to improve relations with her own son in this letter she wrote
to her mother in London: 'I must concede this much to Wilhelm,
that his relationship to me was systematically poisoned, and that for
years he was lectured that it had been the greatest misfortune that
his Papa had listened to me and had faith in me, and that I was an
enemy of Germany and had dangerous convictions, etc.' And how
revealing in this connection is the opinion of her brother, King
Edward, then Prince of Wales, regarding his nephew who had just
ascended the German throne. After a long conversation with him,
Edward vouchsafed: 'The Kaiser is clever and sensible and only wants
to do what is right,' and went on in parenthesis: 'That means only
when he is allowed to do so.' Later, as King, Edward did not always
express himself in so friendly a fashion.

On New Year's day, 1900, Grandmama wrote to her old mother
in London: 'My first words this morning and my motto for the
century are "God Save the Queen!" ' The Queen, who had put the

stamp of her personality on a whole, long era, died in January, 1901, aged eighty-one. A few months later, in August, her daughter Vicky died. How remarkable it is that Kaiser Friedrich followed his father into eternity in the same year, and that his wife died in the same year as her mother. . . .

As far as the picture presented to posterity regarding the attitude of Vicky towards her son is concerned, a certain English Court official played a not inconsiderable part. He was Sir Frederick Ponsonby, later Lord Sysonby, Private Secretary to King Edward VII. In 1909, when he accompanied the King on his official visit to Berlin, he found that as a godson of Kaiser Friedrich, he was naturally a person of some consequence. It was known that he was the son of the Queen's long-standing Private Secretary, General Sir Henry Ponsonby, and one was also aware that there had existed a friendly relationship between his mother and the Empress. Sir Frederick, who spoke fluent German, was a courtier to his fingertips, and he was very proud of his position. Outwardly, he was plausible and not without dignity. 'His ability, his conversational powers, his wit and his impeccable manners,' so they said, 'contributed essentially to make life in Court circles easy and agreeable.'

However, Sir Frederick had another side to him. A well-meaning biographer wrote: 'His character was full of contradictions, he lived well and right up to the limit of his income—which was never very high.' That is a refined way of saying that Ponsonby lived beyond his means, and so found himself notoriously in financial difficulties.

We were not aware of these characteristics of King Edward's aide and besides, we would not have been particularly interested. Notice was first taken of him in 1928 when, under suspicious circumstances, the contents of the Empress' letters to Queen Victoria were published—and they were documents of great historical importance. With a prodigious literary fanfare, Ponsonby revealed how he had come into possession of the letters and of his right to publish them, despite the fact that they did not belong to him and they were the property of the British Crown. The story he concocted showed not only his audacity but his untruthfulness as well. Nevertheless, it was accepted as genuine and went into the history books where it appeared to belong—that is, until today.

The tale told by Sir Frederick Ponsonby had its scene set in Kronberg Castle, where King Edward was visiting his sister, the Dowager Empress, and Ponsonby was in the King's retinue. My father was then in Homburg, from where he came to Kronberg to visit his mother. Sir Frederick reported:

'Soon after King Edward came to the throne in 1901, the accounts of the Empress Frederick's health began to be alarming, and as she was his favourite sister, he decided to go along and stay with her for a week at Friedrichshof near Cronberg.

'After I had been in Friedrichshof for three days, I received a message that the Empress wished to see me in the evening at six o'clock. At the hour named I went upstairs and was shown into her sitting room where I found her propped up with cushions; she looked as if she had just been taken off the rack after undergoing torture.

'I sat down feeling very helpless in the presence of so much suffering, and waited. Suddenly the Empress opened her eyes and began to speak. How did I like Friedrichshof? What did I think of it? Had I seen all her art treasures? The impression that I was talking to a dying woman vanished and I was suddenly conscious that I had to deal with a person who was very much alive and alert. But after a quarter of an hour this intense conversation and hurricane of questions seemed to tire her and she closed her eyes.

'I remained silent, uncertain whether I ought not to leave the room. Just then the nurse came in and said I had been over twenty minutes and that I really must go. "A few minutes more," said the Empress, and the nurse apparently consented, for she left the room. After a pause the Empress opened her eyes and said: "There is something I want you to do for me. I want you to take charge of my letters and take them with you back to England."

'When I expressed my readiness to undertake their custody she seemed pleased and went on in a dreamy sort of way: "I will send them to you at one o'clock tonight and I know I can rely on your discretion. I don't want a soul to know that they have been taken away and certainly Willie must not have them, nor must he ever know you have got them.''

'Our conversation was again interrupted by the entrance of the nurse, who explained that the Empress had said "a few minutes conversation" and I had been with her for over half an hour. This time there was no doubt I had to go and so I retired to my room wondering if the Empress had said all there was to be said on the subject.

'I dined as usual with King Edward. On this occasion the German Emperor, the Duchess of Sparta (afterwards Queen of the Hellenes), Princess Frederick Charles of Hesse (both daughters of the Empress), Countess Perponcher, Count Eulenburg, General von Kessel, General von Scholl, Rear-Admiral von Müller, Count Hohenau and the German doctors Renvers and Spielhagen were also present. After dinner we talked till about eleven, when everyone went to bed. I went to my bedroom and started work. There was so much to do that the time passed quickly.

'The castle clock boomed one and I waited expectantly, but there was dead silence, and I was coming to the conclusion that I had either misunderstood or that some unforeseen obstacle had prevented the letters reaching me, when I heard a quiet knock on my door. I said "Herein", and four men came in carrying two boxes about the size of portmanteaux and covered with black oilcloth. The cords around them were quite new and on each box was a plain white label with neither name nor address. I noticed that the men wore blue serge breeches and long riding boots and I came to the conclusion that they were not trusted retainers but stablemen quite ignorant of what the boxes contained. They put the two boxes down and retired without saying a word.

'It now dawned on me that I had undertaken no easy task, and I began to wonder how I was to get such large boxes to England without anyone suspecting their contents. I had assumed, perhaps not unnaturally, that the expression "letters" meant a packet of letters that I should have no difficulty in concealing in one of my portmanteaux. But these large corded boxes were quite another matter and the problem of getting them back to England required careful thought. To adopt any method of concealment and to attempt to smuggle them away was to court disaster, as the whole place was full of secret police, but on the other hand, to account for these boxes which had apparently dropped from the skies was no easy matter. I therefore wrote on the label of one "Books with care" and on the other "China with care", with my private address, and determined to place them in the passage with my empty boxes without any attempt at concealment.

'On March 1, 1901, we left Friedrichshof to return to London. That day a party of soldiers from the garrison was employed to carry all the luggage down. I was talking to the Emperor in the hall at the time and out of the corner of my eye I could see the procession of soldiers carrying portmanteaux, suit-cases, despatch boxes, etc; when these two black boxes came past they looked so different from the rest of the luggage that I became nervous lest someone should inquire what they were, but no one appeared to notice them, and the Emperor went on talking. When they disappeared from the hall, I breathed again, but not for long because, as ill-luck would have it, they were the last to be placed on the wagon which stood in front of the windows of the great hall. The other wagons were covered up, but this particular wagon remained uncovered with these two boxes with their new cords and labels staring at me. The Emperor, however, was holding forth on some subject which interested him, and naturally everyone, including myself, listened attentively. It was a great relief when I at last saw the tarpaulin cover drawn over the luggage and a few minutes later heard the wagon rumble away.'

That is Sir Frederick Ponsonby's report. It reads not only like a crime novel, but has the merit of being one—it is clearly fabricated. In this sort of light reading, how often does the culprit fall foul of the law because he has overlooked something? The author here fell into that trap. What Ponsonby did not know was that my grandmother kept a diary.

It was on the third day of his stay in Kronberg, Ponsonby wrote, that his conversation with the Dowager Empress took place. That was on 27 February 1901. On that day the entry in my grandmother's diary (which is now in the possession of the Hesse family) reads: 'Saw Fritz Ponsonby later in the day in the sitting room. Went downstairs. Mossy and Sophie played the piano.' Whereas Ponsonby related that the Dowager Empress had looked so weak that a nurse had had to stop her conversation with him, in reality, after the end of the conversation, she actually went downstairs to listen to her daughters Margarethe and Sophie play the piano.

It is even more irritating to read what Ponsonby wrote further about this affair when he relates that on that evening, he dined with my father then went to his room to await the Empress's emissary. In my grandmother's diary for the previous day, 26 February, she wrote: 'William came here to luncheon and left Homburg for Berlin in the evening.' That means that my father came to Kronberg on that day, and in the evening travelled from Homburg to Berlin. On that 27th of February my father was already residing in Berlin, and therefore the meal, which Ponsonby described and in which he named its participants, definitely never took place.

My father left Homburg at 1945 hours on February 26th and arrived in Berlin at 0800 hours on the 27th—my parents' wedding anniversary. On the following day the papers reported:

'Berlin, 28 February. This morning the Kaiser went for his usual walk in the Tiergarten, listened to a report from the Reich Chancellor, Count Bülow, at the Foreign Office, and at 1030 in the Royal Palace received reports from the War Minister, von Gossler, and the Chief of the Military Cabinet von Hahnke. On his return to the Royal Palace, the Kaiser narrowly escaped collision with an electric tram. The Imperial carriage was going at a fast pace down the Unter den Linden from the Brandenburg Gate. As they passed the Opera House, a tramcar came from the direction of the Kastanienwäldchen on the Danziger Strasse-Rixdorf line on to the Linden. Whether the driver did not see the Imperial carriage or could not brake sufficiently on the slippery rails, the tram rushed straight towards the Imperial carriage and a collision seemed unavoidable. But at the last moment the Imperial Coachman reined the horses and stopped and the electric car struck the carriage only lightly. The Kaiser leaned out of the window and took in at a glance the dangerous situation in which he had been involved, exchanged friendly greetings with the crowd which had gathered, and resumed his journey to the Palace.'

On the proceedings of the following day the papers reported:

'Berlin, March 1, Evening. This morning the Kaiser went for his usual walk in the Tiergarten then listened to a report from the Reich Chancellor, Count von Bülow, at the Foreign Office. Between half past ten and midday the Kaiser visited the studios of the sculptor Ludwig Cauer and the painter, Professor Hertel, then went to see the French Ambassador, the Marquis de Noailles. Afterwards, in the Palace, the Kaiser received the Württemberg Minister President, General of the Infantry Baron Schott von Schottenstein in audience.'

Sir Frederick Ponsonby on these particular days unconcernedly had the Kaiser staying at Kronberg Castle. Yes, and he had him as one of the principal figures painted in a detailed scene on March 1 in which the boxes full of secrets were being carried away from the castle. And he conversed with the Kaiser during this time, too—'. . . and the Emperor went on talking. . . .' and '. . . the Emperor was holding forth on some subject which interested him, and naturally everyone listened attentively. . . .'

The supposition that 'the whole castle was full of secret police' is also the product of an unfettered imagination, for Kronberg Castle was never even supervised. But it is certain from where and from whom the author gets his lies in this particular part of the story. An historian who considers these matters of the Ponsonby story, as a matter of fact, wrote recently: 'At that time the castle was already ringed by secret police, and Sir Frederick Ponsonby had to use extraordinary resourcefulness to get the boxes out of the strongly guarded castle.' In the event, Ponsonby had to use his extraordinary resourcefulness to invent his story. It was only the truth he ignored.

It is deplorable that such historians should use Ponsonby's report without checking the facts first. He did not even see fit to look at my grandmother's diary. One look at a newspaper of the time would have been sufficient. Then they could quickly have read when the Kaiser had left Homburg and at what time he had reached Berlin. From the Homburg newspaper *Taunusbote* they could have had details of his departure. The item read:

> 'The Battalion Commander von Uthman, Lord Mayor Dr Tettenborn, Architect Jacobi, and Prefect Dr von Meister were at the station to bid farewell to His Majesty. They talked in friendly fashion and shook hands, and as the train moved away His Majesty nodded to those who remained behind.'

The Ponsonby story did achieve its aim: it helped its author out of his financial straits, illustrated how it apparently gave him authority to publish other people's letters, and enabled my grandmother's correspondence to 'reveal' to the public the attitude of the German Kaiser *vis-à-vis* his mother.

But one simple, trivial fact spoiled Ponsonby's fabrications. My grandmother had collected material for a life story of her husband, and had asked the Queen if she could have extracts from the letters she had written her. As the Queen died in the meantime, she turned to the competent authority—the King's Private Secretary. That's where the letters could have been obtained, for they belonged in the Royal Archives at Windsor. But it was evident they never reached there since, nearly three decades later, long after Edward VII had died, too, they were brought on the book market—by Ponsonby.

3   Constitutional Crisis

As I have already written, my family connections were close and wide-ranging, encompassing practically every European House. For example, our relationship with the Russian Czarist family was as close as that which we had with the English Royal House, and the whole tragic story and the dreadful fate which overtook these Russian relatives of mine was only brought back to mind when I recently attended a German Boy Scout meeting near Bad Kreuznach. Wandering through the beautiful forests one day, I met one of the foresters who showed me where my father and Czar Nicholas II of Russia had once stayed. Here, they had discussed the Czar's marriage plans, and my father had agreed to act as go-between with the House of Hesse, so that Nicholas could marry Princess Alix. She was the daughter of Grand Duke Ludwig IV and his wife, Alice, the second daughter of Queen Victoria. One of Princess Alix's sisters, Princess Irene, was the wife of Prince Heinrich, my father's brother. The Czar's marriage, when one discounts all his troubles and illness, was very happy. He was a loving husband and father, and they led a wonderful family life. My own impression of the Czar was that he was a lovable and highly esteemed human being.

My father wanted close and friendly relations with England, and he had promised Kaiser Wilhelm I, his grandfather, on his death bed, that he would also maintain his friendship with Russia. He took this promise very seriously. Both the Czar and my father met often to exchange thoughts and ideas. Earlier, my father had come to recognise the danger developing in the Russian social and political structures. He called for liberal reforms to ease the internal political pressures, and there was a great interchange of letters between the Kaiser and the Czar. 'I had no intention of interfering in Russian internal affairs,' my father said later. 'In Germany's interests I wanted to remove the danger of inner ferment which could lead to external conflicts. I wanted merely to help remove the danger of war inherent in the internal Russian situation.' Resignedly, my father added: 'I went to no end of trouble with Russia, but the Czar did not listen.' Today, we know that Nicholas was in a difficult position, that he could not often have his way—in direct contrast to the attitude of Edward VII towards us.

A remarkable example of the generally close affinity between the European Royal Houses was that of Denmark. Fittingly, King Christian IX was known as the Father-in-law of Europe. His mother was a Princess of Hesse, his eldest daughter, Alexandra, married Edward VII of England, and his second daughter, Dagmar, married Czar Alexander III of Russia. His third daughter, Thyra, became Duchess of Cumberland and my mother-in-law. Christian IX's second son became King George I of Greece, the third, Waldemar, married a Princess of Orleans, while the eldest, who ascended the Danish throne in 1906, wed a Swedish Princess and their son, who became King Christian X in 1912, married Duchess Alexandrine of Mecklenburg, a sister of the German Crown Princess Cecilie, my sister-in-law.

While still on the subject of relatives, I had known Dagmar—King Christian IX's daughter—since childhood when we called her Aunt Minni, but when she married she became known as Maria Feodorovna. As a very young Princess she had been engaged to Crown Prince Nicholas of Russia, but he died and she married his brother who later became Czar Alexander III. Anyway, she brought a whole host of resentments with her from Denmark which really had their basis during the time of the German unification conflicts.

One of the repercussions of the German-Danish conflict, which had arisen in the middle of the previous century was when Maria Feodorovna's sister, Alexandra, was being talked of as a future bride for the Prince of Wales, Bertie, as he was known in the family. Queen Victoria and Prince Albert had for some time been apprehensive that an alliance between their eldest son and one of the Danish Princesses would draw them into the controversy which was raging between Denmark and Prussia over the thorny Schleswig-Holstein question.

On the other hand, they believed there was scarcely any other choice. Prince Albert was quoted as saying: 'We have tried to give Bertie the opportunity of seeing Princess von Meinigen as well as the daughter of Prince Albrecht of Prussia, but both displeased him. Vicky has racked her brains to search on our behalf, but without success. Prince Friedrich of the Netherlands' daughter is too ugly; otherwise there is no one else with the exception, perhaps, of Louis's sister, and she's got bad teeth.'

I discovered these portentous words in a letter written by my great grandfather to his brother Ernest, Duke of Saxe-Coburg Gotha. From that letter, too, I gathered how Bertie's interest in Princess Alexandra had been aroused: 'Reports reached him from all sides regarding the young lady's beauty, reports which were further confirmed by a portrait he saw hanging at the Duchess of Cambridge's house,' my great-grandfather wrote.

It was Vicky's mention of her to Prince Albert and her own choice of Alexandra which finally gave the prospects of this marriage a real chance. Alexandra had also been brought to my grandmother's notice, and she had seen her, too. However, she arranged that she should be invited to the home of the Grand Duchess of Mecklenburg-Strelitz, a daughter of the Duke of Cambridge and one of the relatives, at the same time as Princess Alexandra. When they met, my grandmother was simply enchanted by her. 'I have never seen such a sweet creature,' she enthused. 'She is delightful and though no dazzling, eye-catching beauty, she has indescribable charm. Her voice, her bearing, her deportment and her behaviour are perfect, and I have seldom seen such an accomplished feminine and aristocratic person. One would have to go far to find such a Princess—she is one in a thousand.' My grandmother only saw one disadvantage in her: 'Oh, if only she were not a Dane!' she complained.

Queen Victoria and Prince Albert allowed themselves to be convinced. Yet, in a letter to Coburg, the Prince Consort wrote how seriously they had both reflected on the fact that they would rather not have let their son know of the existence of Princess Alexandra—

'this forbidden fruit', as he described her—since they had informed him of all the other possibilities.

The story of the acquaintanceship of the Prince of Wales and the Danish Princess was a real example of old-fashioned theatrical Court intrigue. My grandfather, then the Prussian Crown Prince, and my grandmother arranged the scenario. It so happened that the autumn manoeuvres that year were to take place in the Rhineland, and the Prince of Wales was invited to take part—as a guest, of course. At the close of the military exercises my grandparents, together with Bertie, went on a trip that took them from Coblenz via Mainz to Speyer. Rumpenheim Castle, on the River Main, was one of the seats of the Hesse family, and it was here that its far-flung members traditionally gathered. On this occasion, each set out from their original base travelling by the latest fashionable means of transport, the railway. Among them were Prince and Princess Christian of Schleswig-Holstein-Sonderburg-Glücksburg and their daughter, Alexandra. Their destination, of course, Speyer.

A visit to this old episcopal town invariably entails a tour of the venerable Roman cathedral, burial place of the German kings and emperors, and the parties naturally met there. 'What could have been more natural,' said my grandfather, 'for their first meeting to have taken place "accidentally" in front of St Bernard's altar in this glorious cathedral?' For it was here he introduced Edward to Alexandra, and then left them discreetly alone.

After a while, Nicholaus Weiss, the Bishop of Speyer, took charge of the two and showed them the sights, but my grandfather never let them out of his sight. 'I kept myself at a little distance from them, apparently having a look at the wonderful frescoes,' he said later, 'but really I wanted to watch the outcome of their conversation.' They spent two hours in the cathedral, which naturally pleased my grandfather. 'Of course, initially, there was some inevitable embarrassment, though it was soon obvious that both of them were scarcely indifferent to one another,' he said. 'While our good Bertie seems to bring an ardent heart to England—à sa manière—she, in her way, became quieter and more serious. . . .'

After such a good beginning, the two sides of the family joined together in a trip to Heidelberg where, next morning, they break-

fasted together, then went on a joint picnic in the country. On the
following day, they separated, the Glücksburgs going back to
Rumpenheim while my grandparents and Edward went to visit my
great aunt Louise, Grand Duchess of Baden, at Baden-Baden.

To my grandfather's great satisfaction, he saw the two young
people exchange photographs as they parted, and remarked: 'Before
he finally left her, they shook hands twice when they said farewell to
each other, the second handshake, Bertie said, being Alexandra's.'
After this, my grandfather paused and added: 'May God give this
tender, budding affair the same heights of happiness he granted
us.'

Two years later, my grandfather took the place of the late Prince
Consort at the Prince of Wales's wedding, in accordance with English
custom and at Queen Victoria's special request. During the time that
the marriage was being discussed, Prince Albert had strongly emphasised that no feelings of sympathy should be instilled in his son for the
wrong—Danish—side of the question. Yet, only a few months after
the wedding, when my grandfather visited Windsor, he found that
both Edward and his wife were already thoroughly pro-Danish—
which he deplored.

That was in 1863. In the following year Denmark lost Schleswig-
Holstein to Germany and two years after that Prussia annexed the
Electorate of Hesse-Kassel. Queen Luise of Denmark, Alexandra's
mother, was a Princess of Hesse.

The antipathy for anything German, particularly for Prussia and
its rulers, dominated the thoughts of the Princess of Wales, later
Queen of England. Foreign policy always remained to the forefront
of her interests, and she made no secret of her feelings, at times, even,
actively demonstrating them, as happened during our visit to England
when my father attended the unveiling of Queen Victoria's memorial.
She stayed right away from the ceremony. She and Edward even
allowed eight years to pass after Edward ascended the throne before
condescending to pay their first official visit to the German Kaiser in
Berlin. It would have been an even worse affront had they delayed
that any longer! I must say, however, that the Queen's courtesy was
otherwise perfect, her amiability and charm were such that it was

impossible to gauge her true feelings, which she managed to hide adroitly. Truly brought up in a good school, one would say.

After the outbreak of the First World War, she was on the side of all those who wanted to see the once-close relationship between the English Royal House and the Hohenzollerns extinguished altogether. She took offence at the black and white flags of Prussia, and those of the German holders of the insignia of the Order of the Garter, which hung at Windsor. She turned to her son, King George V, and said: 'It is only right and proper that you should have these hateful German flags in our holy St George's chapel at Windsor taken down.' The pressure of public opinion which followed forced the King to haul down the flags of all of the principalities with whom England was at war, but Alexandra went even further in reference to them. 'They are just mere soldiers or vassals who are forced to obey the brutal German Kaiser,' she wrote to her son.

She always remained anti-German, and despite being Queen of England she still felt Danish. When Flensburg was not ceded to Denmark after the end of the First World War, because the people had opted for Germany, she protested harshly and passionately to her son, blaming the Germans, 'who, for years, have been preparing for the seizure by expelling every Danish-speaking person. Look at the map and you will see just what Flensburg does mean to that loathesome German nation!'

Alexandra's sister, Dagmar, the Czarina of Russia, was equally anti-German. Both were lovely women, the Queen of England in particular a picture of beauty, while Dagmar was known as the most beautiful woman at the Russian Court. I also think Dagmar was the cleverest and the most singleminded of the Danish Princesses. In the same way that Alexandra spread resentment of Germany at the Court of St James, so equally did Dagmar at St Petersburg. Her influence both with the State and in society can hardly be underestimated. Her enmity of Germany was such that she energetically opposed her son Nicholas's wish to marry Alix of Hesse, and she did so deliberately because my father supported the alliance. As she could not very well ignore either the English descent or the English education of the intended bride, she argued against the alliance by bringing into play the allegedly typical German characteristic peculiarities of Alix's father, the Grand Duke. The Czarevitch, deeply in love as he was, declared furiously in riposte: 'It will be this one, or no one!' He got his way, this time, though it was not a common occurrence.

When, in later years, my father tried to form an alliance between our family and the Russian—such as a marriage between my brother Adalbert and one of the Czar's daughter's—the Russian family remained deaf. When one considers what had gone on in the past, their silence was not to be wondered at. Maria Feodorovna's influence over her son was maintained even after he ascended the Throne on her husband's death. In Nicholas II's letters to his mother, he seems always to be turning to her for her sanction. 'I hope, dear Mama, you approve of my decision and do not consider I have handled the matter too tamely. . . .' he wrote. Or, 'My dear Mama, you cannot imagine how worried I was before I had to act. . . .'

From another world altogether, though at a somewhat earlier date, came some sympathy and understanding for Germany. From far away America—at least we thought it far away in those days—a distinguished visitor came to see us in Potsdam: Theodore Roosevelt. During the period of his Presidency there had been several interchanges of ideas between him and my father, not only in the political but cultural fields, one result of which was the establishment of the Roosevelt Professorship in German universities, which enabled some of the foremost American philosophers to lecture here on the various problems facing the United States. The founding of these Chairs pointed the way to an historic friendship between the U.S.A. and Prussia, which resulted in so many students from the North American States receiving their education in Germany. Later on, these students headed many of the higher educational institutes in their country.

In 1910, a year after the expiration of his term of office, Roosevelt accompanied my parents to Berlin University where he was to receive an honorary doctorate. He made a superb speech on the theme of a world cultural movement, and afterwards the Dean of the Faculty of Philosophy, Professor Roethe, turned to him and said in a speech which I have always remembered:

'Mr Roosevelt, you are a democrat, a democrat of the purest water, but you also understand perfectly that we Germans look upon our Imperial House and particularly on our Emperor with pride, reverence and love.'

Theodore Roosevelt came to stay with us at the New Palace where we gave a dinner in his honour. I thought him an interesting personality. Later, he took part in the army manoeuvres at Döberitz, and followed the military exercises with particular interest. I must say he and his son, who accompanied him, were first-class horsemen.

I have rarely witnessed such intensive conversations as the ones my father held with Theodore Roosevelt. I considered him as a person of considerable originality, very straightforward, and very open. My father said of him: 'He is the incarnation of every good attribute of his people and I esteem him as a practical, reasonable man. What I admire most about Roosevelt,' my father declared, 'is the fact that of all the men I have known, he is the one who has shown the strongest moral courage.' In short, my father liked him. And, as far as I could see, the admiration was mutual. Roosevelt said to my father, 'Back home they say of you that if you lived with us you would have your constituency right behind you and at the national convention of your party you would stand right at the top of your delegation—and that is more than I can say of any other one of your crowned colleagues.'

My father was very interested in manoeuvres. He felt personally responsible for the high state of readiness of the army, which was there to guarantee Germany's frontiers and her central position geographically and geopolitically—a point of view which, strictly speaking, even the non-military minded had to understand. Field Marshal Baron von der Goltz, who was an expert, fully agreed with the Kaiser's stand. 'Kaiser Wilhelm II's energetic participation in his troops' manoeuvres invigorated them exceptionally,' he said. 'The old conception of strain vanished and the training of each individual improved, for they were stimulated by the monarch's special incentives inducing friendly rivalry which enhanced their performance.'

My father often sat in the saddle the whole day long during these manoeuvres. 'I want to show the people I am actively taking part,' he told me once, 'otherwise they will think "there he is, sitting at home, while we wear ourselves to death." ' Besides such thoughtfulness, he also had the genuine desire to honour his soldiers and their commanders. Hour after hour during the parades he would remain in the saddle while companies, squadrons, and batteries marched past, regiment after regiment, brigade after brigade, division after division. He saluted every new unit and every single flag. This was no basking in his own power. Whoever knew him knew that he was there because he wanted to honour every officer and every man with his presence.

Besides the manoeuvres there were other inspections and ceremonies. There were various authorities to be visited, officials to be received and speeches to listen to.

Winston Churchill, at that time an Under-Secretary of State and just thirty-two years old, took part in the Imperial manoeuvres in Silesia as my father's guest. Wearing British officer's uniform he accompanied my father all over the terrain where the exercises were under way and sat, like everybody else the whole day in the saddle. Later, he visited the battlefields where Frederick the Great had fought his campaigns, then took part in further entertainments in connection with the manoeuvres. Churchill was an interested and attentive observer, and on several instances had the opportunity to talk with my father. 'The Kaiser spoke to me with his usual ease,' Churchill reported, 'but still with a majesty that no one can deny him.'

1908 brought my father and our family a fatal blow which was to have far-reaching consequences. In the notes my mother made in her journal of my life, she wrote: 'In November this year there arose very many difficult and serious political repercussions for her father. First of all one of his best friends, Count Hülsen, died quite suddenly while hunting in Donaueschingen. I went to Baden-Baden, found my husband very depressed and we returned to Potsdam together. Suffering from overwork and assailed by many mental conflicts at this time, he fell ill.'

What, then, had happened?

During the reign of Edward VII, public opinion in England had turned more and more against Germany, and when talks regarding the German naval programme grew more acrimonious, my father decided to go over there to mediate and to clarify matters. During November/December 1907, he spent several weeks there with my mother, exchanging ideas with the King. He also spent some time in discussion with various politicians, professors and journalists, attended a reception given by the Lord Mayor of London, was host to the London County Council, and was finally honoured by Oxford University with a Doctorate of Civil Law. The underlying motives of friendship ran like a thread through all his conversations, and in a speech to English journalists he declared his innermost conviction that:

> 'We belong to the same race and have the same religion, bonds which must prove to be strong enough to create lasting harmony and friendship between us.'

In the Guildhall, the Kaiser, considering all that has happened since, spoke these prophetically macabre words:

> 'My endeavours are above all directed to the maintenance of peace. History, I hope, will give me my due in recognising that I have unflinchingly pursued this goal. The mainstay and foundation of world peace, however, is the maintenance of good relations between our two countries. I will, furthermore, strengthen these as far as it lies in my power to do so. The wishes of the German nation are identical to my own.'

In an address to King Edward later, my father emphasised:

> 'It is my most earnest wish that the close relationship which endures between our families should be reflected in the relations between our two countries and so strengthen the peace of the world.'

During his goodwill tour my father also visited Highcliffe Castle on the Isle of Wight, where he had talks with General Sir Stuart-Wortley and invited him to our grand manoeuvres in Germany the following year. Stuart-Wortley accepted the invitation to attend, and while there made certain proposals which would serve to better Anglo-German relations, and suggested that the essence of his conversations with the Kaiser in Highcliffe Castle should be published in England in the form of an interview. My father agreed, and Stuart-Wortley prepared the text with the help of Harold Spender, a well-known English journalist. The *Daily Telegraph* was selected for its publication, and my father received a copy of the text for approval.

The Kaiser handled the affair with every care. He sent the draft to the Reich Chancellor and added remarks referring to certain passages, which he recommended should either be changed or deleted. Baron von Jenisch of the Foreign Office insisted in an accompanying letter to the Chancellor that the article had first to be thoroughly checked in every respect. The Reich Chancellor, Prince Bülow, was on Nordeney on holiday when he received the dispatch, but read the article and sent it back to the Foreign Office for even further checking. There, it was again examined by Under-Secretary of State Stemrich and Counsellor Klehmet.

'The article was re-submitted to Bülow in Nordeney by Stemrich with few alterations', wrote an historian who studied this particular affair. 'The Chancellor, in holiday mood, left the file lying about for a few days, then informed the Kaiser that the contents had been officially approved and that there were no objections to its publication.'

It was only then that my father gave his own sanction for publication, and the article appeared in the *Daily Telegraph* on 28 October, 1908. Immediately afterwards, a political storm broke over the Kaiser's head. The Reichstag was furious, and waves of Press criticism thundered noisily and threateningly against the Throne.

In the *Daily Telegraph* article, the readers were told that the Kaiser had always been a reliable friend of England and added quite a few facts in support. The purpose of the article, however, came to nothing and the remainder of the English Press generally was heavily antagonistic towards the Kaiser. In Berlin, the newspapers there seemed only to have been awaiting this cue. Unrestrained criticism overwhelmed the Kaiser and phrases like 'despotic ruler', 'autocrat' and 'abdicate!' flew all around his head. He was accused of playing personal politics as well. The Reichstag met on 10 November and debated for two days. Every party criticised the Kaiser's behaviour. Never before had there been such unbridled censure of a German

Head of State. But it was Chancellor Bülow who betrayed his Emperor. Yet, my father had never publicly proclaimed his own views of Bülow's handling of affairs, and had always treated with consideration the man who for years had been his Chancellor. The total ignorance to this day of the truth concerning the so-called 'Daily Telegraph affair', and the consequent attacks upon my father, have forced me to disclose the details and to name the people more directly involved:

Even in the Official Gazette, Bülow tried to cheat his way out of the whole business by publishing a declaration that he had never known about the controversial article and, had he known, it would never have been published. He even confirmed this assertion before the Reichstag. Peculiarly enough, he also went so far as to tell Parliament that he had advised the Kaiser 'to exercise greater caution, otherwise neither I nor my successor could be held responsible for the consequences'. This from the man who had not only read the article *twice*, but who had also personally decided on its exact form and content for publication. An expert later concluded that 'the Reich Chancellor clearly knew of the Kaiser's conversation with Stuart-Wortley, and was aware not only of the substance but also the entire subject-matter of what had been discussed at Highcliffe Castle. Yet, he professed afterwards that he had been unable to recollect anything about it. At the Foreign Office, no one doubted that Bülow had played false, and that he had knowingly played false because he himself was a perfidious man.'

My father had believed in Bülow, but the unprincipled manner in which the Chancellor stabbed him in the back was for him a dreadful disillusion. In fact, the tumult which raged around him over the 'Daily Telegraph affair' was more than he could bear, and he suffered a breakdown as a result.

4   *End of an Era*

I was seventeen at the time of the political crisis which enveloped my father in November 1908, and which I described in the preceding pages. It was the year of my confirmation, too, and a period of intense religious preparation, all of which had to be taken very seriously. My parents were pious in every meaning of the word; the Kaiser himself being strongly religious. His life was directed by Christian principles which had to be followed both by his family and his immediate entourage. On board his yacht, the *Hohenzollern*, for instance, he led the devotions himself.

My mother had the important duty of deciding who, for example, was going to undertake my confirmation lessons. At first she thought the Court Chaplain, Dryander, would do, but finally chose the Super-intendent (rural dean) of the Church of St Nicholas in Berlin, Händler, as she believed he would not only have a closer affinity with me but would be better able to gauge the things which would be more important to a girl.

I was confirmed at the festively decorated Friedenskirche in Potsdam on 18 October 1909. It was a fine, sunny day and my parents accompanied me to the church in an open carriage. At the doors I was ceremoniously greeted by the various ecclesiastics, and led to the altar to the accompaniment of hymns sung by the cathedral choir. It was good to see my beloved godmother, the Grand Duchess Luise of Baden, there with the other members of my family. Naturally, my tutors were present, too, to watch the ceremony conducted by the Court Chaplain, Dryander, who also preached the sermon.

Then, inwardly shaking, I read out the confession of faith which I had prepared. My face lost all colour, but nevertheless I managed to read the Creed loudly and distinctly, much to my parents' delight. That evening we held a celebration party to which only the nearest relatives were invited, including, of course, my great-aunt Luise of Baden.

Confirmation for me meant the end of an era. I was eighteen now, and my girlhood was over. It meant saying goodbye to my governesses, and a feeling of depression overcame me when I realised I would have to part from Fräulein von Saldern, Mademoiselle Lauru and Miss Topham. My mother, too, found the parting difficult; they were all so very nice. However, my father asked the three ladies and Mathilde, Countess Keller, one of my mother's ladies-in-waiting, all to come and see him, thanked them for what they had done and gave each a present as a token of his appreciation of their work which, to my mind, had not always been easy.

Another development now emphasised the fact that I was no longer a young girl. A few days after my confirmation, on my mother's birthday, my father unexpectedly made me Colonel-in-Chief of the 2nd Guards Hussar Regiment—the Death's Head Hussars as they were known—which filled me with joy, naturally. But let the Countess Keller tell how it happened:

> 'His Majesty had made all the arrangements for the Princess's promotion very secret, so that when it came it would be a glorious surprise. On the day, he said: "Go upstairs and put on your uniform, for the officers of your Regiment are shortly to report to you!" Surprised, the Princess hurried to her room and there, right in front of her, was a truly splendid uniform. Father Schultz, the Kaiser's old servant—he had also served Emperor Friedrich—had been instructed to exercise every caution in finding out from the Mistress of the Robes the names of Her Royal Highness's seamstress and shoemaker, and to keep secret the reason for his inquiries so that the uniform could be made without the Princess or anyone else knowing.'

But that was not all. Good old Father Schultz's mission was not yet over. He had to help in other ways, for none of my maids knew how to arrange all the trappings of the Hussar uniform, so it was he who had to undertake the delicate task of buttoning me up and fixing the various accoutrements. Dressed according to regulations and fully equipped, I reported dutifully to my father. With a flourish, he handed me the famous blue document issued by the Cabinet which authorised my appointment. My mother said afterwards she never knew which of us looked the prouder—my father or me.

The 2nd Guards Hussar Regiment had previously had my grandmother, Empress Victoria, as its Chief and part of its title embodied her name. The year before my appointment the Regiment had celebrated its hundredth year of existence, though its traditions went back to 1741 when the Guards had been founded by Frederick the Great. However, after reporting to my father I received the officers of what was now *my* Regiment and the Commandant, Colonel Krahmer, introduced each one to me. The Commander of the XVII Army Corps, Cavalry General August von Mackensen, who had begun his career in the Guards Hussars and later commanded the Guards Hussar Brigade, was also present. Both von Mackensen and Krahmer—who later became a General—reached a venerable old age, each exceeding ninety, and both survived beyond 1945 to witness the destruction of the German Empire. Krahmer was in Potsdam when the Russians came; von Mackensen died in a farmyard near Celle after fleeing to Lower Saxony. It was there that this great cavalry leader and true servant of his Kaiser found his final resting-place. I kept in constant touch with them both until they died.

In August 1910, I had to lead my Regiment in a march past before my father, but it was not as easy as it sounds. I had endlessly to practise the proper pace on my two horses, Rosi and Portas, riding side saddle, too. I regretted being a female. Just beforehand, I wrote to my father:

'When I lie in bed at night my heart beats with joyful excitement at the thought that in four weeks time I am to lead my Regiment past you. I can never thank you enough, and I kiss your hand for bestowing me this great favour. I have always regretted not having been a boy, so as to be able to join your army, but now at least I have been consoled by your gesture.'

At last the day arrived. The sun shone brightly over the parade ground and I led the 2nd Guards Hussars, riding ahead of its commander, past the Kaiser. The first march past was at walking pace, the second at the gallop. It was terribly exciting for me—and very exacting, for we had mounted at half past nine in the morning, and with only a brief rest of twenty minutes we rode until a quarter past three in the afternoon. After that we had a meal in the Mess, and although I didn't have to make a speech, I did have to give the toast to the Kaiser which made me extremely nervous. Finally, it was all over and I had the feeling that it had been the most wonderful day of my life.

My close connections with the Regiment have remained with me right to the present day, right through all of these fateful years, though the Regiment was disbanded after the First World War. But its traditions were maintained by its successor, the 5th Cavalry Regiment, which kept the Death's Head emblem to wear on their peaked caps. They were based in Stolp and they hung my portrait, which had formerly been displayed in Danzig Langfuhr, in the Mess.

On the day that I took over as Chief of the 2nd Guards Hussars Regiment, my father gave me, in addition to the uniform, a riding-crop with a silver knob on which my initials and the date, 22.10.1909, were engraved. In 1964 I gave it to Hermann Schridde at his home in Meissendorf, after he had returned from the Tokio Olympics with two medals. He, together with Hans Günter Winkler and Kurt Jarasinski, had won the gold medal in the equestrian team event, the Nations' Cup, and Schridde had come second in the Show Jump. I was very happy to have been able to please this young horseman, because riding had always been my passion. Unfortunately, I had not been able to ride as often as I wished when I was young, particularly at the hunt, because my father was always worried that I might have had an accident. I could only hunt when I had his express permission.

My father himself was a first-class rider. He rode wonderfully, unbelievably well, particularly when one considers he had a fore-shortened arm. I was always wanting to go out riding with him and a little game developed between us. 'What's the weather going to be like?' was the invariable question between us, for my father never went riding in bad weather since he couldn't risk catching a cold. It was old father Schultz's duty to forecast what it would be like, and I always tried to make him give me a favourable outlook. My window overlooked the area where he usually made his so-called meteorological studies, sometimes stretching out his hand to feel what the weather was like. Then I looked down and called to him:

'Father Schultz, it's not going to rain.'

'It *is* going to rain,' he replied.

'No, it is *not*.' I was persistent.

'The Kaiser must not get wet.' He was equally insistent.

'Please, Father Schultz, say it isn't going to rain.'

Eventually Father Schultz gave in and he reported to the Kaiser that the weather was suitable for him to go riding. So, my father got dressed and we rode off to Döberitz. And, of course, it poured!

'I just don't know what's the matter with Father Schultz,' my father grumbled. 'What did he mean, it wasn't going to rain?'

So we rode on in the rain and I felt radiant because I was out riding with my father and I knew that he was happy to be with me. However, every now and again he would mutter pensively, 'Funny, very funny. Don't know what Father Schultz was up to today.'

There were difficulties, too, for other members of the Royal Family, since the Kaiser would not allow anyone to take part in riding competitions. My cousin, Friedrich Karl, one of Prince Friedrich Leopold of Prussia's sons, was the first to be allowed to take part in a race, mainly because I put in a word for him with my father, and permission was given for him to go to a meeting in Sweden. He was certainly the first outstanding sportsman in our Prussian family. He was a captain of cavalry and Squadron Leader of the 1st Guards Hussars. A flyer, he fell over the Western Front in 1917. For my brother Wilhelm, the Crown Prince, who was also fascinated by the sport, the Kaiser had additional matters to consider apart from the dangers of horse racing. If Wilhelm won, there was the possibility that people would say it had been fixed beforehand, and if he lost, there was the risk of exposure to public ridicule.

One of the sensations of the first decade of this century, comparable to the first space flight later, was the attempt at airship and aircraft

construction in Germany. At the beginning of November 1908, the
builders announced that an airship had actually been built, had risen
into the air and had come down again safely at Bodensee. We read in
the papers that the airship had behaved superbly and had responded to
every command. Proudly, it was recorded: 'Experts estimate that
the speed of Zeppelin I would exceed 50 k.p.h.'.

My father, who had very much encouraged the work of Count
Zeppelin, went to the site to find out at first hand. At Manzell he
visited the works and watched the first take-off of the airship Z.1.
After it had landed he decorated Count Zeppelin with the Order of
the Black Eagle and extolled him as 'the man who, through his
discovery, has taken mankind further along the road of his development'. It is interesting to note that this scene took place on the very
day that the tumult broke out in the Reichstag over the *Daily
Telegraph* affair.

In May 1909, Count Zeppelin took off in his airship on a flight to
Berlin. The whole city was in a state of great excitement. People
crowded the streets, packed every window, all on the lookout for
this new wonder of the air. We, too, travelled to Berlin to see it and
waited tensely for its arrival. Hours passed and nothing happened. At
last, very late that night, news came that Z.1 had had to change course
and could not fly over Berlin at all. It was a great disappointment.

Three months later we waited once again in feverish anticipation
as the news flashed—the Zeppelin's coming! Everybody was alerted
and people could be seen running in the streets and looking skyward.
Schools closed, business and office and factory workers streamed
outside crying, 'The Zeppelin's coming!' It seemed the whole of
Berlin was on its feet. Once more they waited: not a single sign of the
huge airship. Hours later came the announcement that it had lost a
propeller, and had had to make an emergency landing.

The next day, Sunday, there was more anxious waiting. Would it
come this time? It did. We jumped into a car and hurried—as much
as we could in such a vehicle in those days—to Tegel. The Kaiser
was absolutely beside himself—I can hardly describe it. Highly
excited, he shouted to everyone as we passed: 'The Zeppelin's
coming, the Zeppelin's coming! To Tegel! To Tegel!' Finally, the
airship appeared, cruising majestically above us. Shortly afterwards

we watched it land, and my father hurried forward to greet and congratulate Count Zeppelin and his crew. Later, still clad in their leather jackets and flying gear, they were our guests at home.

A few weeks after the airship's landing, the aviator Orville Wright flew into Berlin in one of his aircraft. It was called an airplane and certainly looked like one. I followed Wright's exhibition with passionate interest, and though the aircraft certainly did not rise very high, it stayed quite a time in the air, thus creating a record.

To my intense surprise my great enthusiasm for air travel was rewarded by the naming of one of the Zeppelins after me. It was with tremendous pride that I watched the airship *Viktoria Luise* cruise above the boats during Kiel Regatta Week in 1912 before commencing its journey to Heligoland. In July the same year LZ.XI, the *Viktoria Luise* took part in the great 'Zeppelin Day' in Hanover and was triumphantly greeted by everyone.

My name was also bestowed on one of the great international passenger steamships, and in 1911 I was invited to be present at Kiel for the naming and launching ceremony of one of the newest ships of the Imperial Navy, the *Kaiserin*, built by the Howaldt shipyards.

In May that year I accompanied my parents on a State visit to England, one of the purposes of which was to attend the unveiling of the Queen Victoria Memorial. My parents had been invited by King George V, who had succeeded his father in 1910. The Kaiser had already attended King Edward VII's funeral, and that event had claimed a great deal of interest not just in England but also in Germany. My father had walked beside King George at the cortège, had laid a wreath, and had uttered a silent prayer. After that, both Monarchs solemnly shook hands. That evening, a member of the English Royal Family told my father:

> 'Your handshake with our King is all over London. The people are deeply impressed by it and take it as a good omen for the future.'

My father replied: 'That is the sincerest wish of my heart.'

In Germany itself everyone believed in an improvement of relations with England, but what was certain was that the climate between the two Royal Courts was now much healthier. The relationship between the two cousins, King George and my father, was more harmonious than it had been between uncle and nephew. And the new Queen, too, born a Princess of Teck, was on very friendly terms with us, so it was under these happy auspices that our visit to England took place. The outcome, too, was pleasing. We were heartily welcomed both by the Royal Family and by the people and at the unveiling of Queen Victoria's Memorial the King, in his speech, had some warm words of friendship for my father.

The absolutely precise display given by the British troops at the unveiling ceremony showed that military exhibitions of this sort were not the sole prerogative of the Germans. My father remarked afterwards:

> 'That unveiling ceremony was very skilfully staged and a magnificent show. The broad circular area in front of Buckingham Palace was surrounded by stands filled to overflowing with people who had been invited. In front of them stood lines of troops of every arm and regiment of the British Army in full dress uniform with both the cavalry and the artillery on foot. Round the Memorial itself were the regimental flags in a blaze of colour. The Royal Family, with their guests and attendants were grouped in front of the Memorial. King George then made a very effective dedicatory speech and unveiled the marble Memorial to the accompaniment of salutes and cheers. And there was the Queen in marble, sitting on a throne overlooked by a golden statue of Victory—a very impressive moment indeed. Then came the march past of the troops, headed by the Guards and followed by the Highlanders in their colourful kilts lending a wonderful splash of colour to this military occasion, and finally, the other troops. The march past went round this circular area, wheeling seemingly endlessly. It was a very difficult manoeuvre for the soldiers as the outer ring had to lengthen their stride while the inner had to shorten theirs. It was all superbly executed; not a man fell out of line.'

The Duke of Connaught had been responsible for the organisation of the military side of the ceremony and his skill was commended by everyone, but for me, he was just my very charming uncle. He was a *grand seigneur* of the old order, full of natural amiability and great good nature. He looked splendid and bore a very close resemblance to his great uncle King Ernst August of Hanover. The Duke asked me afterwards which part of the ceremony had impressed me most and I replied: 'The Highlanders, of course!' I was really very taken with them.

That evening there was a grand ball, and King George danced with me. My mother was of the opinion I had been very highly thought of by everybody, and said that there were all sorts of rumours flying around about my engagement 'which, fortunately, were not true'.

Whispers had been going about that a marriage was being arranged between the Prince of Wales and myself. David, later King Edward VIII and then Duke of Windsor, was only seventeen years old at that time. He was very nice, but looked so terribly young, younger than he actually was; he always looked youthful.

Even the *Daily Express* went so far as to comment upon my marriage prospects:

> 'Truthfully, she has created havoc in the hearts of many young German nobles, who can only sigh from afar as they gaze at the unattainable. . . . Rumour has more than once been rife as to the future of the Princess. Certainly her marriage would be one of the most important events imaginable, fraught with tremendous consequences for the whole of Europe. One thing is certain and that is that the Kaiser would have some weighty words to say on the subject. . . . The Kaiser's daughter has taken London by storm, and everywhere is reaping golden opinions by her winning smile and abounding interest in everything and everybody with whom she comes into contact.'

That autumn I took part in the Imperial manoeuvres in the Mecklenburg area. The armies involved were commanded by Prince Friedrich Leopold and Baron von der Goltz, and what was particularly remarkable about the exercises was the introduction of airships and aeroplanes. Aircraft techniques had been so far advanced by now that these craft could now form part of the armed forces. Two airships and eight planes were in action during these military operations.

The manoeuvres over, there occurred for me not long after an event which was to have far-reaching consequences. I undertook my first journey alone. My mother agreed that I should accept an invitation to stay with Princess Knyphausen, at her estate in the country at Lütetsburg in East Friesland.

'The Princess has such a good influence on the little one that I can let her go without disturbing my peace of mind,' my mother wrote in self-vindication.

I, 'the little one', may I say, was already twenty years old.

5   *Ernst August*

As it turned out, 1912 began for me with a severe attack of bronchitis which set me back for some time, and I had to have four weeks of recuperation at St Moritz. After that August Wilhelm and I accompanied father to Corfu, while my mother remained at Bad Nauheim owing to her heart condition. On our return we joined her at Bad Homburg and it was here on the 20th of May that we received news of the death in a car accident of Prince Georg Wilhelm of Hanover, the eldest son of the Duke of Cumberland. The young Cumberland, an Austrian officer, had been on his way to Denmark to attend the funeral of his uncle, King Frederick VIII, when his car skidded off the road near Nackel in Mark Brandenburg. The Prince, who was a good driver, was at the wheel and both he and his valet, who was sitting at the back, were killed outright while his chauffeur, sitting next to him, survived. On my father's orders my brothers Eitel-Fritz and August Wilhelm together with a deputation of Hussars went at once to the estate where the Prince was lying in state and formed a guard of honour round the bier.

It was a remarkable caprice of fortune that the eldest son of the Hanoverian Pretender to the Throne should die on Brandenburg soil, in Prussia, from which the Guelphs had so singularly severed themselves since 1866.

The task of informing the Duke and Duchess of Cumberland of their son Georg Wilhelm's death fell to his brother, Ernst August, but the ducal pair were on their way from Gmunden to Dresden, therefore the Prince told his parents' personal physician of the tragedy on the telephone so that the doctor could inform them. Suddenly Ernst August realised that he had heard all this story before. My God, he thought, I know it all already! Astonished at this sudden recollection, he went to his servant and he knew the story, too. Yes, he said, when Prince Georg Wilhelm had returned from the Coronation ceremonies in London the year before, he had told his valet, old Grewe, and his own family, of a dream he had had and how they had all laughed heartily about it.

Georg Wilhelm had dreamed that he had been killed in a car accident in Prussia, somewhere near Berlin.

Prince Ernst August could not bring himself to believe that this dream had now actually come true. Even less could he believe in the rest of the dream, details of which were also to become fact:

Georg Wilhelm had related how he had dreamt that two Prussian Princes would be present at his funeral, and that soldiers in red uniforms would be carrying or escorting his coffin. It is extraordinary how that picture really took shape.

In Homburg, my father gave orders for my brother, Eitel-Fritz, to go right away to the spot where the accident had taken place. However, my brother was uncontactable as he was on manoeuvres in Döberitz, so my father ordered August Wilhelm to take his place and he went. Auwi went immediately to Nackel. He had hardly arrived when Eitel-Fritz, who had in the meantime received my father's orders, appeared on the scene. So now there were two Prussian Princes at Georg Wilhelm's bier! Still in Homburg, the Kaiser then ordered that an infantry company from a certain regiment should be dispatched to escort the coffin, but they, too, were uncontactable as they were on duty out in the country. The order was then switched to the Zieten Hussars. They took over the funeral escort instead— dressed in their red uniforms! Really a very remarkable coincidence indeed, almost unbelievable that such a premonition should actually become fact.

Prince Georg Wilhelm was taken back to Gmunden and buried there. My father telegraphed the Duke and Duchess his heartfelt condolences and we left Homburg for Potsdam. There we received a call from Prince Max of Baden who asked my father if it would be convenient for the younger son of the Duke of Cumberland, Prince

Ernst August, personally to come to thank and pay his respects to the Kaiser on behalf of his parents for the goodwill which he had shown them. My father, of course, agreed. For the first time in nearly fifty years now, there would be a Guelph at the Prussian Court.

Prince Max's intervention was well received; he was on very friendly terms with my father and was also married to the Duke of Cumberland's daughter, Princess Marie Luise. Max accompanied his brother-in-law in what we might call this diplomatic mission.

Prince Ernst August's visit took place in circumstances which would become very familiar. We sat outside and strolled around as we pleased while we were waiting for our tea. Until that moment I hadn't the slightest inkling of the existence of this Hanoverian Prince. We had, of course, spoken of Georg Wilhelm, whom we called the young Cumberland, but nothing else. Countess Bassewitz, later my sister-in-law and one of the Kaiserin's maids of honour, was staying with us at the time, and I learned some of the details about him from her.

An air of excitement pervaded my home circle as we waited for the Prince's arrival, for the fact that a member of the Hanoverian family was actually to visit us was a rare occurrence indeed. Finally, Ernst August arrived together with Max of Baden. Max eased the tense atmosphere quite adroitly and helped to brush away the anxieties attending this first confrontation. Ernst August, however, proved very quiet and aloof, and the whole conversation was stiff and solemn. My parents tried to make things easier for him by asking where his interests lay and showed him various things which they thought might stimulate him. It turned out he was a cavalryman, a Lieutenant in the Bavarian 1st Heavy Cavalry Regiment, and he seemed keen for us to show him our horses. I asked my parents if I could, then took him to see my beautiful thoroughbreds. Ernst August at once became animated; the ice had melted. From then on the conversation became light-hearted and the tea a cheerful affair.

Prince Ernst August made an excellent impression, looked absolutely splendid, and had a distinguished appearance. That was our unanimous verdict. My mother remarked that he had an outstandingly sympathetic nature and she was struck by his beautiful eyes which were so like his mother's.

The Kaiserin with her three-month-old daughter, January 1893.
The Empress kept a book on the birth of each of her children.
Princess Viktoria Luise was the seventh child, after the birth
of six sons.

Our great-grandmother Queen Victoria, in Coburg in 1894 for the wedding of Ludwig of Hesse and Victoria-Melitta of Sachs-Coburg. Back row, from left: Prince Ludwig of Battenberg, Grand Duke Paul of Russia, Prince Heinrich of Battenberg, Prince Philip of Coburg, Count Mensdorff (in top hat), Grand Duke Sergei of Russia, Crown Princess Marie of Rumania (half hidden), Crown Prince Ferdinand of Rumania, Grand Duchess Elizabeth of Russia, Grand Duke Vladimir of Russia (with mutton chops), and Duke Alfred of Coburg. Second row, from left: the Prince of Wales (later King Edward VII of Great Britain; light-coloured coat), Grand Duchess Vladimir of Russia, Princess Luise of Coburg (profile), Princess Alexandra of Coburg, Crown Princess Charlotte of Sachs-Meiningen, the Duchess of Connaught, and the Duke of Connaught (standing directly behind his wife). Third row, from left: Crown Prince Alfred of Coburg (young man), Czar Nicholas II of Russia, Czarina Alexandra of Russia (with boa), Princess Ludwig of Battenberg, Princess Irene of Prussia (with boa), Princess Heinrich of Battenberg, and the Duchess of Coburg. Seated, from left: Kaiser Wilhelm II, Queen Victoria, and the Empress Friedrich of Prussia (née Princess Victoria of England, the Princess Royal). The little girls, from left: Princess Beatrice of Coburg and Princess Feodora of Meiningen.

The Imperial family, 1896. From left, seated: August Wilhelm, Joachim, Oskar. Then from left: Crown Prince Wilhelm, Viktoria Luise, the Kaiser, the Kaiserin, Adalbert, and Eitel-Friedrich.

The New Palace, in Potsdam, *circa* 1900.

Princess Viktoria Luise, at the age of ten.

A ride on the Tempelhofer Field, Berlin, 1911. Princess Viktoria Luise, Prince August Wilhelm, the Crown Prince, and Colonel-General von Scholl.

Guests for military manoeuvres. Above: Winston Churchill with Lord Lonsdale (left) and an English Military Attaché to Berlin (right), 1906, in Silesia.

Theodore Roosevelt with the Kaiser,
May 1910, in Döberitz.

The zeppelin *Viktoria Luise* created a sensation in June 1912, when it flew over the yachting races of the Kiel Regatta in the Baltic Sea, en route to Heligoland, from the Elbe River. This was the first voyage of a zeppelin over the ocean.

The day of the engagement of H.R.H. to Ernst August, Duke of
Brunswick, 10 February 1912, in Karlsrühe.

Quite apart from the personality of our guest, my mother was fascinated by his light blue uniform. 'How nice it is to see a Bavarian uniform here,' she said. 'It's just like the one in which my father went to war in 1870.'

My mother's family had suffered a similar fate to that of the Hanoverian, for her father, Duke Friedrich von Augustenburg, commonly known as the 'Augustenburger', had been outmanoeuvred by Bismarck in the struggle for the succession of the Schleswig-Holstein Throne; Prussia had subsequently annexed the Duchy in 1867. The distinction between him and the Hanovers, however, was that in 1870 he fought against France side by side with the Prussians, but did not enter the Prussian army again—although he had been in the Guards yet chose to serve in the Bavarian forces as a Major-General. Later, in France, he was reconciled to the Hohenzollerns, and took part in the ceremony in which the King of Prussia was acclaimed German Emperor by the assembled German Princes in the Palace of Versailles on 18 January 1871. 'Such a time,' he told Gustav Freytag [a German poet of the time; Ed.], 'changes the opinions of men and imposes new allegiances.' It was understandable that with such similar family backgrounds my mother should feel an affinity to the Hanovers, which the Hohenzollerns did not, and this feeling was reciprocated by Prince Ernst August.

For me, it was love at first sight. Suddenly, I was all fire and flame. My mother must have noticed it because, as I was able to read later, she confided to her diary, 'He certainly made an impression on my child from the first. God knows whether it will ever come to anything.' I had no idea at the time that my feelings had immediately been perceived by my mother.

My mother asked me whether I thought Prince Ernst August was nice and what I felt about him. I made no secret of my feelings, being only too glad to be able to discuss him with her at last. My father, too, I heard, knew about my enchantment for the Prince, but asked no questions. He knew exactly what a ticklish problem it posed, and no one knew how the Duke of Cumberland would react. As head of the House, it was he who would have to make the decision. My father then had a word with Prince Max of Baden who undertook to sound

c

out the Duke, his father-in-law, using all his tact and discretion, because the Kaiser did not wish to risk a rebuff.

During the Imperial manoeuvres in the autumn, my father came across Prince Ernst August quite by accident, when the latter was on patrol and had to report to him. All my father could do was to wish him well in his military career.

Meanwhile, Prince Max of Baden's soundings were not resulting in any definitive answers. No one knew if the feelers put out to the Duke of Cumberland were having any effect. As far as we could see, the matter could go either way. Prince Max and his wife had put in some warm words on our behalf, for they wanted to establish a suitable climate at which the question could be broached, but these did not get very far. The barrier at which each attempt was foiled was the claim to the Hanoverian Throne, for the Duke appeared determined on no account to relinquish it.

At the beginning of January 1913, Max came to Potsdam and reported that the outlook wasn't very favourable. I was in despair, but managed not to show it. 'The little one remained very calm and brave,' my mother remarked in her diary.

In order to bring a little light into the darkness surrounding the success or failure of the negotiations, I took my sister-in-law, Crown Princess Cecilie, into my confidence. She was, after all, related to the Hanoverian family through her brother, the Grand Duke of Mecklenburg-Schwerin's wife. Cecilie undertook the task of having a word with Prince Ernst August himself, since it could easily be done as the Crown Princess often went to Partenkirchen and Ernst August lived in Munich not far away. A meeting could thus be arranged.

The fact that Cecilie could assume the role of *postillion d'amour* gave my romantic thoughts and dreams a certain nuance. Cecilie had been the first bride I had been close to. For a young girl like myself, her wedding was an exciting event. I was twelve years old when my brother Wilhelm and Cecilie got engaged, and Wilhelm had sent me a telegram from Potsdam announcing his betrothal. I don't know what impressed me most, the fact that my brother had personally given me the news or the surprise that I was to have a sister-in-law. And to be her sister-in-law seemed to me to be an advance in my status. In any case, I was very proud.

When the reception for Cecilie was held at the New Palace, I was overwhelmed with curiosity as to how a proper bride should look. The two of them sat in my parents' anteroom and I went through to have a look. Cecilie's beauty, grace and charm filled me with astonishment. So that was what a bride looked like! I went through the room several times more in order to have a good look at her, and my brother scolded me severely for so doing. My curiosity in going in and out of the room thoroughly displeased him. However, I now knew what a bride looked like. Cecilie's bewitching appearance at least conformed to the picture conjured up by my girlish fantasy, and it was she who now fulfilled all of my longings.

My sister-in-law's endeavours on my own behalf were supported by my brother Adalbert, who joined Ernst August in Partenkirchen. So, while the three of them were there together, I waited with rapidly-beating heart, in Potsdam. The first news I received was a telegram from Cecilie, sent in English, with Prince Ernst August's name discreetly omitted:

'Just had tea and long talk with somebody dining with Adalbert only stop we three thinking all the time of you darling stop tender love Cilly.'

When I eventually learned the details of this talk, I knew that Ernst August had the same feelings for me as I had for him—which was wonderful. On the other hand, he had also spoken very temperately about the dynastic difficulties which confronted us, and was in no way pessimistic, but emphasised that everything would have to be thought out carefully in Gmunden, and that would take some time.

It was Adalbert who sent me the first photos of Ernst August, and it was he who enabled me to have my first telephone conversation with him. It was all kept very secret and nobody else knew about it, not even my parents. Adalbert also used all of his powers of persuasion in Partenkirchen and Karlsruhe to further my ends, but I must say that without Prince Max's preliminary diplomatic efforts, he would not have got very far, and we would have never reached our goal.

The decisive advance to the old Duke was made by Prince Ernst August himself. Against all opposition, he put forward his proposals to his father and found it was no easy going. Then, on 20 January 1913, we received a telegram from Adalbert giving us the happy news that the difficulties had been overcome. At last, all of the uncertainties were over and my mother wrote in her diary, 'My child, her father, and I were radiantly happy.'

The solution to the dynastic, constitutional and political impediments which Adalbert, Ernst August and Max had found resembled Columbus's Egg.[1] The Duke of Cumberland would renounce the Throne of the Duchy of Brunswick in favour of his only son—the renunciation of that of Hanover was not mentioned—and Ernst August would enter the Prussian Army, take the oath to the King of Prussia, and would refrain from making any move for the Hanoverian Throne. That was the plank whereby the famous renunciation question would be bridged.

On 24 January Adalbert returned to us once more, bringing with him the proposed announcement. Then he went to inform the Chancellor, Bethmann Hollweg, to put him in the picture. Both as Chancellor of the Reich and as Minister President of Prussia, Bethmann Hollweg was very interested in the proceedings and took the necessary official steps. The Prime Minister of Brunswick, Adolf Hartwieg, too, was informed—everything was done under the strictest secrecy. That secrecy was even maintained at Court, so much so that when the Countess Keller was finally put in the picture, in the first week of February, she expressed 'great surprise' at the turn of events.

Feverishly, my parents and I made the necessary preparations, but for me, nothing could go fast enough. I had wished the engagement to take place at my sister-in-law's in Partenkirchen, and in complete quiet, but my father decided it should be in Karlsruhe. He had in mind the familiar and historic colour that this place would have, for the Baden House would be the more suitable in which to bind the Houses of Hohenzollern and Guelph together. In particular, my

---

[1] Columbus, one evening at a banquet in his honour, and in reply to a suggestion that other pioneers might have discovered America had he not done so, is said to have challenged the guests to attempt to make an egg stand on its end. Everyone having failed, he flattened one end of the egg by tapping it against the table, and stood it up—thus indicating that *others might follow, but he had discovered the way*.

father considered that here, the Dowager Duchess Luise, as representative of the older generation of our House, would best give her blessing to this engagement.

So my parents, my brother Oskar, and I went to Karlsruhe where we arrived on 10 February. Adalbert could not accompany us as he had become ill. We thought we would keep the reason for our journey secret and Ernst August himself arrived incognito. Even my great-aunt Luise acted with great circumspection, for she did not inform her ladies-in-waiting of our arrival until 11 p.m. the previous night. Despite all the precautions, the news leaked out. When we arrived in Karlsruhe a mass of people had gathered and we were cheered. Huge headlines in the morning newspapers announced my forthcoming engagement.

Soon after our arrival, my father asked Prince Ernst August to come and talk to him. They were together a good threequarters of an hour and walked up and down in the castle gardens in close conversation, discussing personally for the first time the question of succession. Then they were joined by my mother and me. I was very excited and in contrast to my shining, bright red silk gown, my face was pale. My parents spoke only a few sentences to Ernst August and me, and then left us. For the first time we saw each other without anyone else being present. Alone. An indescribable moment.

My mother, who had been waiting in a nearby room, 'full of anxiety and agitation' as she told me later, returned to our side an hour later and asked us if we had made up our minds. There was no need for us to say yes, as she could obviously read the answer in our eyes. A few minutes later, my father entered and I ran to him and told him I was now engaged.

Suddenly, there was an almighty crash. Ernst August had knocked down a huge vase containing some big, long-stalked flowers which had been standing on one of those small, elaborate tables which cluttered the salons in the last decade of the 19th century. My mother, scared by the noise, gave a mighty shriek but, looking at the scene, all we could do was smile in great amusement. My freshly-new fiancé, however, just stood there amid the heap of fragments, visibly embarrassed, holding the bunch of flowers from the broken vase in front of him, not knowing what to do.

Then we went to dinner, Ernst August and I going hand in hand and everybody could see how happy we were. My great-aunt, who still lived with her conceptions of the past and was very aloof, looked somewhat shocked at our behaving at table like lovers. That immediately knocked one part of our plans awry, for we had decided that our engagement would first be announced after our return to Berlin. Our attitude, which spoke volumes, as well as the expression on my great-aunt's features, forced my father to tell the Grand Duchess the news *tout de suite*. Our happiness simply could not be kept secret—and on the same day our engagement was made public.

What followed seemed like a fabulous dream. That evening there was a reception given by the Courts of Prussia and Baden. My parents, together with Ernst August and I, went round the whole circle of people gathered in front of my great-aunt's chamber where the reception was being held, and received the good wishes of everyone. At the end my father said: 'Now we really must leave the young people alone.' They were the same words spoken almost thirty-three years before, to the day, at my parents' engagement and which led to their peaceful life together.

Joy, good wishes, flowers everywhere. And from Gmunden came a telegram from my parents-in-law. The Duchess also insisted on telephoning her congratulations and for the first time I heard the kind, loving voice of my mother-in-law. Ernst August and I went for walks and outings, accompanied by Oskar and occasionally by my mother and Prince Max, while my father went back to Berlin next day. The rest of us followed the day after. Before we left, a telegram was rushed to us. It was from the Adjutant General, Baron Moritz von Lyncker:

'Tomorrow February 13 at 0830 hours H.M. The Kaiser will meet the special train arriving at Berlin Potsdam Station and greet H.M. the Kaiserin, H.R.H. Princess Viktoria Luise of Prussia, and H.R.H. Prince Ernst August Duke of Brunswick and Lüneburg. In attendance at the station will be:

1. The Royal Princes who insofar as can be ascertained are either in Berlin or Potsdam; (b) Members of the Cabinet; (c) H.Q. staff; (d) The Governor and Commandant of Berlin;

(e) President and members of the State Ministries; (f) The Lord Mayor of Berlin.

2. The Guard of Honour of 2nd Foot Guards Regiment with their Colours will be on the platform together with the regimental band.

3. In front of the station, ready to escort their majesties and the royal bridal pair to the Royal Palace will be No. 1 Squadron (Brandenburg) Hussar Regiment, half of which will ride in front of the procession and half behind.

4. The remaining four squadrons of the Hussar Regiment—mounted—at Lustgarten.

5. Dress: His Majesty, Royal Princes, officers named in 1 (b)–(d) above, service dress, 1 (e)–(f) gentlemen in overcoats, Guard of Honour and Hussars in parade uniforms.'

Amid the clang of the ceremonial bands, our train rolled into the gaily decorated station where my father awaited us. As I stepped on to the platform, he handed me a gorgeous bunch of Marshal Niel roses. Then we got into a carriage-and-four where I sat with my mother, while Ernst August sat next to the Kaiser in the back seat. The weather wasn't very good to us: clouds hung over the city and it rained, but the Berliners had nevertheless insisted on turning out to greet us. Of course, this was a noteworthy procession, for not only were they greeting a bride-to-be as of old, but greeting the groom, too. Our cavalcade made its way along the Charlottenburger Chaussée, through the Brandenburg Gate, over the Pariser Platz and along the Unter den Linden to the Palace to the great jubilation of the crowd, whose enthusiasm knew no bounds. They even broke through the police cordons. On arrival, the officers of the Hussars Regiment which he was to join as Captain were presented to Ernst August.

On the same day Prince Ernst August took the oath and was invested with the Order of the Black Eagle. He had previously requested the Prince Regent of Bavaria's permission to be released from the oath which bound him as a Bavarian officer and it was graciously granted. So now we had a situation in which the heir to the Guelph Throne was actually taking an oath of loyalty to the King of

Prussia. The investiture, which was ordered by my father to be held with few present, was an impressive ceremony. Everyone realised the historical importance and meaning of that moment. Yet as incomprehensible as it was, Colonel-General von Plessen was tactless enough to turn to the Prince and remark: 'I hope Your Royal Highness fully realises what you have done?' Ernst August was beside himself with anger. With that remark, we had received but a foretaste of what was yet to come.

One could perceive how new and unaccustomed Ernst August was to the life and activities in Berlin and at the Imperial Court. It wasn't just that it was a new dimension for him. Above all it was the strangeness of his surroundings which he had to get used to, and which my father gallantly tried to ease for him. In the same way, my mother solicitously took care of her future son-in-law. He had fully won her affections. She was absolutely certain she had found a thoroughly trustworthy man for her daughter, and therein lay her consolation for the day when she thought she would finally lose me.

Ernst August stayed in Berlin for four days, then went to his parents in Gmunden where he was to remain until he returned to us on February 27, my parents' wedding anniversary. He wrote me from there expressing the earnest wish that our reunion would not take place in the presence of a third party. 'I don't like people to be there and stare,' he wrote, 'for they are all kill-joys. You don't like it either when folks say, "oh, how touching, etc." ' I felt exactly the same way as Ernst August.

Later, he and I and my mother left Berlin for Gmunden, but her enthusiasm for the visit waned, for we had never met the Hanoverian family and as we neared the Guelph residence we were filled with anxiety. I perceived it clearly in my mother and I, too, felt tense at having to come face to face with my in-laws. However, all our tremulous expectations proved groundless. The Duke and Duchess came to meet our train accompanied by Princess Friederike, a daughter of the late King of Hanover, by Princess Olga, Ernst August's unmarried sister, and by their sons-in-law Friedrich Franz of Mecklenburg and Max of Baden, both with their wives. In fact, the whole family appeared.

We were affectionately received by the Duke and Duchess, and from the first there was a marvellously close harmony between us. The Duchess, Thyra, was a small, elegant and efficient woman with proverbially beautiful eyes reflecting perhaps a somewhat sad expression. One loved her immediately. The Duke wore Austrian General's uniform. He was tall and slim, was softly spoken and his face exuded friendliness.

The greetings over, we went on to Gmunden where we were received by the Prince's Court and State representatives. We then proceeded through the district to the castle in a procession of one carriage drawn by six horses and six carriages-and-four—the two mothers and Prince Ernst August and I in the same carriage—escorted by Court personnel in red English livery. It was the first time I had set eyes on the enchanting landscape of the Trauensee and the mountains which would become so close to my heart. They were covered in light snow which glittered in the March sunlight and on top of the castle the German Empress's standard and a Prussian flag fluttered in the breeze.

The Duke and Duchess lived a peaceable, delightfully model life together and their genteel character impressed itself on the Gmunden milieu. Tactfully, they both helped us through the various difficulties, though there arose precarious situations which we would rather have avoided. There were, for instance some strict Guelphs who made no secret of their reservations concerning the Prussian presence at their Court. Typical of these was Fritz Freise, an old valet and a splendid little man who, when approached by Ernst August and told that he had just become engaged, Freise merely countered with, 'Have you renounced your claims, then?' When the Prince denied having done so, Freise retorted, 'Then I congratulate you!'

Less amusing was a suggestion made by Princess Friederike, who encountered me quite unexpectedly one day. She conversed with me for a while, then suggested that I knew that I also had to get married the English way. I was more than slightly shocked. 'English way?' What was that? No one had spoken of it before. I rushed to my fiancé and asked him what his aunt had meant. Ernst August immediately sought out my father-in-law and both were beside themselves with irritation at the Princess's meddling. The old Duke made a decision on the spot: there was to be no question at all of marriage the English way. Slowly, I calmed down again and my mother, too, soon recovered from the shock.

Then the Duke explained what it all meant. Marriage the English way, he said, was the way of indicating that even the House of Hanover belonged to the English Royal Family. In English law, according to the Royal Marriages Act of 1772, the King had the right to signify his approval or rejection of all marriages of Princes and Princesses who were descendants of George III even if they lived abroad. The English Ministers responsible had to investigate each case then advise the King. The Royal Marriages Act also laid down in detail what should be done should any Prince refuse to submit to the regulations, even to the extent of the punishment to be meted out if somebody should contract a marriage contrary to the Act. Our minds were set at rest when my father-in-law expressly ordered that consent would not be obtained in its usual form, but that he would send instead a formal notification of the marriage to the King.

When we began our journey back from Gmunden I knew that in the Duke and Duchess I could not have found more loving or affectionate parents-in-law. The parting was painful to me.

Two weeks after our return to Berlin, Ernst August followed. But he had only been with us a few days when he received instructions from Gmunden to attend the funeral ceremonies of the murdered Greek King in Athens. Once more we had to part, and I was afraid that somehow or another Germany would be drawn into the Balkan entanglement and my fiancé with it.

At the beginning of April my parents-in-law, and Ernst August and I gathered at Bad Homburg. It was a meeting of great significance. My father wanted to get to know the Hanoverian family and to finalise the form of my wedding. Both fathers-in-law immediately formed an understanding, just as the two families already had, and I was happy to see my Poll—which is what I called Ernst August— once more.

6   *At the Altar*

Heavy clouds of bitter strife in the political arena concerning my forthcoming wedding lay oppressively over us. Its consequences for the State were debated in passionate, often extremely worded articles in the Press. The extremists among the Guelph partisans trumpeted, 'No renunciation of Hanover! We fight on!' They demanded in thinly veiled terms that Prince Ernst August's accession to the Brunswick Throne should also mark the beginning of a Guelph restoration in Hanover. On the other hand there were those who considered the Guelph Party as notorious enemies of the State, and that an alliance between the two ruling Houses would endanger the whole country. The prudent and temperate attitude of many Guelph leaders, however, became suspect and was considered a blind by the opposition. The extremists also categorically demanded the dissolution of the German-Hanoverian Party. Prince Ernst August's oath, too, was not acknowledged, and it was alleged that it would not hinder him from agitating for the Hanoverian Throne. There were hundreds of such blind, biased polemical articles filling the pages of newspapers.

Interested parties submitted material to my father, which in some way could have been injurious to the Guelphs. They pressed him for additional guarantees and, more specifically, that above all he had to demand the renunciation of Hanover both by the old Duke and his son. Even the head of the Kaiser's Civil Cabinet, Rudolf von Valentini, inclined to this view. In fact, they simply tried everything. They even demanded I persuade my fiancé to sign a declaration of renunciation, but I refused. In Homburg I told Ernst August, 'I have here a document which I'm going to read to you. I'm certain that you won't acknowledge what's in it, and I wouldn't expect anything else of you.'

The altercation between the representatives of the Prussian and Hanoverian claimants overshadowed the Homburg gathering. Reich Chancellor Bethmann Hollweg and Count Eulenburg, who had accompanied us, supported one side. Supporting the other was Baron Georg von der Wense, while Prince Max of Baden steered the middle course. It was a blessing that we were all in the neighbouring area of Saalburg, for the two sets of parents could repair there at times while the protagonists carried on with their controversy.

Had it not been for the great understanding between Ernst August and myself I suppose our prospects of marriage would have been hopeless. After a lot of painstaking and excited comings and goings the parties finally reached agreement. He who makes the final great concession, shows the end solution. Hanover was not to be renounced. Even Prince Ernst August was not compelled to pronounce *expressis verbis*, an absolute renunciation, and so a paraphrasing formula was accepted.

In order to express the understanding reached between the Hohenzollerns and the Guelphs, my father bestowed the Order of the Black Eagle upon the Duke of Cumberland—with the Duke's concurrence—and the Duchess was decorated with the Order of Queen Luise. So it was that the Homburg meeting cleared the way for my marriage. At last!

At approximately the same time, our marriage contract was signed, a so-called marriage pact, which was dignified in its expression, legal and sober in its material parts. Today, it must be a truly cultural and historical document. In it, it said *inter alia*:

'By God's Divine Providence and Dispensation and through the establishment between the two high Houses of a sincere friendship, and after mature advice and reflection, a matrimonial union has been agreed and concluded between Her Royal Highness the Princess Viktoria Luise Adelheid Mathilde Charlotte and His Royal Highness the Prince Ernst August Christian Georg, and we hereby consent to the above-mentioned marriage contract and hereupon royally promise to honour and uphold it. . . .'

'We, Ernst August, Duke of Cumberland, Duke of Brunswick
and Lüneburg, with the consent of our dearly beloved consort,
Thyra, Duchess of Cumberland, Duchess of Brunswick and
Lüneburg, Princess of Denmark, Royal Highness, promise and
betroth our dearly beloved son, the Prince Ernst August
Christian Georg, Duke of Brunswick and Lüneburg, Royal
Highness, to her Royal Highness the Princess Viktoria Luise
Adelheid Mathilde Charlotte of Prussia, and We Wilhelm,
Emperor of Germany and King of Prussia, with the consent of
our dearly beloved consort Her Majesty the Empress and Queen,
promise and betroth our dearly beloved daughter the Princess
Viktoria Luise Adelheid Mathilde Charlotte, Royal Highness,
to the Prince Ernst August Christian Georg, Duke of Brunswick
and Lüneburg, Royal Highness, as legitimate consort and as
legitimate husband, and We Prince Ernst August Christian
Georg, Duke of Brunswick and Lüneburg, and We Viktoria
Luise Adelheid Mathilde Charlotte, Princess of Prussia, hereby
mutually promise to take and to hold one another in matrimony
and also to ratify this marriage on a specially appointed day and
at a specially appointed place before the registrar for the serene
members of the Prussian Royal House and there to be married
in accordance with the rites of the Evangelical Church and thereafter with the holy help and blessing of God remain true and
upright and loving throughout our lives, and may the Almighty
grant us His Blessing and everlasting prosperity.'

Then came the material part. A dowry of 150,000 Marks was
settled. My father promised to provide his daughter with 'princely
dresses, jewels, gems and other things executed in such a manner as a
Princess of Our Royal House selects or is her due'. Apart from the
dowry and the paraphernalia to be provided for a married woman, I
was given 450,000 Marks as a 'special fatherly favour' from the
Kaiser's Privy Purse.

Now it was time to prepare for the wedding. The first thing that had
to be done was to find a house in Rathenow, the garrison town where
Ernst August would be stationed and where we would live until he

assumed control of the Government of Brunswick. We found one to rent. It was very nice but hardly a show place. With eight rooms for us and the servants as well as a lady-in-waiting, it certainly wasn't much. It was Baron von Lichtenstern, my fiancé's adjutant and the old Duke's valet, who chose the house and first set eyes on it, and I inspected it with Ernst August and my mother. It really was very small, but I thought it was wonderful. An idea which we cherished, Ernst August and I, was that soon at least we would be by ourselves. 'It would be splendid if we could have the wedding here,' he told me, 'and we could live in peace.'

That wasn't just an expression of our longing, but also a cry from the heart. During those weeks we were beset the whole time by people, particularly by the ladies-in-waiting and Court officials. Everyone wanted to give advice concerning the Princess's wedding, and each had his own opinion and each knew better than anyone else. These counsels were often well meant, but some were given out of sheer vanity or pomposity. My mother just could not escape from them, and her nervousness increased day by day. I myself stood right in the middle of all this hubbub, but at least I had the support of daily letters from my fiancé. Ernst August wrote:

'I'm sorry for your mother. Do try to get her to keep calm. I'm very angry with these ladies for they are to blame for making her so nervous. When you consider that none of these women is married, how can they want to involve themselves in such affairs? Furthermore, they have nothing to do with it and I will not tolerate it. My Mama has always told me never to let ladies-in-waiting meddle in your affairs or in those of your wife, for these matters are the concern of you two only and belong to the holy side of marriage. You know, I understand your mother perfectly. She naturally wants the best for you, but she is an Empress and wants to have you just as she is, but she forgets that she is still an Empress. Do you understand what I mean? I have no use in my life for an Empress as wife, because I'm not an Emperor. I want to stand outside that sort of life, and want my wife to, too. You're going to take your place as my wife, and will certainly fulfil your rôle, of that I am strongly convinced.'

Another time he told me in one of his letters:

'Now you're stepping out into real life and getting to know the world, lit up from a completely different angle, and you'll often be surprised how wicked the world is. That's what I discovered when I went out into it . . . You have been told of such confidential matters so early, because you're going to marry someone who has really no easy life. I'm not complaining about it; on the contrary, because one knows where one is.

You must be sensible and keep calm always, and leave the struggle to me. We will conduct our marriage in the way that we think is right. That is something in which no one has the right to interfere. Listen to everything quietly, without uttering a sound, and at the most say, "that is my future husband's business." Be convinced that I will not tolerate anyone interfering in our personal affairs. . . . Soon we will be together, and we will have peace and quiet.'

The 20th of May was my last day in the New Palace, and on the 21st Ernst August arrived. In his last letter he had told me what arrangements he had made to keep our honeymoon location secret from prying eyes. It was planned that we should go first to the hunting lodge at Werbellinsee, then to the Hubertihaus, my father-in-law's hunting lodge near Gmunden. He made me promise not to tell anyone at all and even in Gmunden itself our plans were kept strictly secret.

The first wedding guests to arrive were the King and Queen of England, and my parents went to the Lehrter Station in Berlin to greet them. George V had put on his Prussian General's uniform for the occasion and, with an escort of Dragoon Guards and Cuirassiers, the Royal couple drove through Berlin. More than half a century was to pass before an English Head of State was to come to Germany again, when Queen Elizabeth II, George V's grand-daughter, came in 1965.

Early on the following day my great-aunt Luise, Prince Max of Baden and his wife arrived, then a little later my parents-in-law and my sister-in-law, Olga. The First Guards Regiment of Foot formed the guard of honour, while the Cuirassiers again provided the escort as we travelled to the castle in three carriages. My father sat with the Duke, who wore his Austrian uniform, in the first carriage; my mother with the Duchess Thyra in the next, while Princess Olga, my fiancé and I sat together in the third.

At midday the Czar of Russia arrived and the colourful welcoming ceremonies began all over again. Wearing the uniform of the Alexander Grenadier Guards Regiment and the tall Frederick the Great cap on his head, Nicholas II's truly imposing appearance drove the waiting Berliners into a frenzy of excitement and wonder.

The arrival of all the wedding guests turned Berlin into a magnificent showcase, a display of Royalty rarely seen before. Masses of people gathered in the streets of the capital to witness the parade of princes. They had come from everywhere to line the route the wedding guests would pass, and the sight of the tremendous throng in Unter den Linden Opera Platz, and in front of the castle was indescribable. 'The police had more than their hands full to protect the lives in the ever-pressing multitude,' the local *Berlin Anzeiger* newspaper reported. 'The great, immeasurable mass of people did not, could not, break ranks . . . every carriage which passed was greeted with tremendous cheers. It was an unforgettable sight. The people's joy knew no bounds.'

For the sightseers, there was more to gape at than just the parade. They saw King George V later visiting the Mess of the 1st Dragoon Guards Regiment, then cheered him on his way to the British Embassy. They looked on when he visited the Berlin garrison's parade ground at Tempelhof, then when he made an extensive ride on horseback to watch the Dragoon Guards at battle practice. They had their view of Queen Mary, too, when she went to inspect the castles and gardens in Potsdam, particularly when she arrived at the Sans Souci which aroused her enthusiasm tremendously. King George also participated in the traditional, great spring parade in Potsdam. Together with my father, he rode past the drawn-up ranks of troops, then, riding at the head of the regiment, my father led the *Garde du Corps* Regiment in a march before the English King.

For my father-in-law it was an opportune moment to get to know Berlin and its inhabitants. He wanted to see everything, but naturally in peace and quiet. He took off his uniform and put on a mountaineering suit so that he could go around unrecognised. I seem to remember he put on a cloak on top of that in case he attracted attention!

Czar Nicholas chose to visit the Arsenal and the Hall of Fame, inspected the Emperor Alexander Grenadier Guards Regiment, then had lunch at the Russian Embassy. The Czar was very pleased to be in Berlin because he could move about much more freely—and clearly enjoyed it—but for us, that gave rise to a great deal of anxiety regarding his safety. Once, without informing anyone, he went for a car ride with Prince Heinrich. Nobody knew about it, and when the Kaiser found out, he was absolutely furious because he felt personally responsible for the Czar's safety, and the police, too, were quite staggered by Nicholas's action.

For me, the wedding celebrations began with the reception of deputations who had come bringing gifts. My father's present to me was a diadem and a pearl necklace, while my mother gave me a diamond tiara. King George and Queen Mary gave me a prodigious gold goblet and a diamond brooch; Ernst August a complete jewellery outfit. The English Queen Mother, Alexandra, gave me an emerald brooch. From the Czar I received an aquamarine and diamond necklace; the Italian King and Queen sent me antique silver vessels and Queen Wilhelmina of Holland an antique pendulum clock. There were presents galore, from the Kings of Denmark and Sweden down to the various cities in Germany, and from Brunswick I received a diadem which had once belonged to the French Empress Josephine. The number of gifts was so great they required several furniture vans to carry them.

One thing which was not on view was my bridal trousseau.

The real celebrations began on the evening of the day before the wedding, with a gala opera when the Royal Court Opera put on Richard Wagner's *Lohengrin*. The Opera House, when I arrived, was bedecked with my favourite flowers, pink carnations, and as we took our places in the Royal Box with our parents, all those present rose from their seats, and Ernst August and I bowed right, left and centre. As one, the entire audience bowed back.

Next day, 24 May, was my wedding day. Early in the afternoon my mother helped me on with my bridal crown and veil. Then we repaired to the Chinese Room, and we found that a unit of soldiers had formed lines throughout the castle and taken up sentry posts everywhere. There was a bodyguard from the 1st Guards Regiment, the Castle Guard in their historic Frederick the Great uniforms, the *Garde du Corps* in ceremonial dress, and the gendarmerie.

At 4 p.m. members of the staff of the Royal Privy Purse came by, carrying the bridal crown of the Princess of Prussia. Then the Mistress of the Empress's Household, Therese, Countess von Brockdorff, picked up the crown and ceremoniously handed it to my mother who carefully placed it on my head. We then proceeded to the chamber deemed the 'Elector's Room' where my father received us, and Count Eulenberg, the Minister for the Royal House, completed the formalities regarding the marriage pact and the official registration of the marriage. As Ernst August and I signed the register, we heard a loud buzzing overhead above the castle. We all rushed to the windows and there above us was the airship *Hansa*, all gaily decorated with colourful pennants. Suddenly, a large bouquet of flowers came floating down from the airship. It was their way of congratulating us.

After the civil ceremony, the bridal procession, led by the Corps of Pages, wound its way through the Picture Gallery and the White Hall to the castle chapel. Behind the pages walked two Heralds with the Brandenburg and Prussian Coat of Arms, then the Chief Marshal, Prince zu Fürstenberg with his big Marshal's staff, and finally Ernst August and me. Behind us were the Kaiser in the uniform of the 1st Guards Regiment, with the Duchess of Cumberland in a lilac-coloured gown, then the Generals and the Admirals, and then the Kaiserin in a light green robe escorted by the Duke of Cumberland in his Austrian uniform. Then the Czar of Russia, in his Hussar uniform, escorted the Queen of England. The King of England, in his Cuirassier uniform, escorted the Crown Princess. Then they were followed by a whole host of Princes, including my brothers, and Princesses, Dukes and Duchesses.

It was 5 p.m. by the time we reached the chapel to be greeted by the sound of music from the organ. All the seats were filled with invited guests, who included the Reich Chancellor, the Ministers of

State and their wives, members of the Federal Council and the Field Marshals.

Bright sunlight filtered through the chapel cupola as Ernst August and I stepped up to the altar which my mother and Crown Princess Cecilie, my sister-in-law, had decorated with roses, carnations and wreaths. Pastor Dryander then delivered his sermon, earnest and worthy words which warned me about the seriousness of life.

After that came the actual marriage ceremony. Ernst August's 'yes' rang out so loudly and clearly that I had to follow suit and when we joined hands in front of the altar he clasped mine very firmly, insisting that his thumbs were on top of mine. You see, there's an old folk-tale which says that if the husband does not have his thumbs above those of his bride at the wedding ceremony then he will have no say during his marriage. Pastor Dryander looked slightly shocked at this little demonstration, but Ernst August and I just smiled at each other. Mary, the Queen of England, however, was so overcome by the whole ceremony that she broke into a flood of tears. Later, they used to say that she had sobbed because she had at that moment foreseen the forthcoming disaster of war the following year breaking over us. That is really out of the question. Queen Mary was very attached to the Guelph family and it was understandable that the ceremony should affect her.

As soon as the vows and rings had been exchanged, the battery of the 1st Guards Field Artillery Regiment fired a 36-gun salute, the chapel bells rang out in loud peals, and the wedding party made its way to the White Hall again, where we stood under the canopy of the Throne and received congratulations from the guests filing past, as the orchestra played the 'Wedding March' from *Midsummer Night's Dream*. My husband and I had my father standing to our right together with my mother-in-law, Queen Mary and the Czar, and on our left my mother, my father-in-law, Crown Princess Cecilie and King George V.

The ceremonial banquet began at 7 p.m. and was attended by one thousand one hundred guests. The remarkable thing about it was that the food was dished up by Lieutenant-General Baron von Süsskind, the Inspector of the Militia, at one end of the table and by Lieutenant-General von Falk, the Inspector of the War Academy, at the other.

They served the food then passed the plates to the lackeys, who handed them to the Court officials, and so on to each guest.

During the banquet my father rose and proposed a toast to us:

> 'My darling daughter,' he said, 'today, as you leave our house, I want to thank you from the bottom of my heart for all the joy you have given me and your mother, and for the ray of sunshine which you have been in our house. You have given your hand and your heart to a man who comes from an honourable German sovereign House and from an old German stock. As long as the German tongue is spoken and as far away as it will sound, it will tell of the prominent rôle played by the Guelphs and Hohenzollerns in the historical development of our Fatherland. You do not have to be told that you are free to follow the dictates of your heart, and to choose the man you love.'

Addressing Ernst August, he went on:

> 'I hereby entrust our child to you. We have the fullest confidence that you will protect her and care for her and that her sunshine will enter into your house. . . . Above all things, however, despite your youth, you will come to serve and care for others. May this duty be the finest accomplishment of your life and may the love of other people warm your heart. May you both, and you, my daughter above all, be loyal to your new House.'

As soon as the dinner was over, the White Hall became the setting for the traditional torch-dance, a sort of polonaise which, in earlier times, was danced with senior Court officials carrying big, heavy candles ahead of the procession of dancers. For these elderly gentlemen then it was certainly no easy task, but in my time these duties were taken over by the pages, who were physically better equipped. My father gave the Chief Marshal orders for the torch-dance to begin. Prince zu Fürstenberg came up to my husband and me, bowed, and invited us to lead the dance. The band of the Guards Cuirassiers struck up a polonaise, the Chief Marshal placed himself at the head of the procession of dancers and, with twelve pages lined up two by two behind him, signalled for Ernst August and me to lead off the dance round the room.

'There was a look of joy and happiness on the faces of the newly-wedded pair and also on the countenance of the Kaiser and Kaiserin', an observer wrote later. 'It was a glittering spectacle, full of dignity and charm, particularly the sight of the Chief Marshal wielding his tall staff, leading the twelve tall, young, and handsome pages in their red coats, jabots and swords behind him, and the bright flaming torches held aloft. Then there was the bridegroom leading his bride by the hand, and the four maids of honour in pink who were carrying her train. After the first round was over, the bride approached the Kaiser, bowed, and invited him and the Duke of Cumberland to join her in the dance. At the same time, the bridegroom approached the Kaiserin and the Duchess of Cumberland and invited them to join him. A new round began. At the next round, the bride asked the King of England and the Czar of Russia to dance, while the bridegroom sought out the Queen of England and the Crown Princess.'

The spectacle of my dancing with the King of England and the Czar of Russia absolutely fascinated everybody present. It wasn't something that happened every day, of course, but there were the rulers of the two mightiest nations on Earth, with the daughter of the German Kaiser between them, all dancing together. At the end of the dance the Czar turned to me and said: 'My wish is that you will be as happy as I am.' I have never forgotten those words: they were the last I was ever to hear from Czar Nicholas.

The torch-dance was over. I left the room on my father's arm, while my husband escorted my mother. The Prussian Princess's Crown was taken away from me and given back for safe keeping to the officials of the Privy Purse. Then my mother lifted off my bridal wreath. The hour of parting had struck.

We changed our clothes and went to the station accompanied by my father and four of my brothers. Adalbert and Oskar stayed with my mother, for at this moment of our parting she could not be left alone. She took it very badly when I left her, but I had written her a letter which she would find on her bed when she retired. My brothers excelled themselves in looking after her after I had gone, and Oskar stayed in her dressing-room all night so as to be on hand if she needed him.

That day my mother finally closed up the book which she had begun about me twenty-one years before. The last sentences she wrote read:

> 'I shall say nothing about myself, except that it seemed that my heart was breaking. I could only pray, particularly as I knelt at my child's bed during the night, God protect my child, my youngest. Make her happy, O Lord'

When we got to the station it was time to say goodbye to my father. I curtsied very low then kissed the Kaiser's hand; he took me in his arms, held me a long time, and kissed me very affectionately. The farewell between Ernst August and the Kaiser, too, was very affectionate. I then embraced my brothers and Eitel-Fritz threw rice over me to bring me luck.

My husband and I then boarded the train, followed by my father, while my brothers remained behind. Once more I kissed my father's hand. Then on the platform once again, he personally gave the signal for the train to depart and, as it rolled slowly away, the Kaiser watched and continued to wave until we vanished from his view.

7 *Clouds of War*

The honeymoon was over. We had spent it climbing in the mountains and walking through the woods around Gmunden. Now it was time to settle down in Brunswick where, during the intervening period, the government prepared for the official hand-over of administration to my husband. As expected, there were constitutional difficulties and political party squabbles all hinging on the enormity that the old Duke of Cumberland had relinquished the Throne to his son who had, of all things, married me, a Prussian Princess. However, by 3 November 1913, the path had been cleared for Ernst August's accession, and we made a triumphal entry into a beflagged Brunswick escorted by a squadron of the Brunswick Hussars.

Back in June of that year it had been the twenty-fifth anniversary of the Kaiser's accession to the Throne, and the whole country celebrated on a vast scale. Congratulations poured in from every part of Germany and the people's enthusiasm knew no bounds. The streets of Berlin were impassable, crammed with festively dressed folk waving innumerable flags. They were rejoicing in twenty-five years of peace and golden economic boom. Our people had experienced a material upswing rarely before seen in the nation's history. Trade, industry and agriculture were many times better off than ever. German trade alone had doubled since the beginning of the century and now led the world, surpassing even that of England, the world's traditional top-trading nation.

How the rest of the world reacted to my father's reign thus far is best seen through the eyes of F. W. Wile, the Berlin correspondent of the London *Daily Mail* and the *New York Times*. He wrote:

> 'Wilhelm II celebrates his silver anniversary. Twenty-five years have brought the Reich to the peak of its national greatness. Under his active leadership the Fatherland has reached the pinnacle in its peaceful pursuit of commerce and industry and has become the mightiest military force in the world . . . These successes combine to equate the name of Germany with progress and power. The whole world, fascinated by his interesting personality, attributes to the Kaiser the exceptional manner by which the Fatherland has been spectacularly elevated to the status of a world power. As Managing Director of Germany Ltd, Kaiser Wilhelm has had a difficult rôle to play yet has succeeded in fulfilling his duties with eminent success.'

My father was a monarch at the time of radical change. 'Another world, a new world!' as Bismarck exclaimed when he appeared once at Hamburg harbour. He perceived then the breezes heralding a new era and it was my father who had to deal with this future. Unlike very many of his contemporaries he understood the meaning of the forthcoming changes. 'We are in a state of transition,' he said back in 1892 and also in 1906 when he was referring in a speech to 'the century of the motor car'. Not a few shook their heads dolefully at what they considered was pure fantasy. 'This is the era of communication,' the Kaiser continued, 'and the big questions which confront us will not be understood. But our times demand a race that does understand . . . freedom of thought and freedom for our scientific research.'

It was he who initiated the integration of polytechnics into the universities, and his endeavours resulted in two institutions, the Kaiser Wilhelm Society for Scientific Research in 1911 and the Kaiser Wilhelm Institute for Chemistry in 1912 being named after him, though the first was changed to the Max Planck Society after the Second World War.

The great strides forward and the successes which attended his efforts during the twenty-five years of his reign vindicated his judgement completely. He had ascended the Imperial Throne when only twenty-nine and now, at fifty-five, was a man of rich experience. He could read the signs of the times. We, who were near to him, were fully aware of the care with which he took all political developments into consideration. My father knew of the dangers which faced Germany as a result of her powerful economic upsurge. In contrast to his Chancellor, Bethmann Hollweg, he suspected that in the event of a European conflict England would set herself against Germany, and that such knowledge would encourage both France and Russia to join the war. He knew that the interests of these great powers were directed against an immensely strengthened German Empire but in the long run there was no way of preventing a concerted military action against us. When Bethmann Hollweg produced a memorandum in December 1912, which suggested that in the event of a war with France and Russia on the one side and Germany on the other, England's participation would at least be doubtful, my father remarked, '*I* don't doubt it for a moment.'

Despite my youth—and sex—I watched the continuous development of these struggles for power. My family were far from unaware of my keeness in what was going on and I found this entry in my mother's diary—'Sissy interests herself a great deal in political events.'

The *Daily Telegraph* affair had shown those, who had wanted to see, which way such things were going. In 1912 there had been an internal political landslide when the Social Democrats won one hundred and ten seats in the elections for the Reichstag whereas they had only had forty-three members elected previously, and the Conservatives and National Liberals had sustained large losses. The latter's total share of the mandate amounted only to approximately twenty-five per cent. This, then, was the state of the parties before the outbreak of war.

The attitude of the Conservatives could be summed up from a remark made by one of their members, Elard von Oldenburg-Januschau who told the Liberal, Konrad Haussmann, in a debate in the Reichstag, 'For you, the Kaiser is an institution, but for us he is a person and we will serve His Majesty the Kaiser personally as long as we live.' Seldom has the essentially different attitude towards Monarch and Monarchy been put so succinctly. On the one side were the feudal conceptions of the Junkers, and on the other the constitutional, thinking citizen. It is instructive that Haussmann had the great majority of the Reichstag behind him in that debate, whereas Oldenburg-Januschau had few friends.

The ceremonial opening of the Reichstag of 1912 took place in the White Hall of the Imperial Palace with glittering pomp, in the same sort of colourful pageant which is still the tradition in England today. There were fanfares as the assembled members of the Reichstag, the Federal Councillors and the various dignitaries awaited the arrival of the Kaiser. Ahead of the Imperial procession were the Castle Guard Company, the Heralds and Court Marshals, then the bearers of the Imperial Insignia. Count Schlieffen carried the Crown, Colonel-General von Kessel the Imperial Standard, Grand Admiral von Tirpitz the Imperial Orb, Field Marshal von der Goltz the Sceptre, War Minister Josias von Heeringen the Sword, and General von Moltke the Privy Seal. Following them came the Kaiser with his sons, the Princes, behind him. He then formally opened the Reichstag with a speech from the Throne. Unfortunately, not all of the Reichstag members were present, the largest faction, the one hundred and ten Social Democrats being conspicuous by their absence.

Just as it was the unfulfilled final aim of my father's foreign policy to preserve the peace among the Great Powers, so he did not succeed in dominating the militant Socialist movement within Germany. Nevertheless he had personally wanted that the best should be done in the interests of the working class. As far back as 1889, at the start of his reign, he had declared that any legislation concerning the working population should aim at their protection in accordance with Christian moral principles, and had throughout maintained this as axiomatic. In his speech from the Throne in 1912, he confirmed that in one generation only social legislation had taken a tremendous step forward. 'This social spirit must be carried further,' he said. 'Evolution does not stand still.' But to demand one man to guide this evolution into other channels, too, meant the exercise of super-human strength, yet that was what was expected of my father. He was, after all, a mere man, and as Kaiser bound by the limitations of a constitutional Monarch.

In March 1914 at five o'clock in the morning, I brought our first child into the world, and we called him Ernst August. Brunswick was jubilant at the birth of an heir and flags hung from every house while never-ending cheers emanated from outside the castle itself. My husband immediately telegraphed our parents and relatives of the news. The first reply we had came from Emperor Franz Josef of Austria. The news had reached his desk at Schönbrunn Palace in Vienna at 6 a.m. when he was already at work. He was so overjoyed that he wanted to go at once to the house of my parents-in-law, who were living in Vienna at the time, to congratulate them personally. His Adjutant-General, Count Paar, could only restrain him with difficulty, saying that such an early hour was hardly the time to pay a visit. However, as the Duke and Duchess laughingly told me later, the old Emperor refused to wait beyond 7 a.m., got into his carriage and was driven post-haste to their home. Fortunately, they had been warned well in advance that he was coming.

Our son's christening took place in May, in the venerable cathedral over Henry the Lion's vault with my parents and all of my brothers in attendance. We had already asked King George V of England and Czar Nicholas of Russia if they would be godfathers and King George cabled from Windsor Castle—'It will give me great pleasure to be Godfather to your little son. I hope Sissy is quite strong again. We send her best love.—George.'

Our son had plenty of godfathers—Emperor Franz Josef of Austria, Czar Nicholas, King George, King Ludwig III of Bavaria, my father the Kaiser, Prince Max of Baden, Grand Duke Friedrich-Franz of Mecklenburg-Schwerin, the Duke of Cumberland, my brothers Adalbert and Oskar, and the 1st Royal Bavarian Heavy Cavalry Regiment. My mother and the Duchess of Cumberland were godmothers. It was probably the last time that such a pageant of royal godparents would be gathered together as in olden days.

The following month my husband and I took part in the centennial celebrations of the 1st Heavy Cavalry Regiment in Munich and then went on a motor trip through the Dolomites to Merano in the Tyrol. It was in a hotel there that we heard from a liftboy the dreadful news of the assassination in Sarajevo of the heir to the Austro-Hungarian throne, Archduke Franz-Ferdinand. This was a Sunday, 28 June.

During our absence Emperor Franz Josef had been visiting my parents-in-law in Gmunden to see my little son. We immediately set out for home and when we saw him he was no longer his serene self: the gravity of the situation was clearly reflected in his whole demeanour. After the meal we had together, he took me to one side, the old Emperor clearly cognisant that he was facing the most fateful trial in his country's history. His last words to me were: 'Tell your father that I am counting on his friendship and loyalty to the Federation at this time.' I executed his commission forthwith.

At the beginning of July my father had wanted to go on his usual Nordic trip, but in view of the crisis which developed as a result of Franz-Ferdinand's murder he decided to stay in Berlin. The Reich Chancellor, Bethmann Hollweg, and the Foreign Office, however, were strongly opposed to his decision. They considered that by carrying out his planned journey he would contribute to the maintenance of international calm, whereas if he stayed he would arouse mistrust and so hot up the crisis even more. My father was not convinced by the cogency of this argument. Bethmann Hollweg told him bluntly that if the crisis developed into a warlike situation and the Kaiser had publicly cancelled his proclaimed holiday, then he would be blamed personally for any outbreak of hostilities. 'Then it is Your Majesty who will be responsible,' he went on. 'The whole world waits only for the redeeming news that the German Kaiser has gone off on his journey.' On the 6th of July, my father went.

The severity of the crisis weighed heavily upon everyone. We decided to break our stay in Gmunden and hurried back to Brunswick, hoping to the very last that the mounting threat of a great war would be avoided at the eleventh hour. But then my husband received his mobilisation orders and reported to the X Army Corps in Hanover.

A few days after my husband's departure I went to see my father, who had returned from his Norwegian trip on 27 July. Whilst on the cruise he had informed the Chancellor and the Foreign Office that he considered it essential he should return. Invariably he received the reply that it was not necessary and that he should carry on. My father was seized with anguished anxieties, all the more so because he was given such sparse news from Berlin and had to rely heavily only on Norwegian newspapers. Finally, when he read in the Press of Austria's ultimatum to Serbia, he took it upon himself to return home at once.

On that August day when I saw my father again, our Ambassador in London, Prince Karl Max Lichnowsky, reported to him. The Ambassador told the Kaiser he was convinced that he personally had been conducive in effecting an improvement in Anglo-German relations, and that he had not believed in a war between the two countries. He was therefore thunderstruck, he told my father, when the English Foreign Minister, Sir Edward Grey, coolly informed him immediately before the outbreak of war that he should not draw political conclusions from his social and personal contacts.

Since I had last seen my father in May, a world had been demolished and my father thoroughly shattered by the turn of events. I could see that at once. His thoughts were concentrated on the depressing fact that all his desperate efforts had not enabled him to extinguish the flames of war, or at least to localise them. That was the essential theme of the conversations he held with me. The bitterness of his words revealed that he, too, despite all the manifest scepticism, had fervently hoped that at the last minute a personal understanding between him and King George V would ward off the great calamity. Regarding Lichnowsky's failure, my father remarked that the Ambassador's use of social contacts to interpret their political views was because 'the German is accustomed to express his aversions or his sympathies even in their outside forms of social intercourse. The Englishman is detached from these things.' A pertinent example the accuracy of which is still being proved by History.

My father told me of the several steps he had taken to prevent the calamity of war. In particular he described his attempts to persuade King George V to keep England neutral, and to keep France and Russia in check. Without England, my father reasoned, both these countries would scarcely be inclined to take the final steps to war. In addition, the Kaiser told me, he had ordered his brother, Prince Heinrich, to talk to King George with this reasoning in mind. My uncle was staying with his family in St Moritz when the Kaiser's request reached him. He hurried to England at once and stayed there for two days. On 26 July he was able to speak to King George. According to Heinrich's report to my father, the King told him— 'We shall try all we can to keep out of this and shall remain neutral.'

Prince Heinrich reassured my father of his own conviction that the King had seriously meant what he said. 'Georgie', he went on, 'was in earnest mood, his reasoning was logical, and he had the most serious and sincerest determination to prevent a world conflagration —and he was counting strongly on your co-operation.' My father had taken King George's words as a promise of neutrality, and they aroused new hopes within him of being able to maintain peace. Admiral von Tirpitz, though, had his doubts. 'I have the word of a King,' the Kaiser lectured him, 'and that's good enough for me.'

That England should now turn against us evoked my father's strongest condemnation. He became very angry with King George who, he believed, had deceived him. My father had manifestly not perceived that his English cousin did not possess the same political weight as Edward VII. George always considered himself a constitutional Monarch, more a figurehead than a politician, while Edward's influence and power reached considerably far afield. My father's wrath also extended to the Czar, but Nicholas's attitude on the outbreak of war was not that which my father would have believed. For that matter the Czar's freedom of action, though not constitutional, was certainly circumscribed. He was well nigh powerless, for instance, against the Pan-Slavonic warmongers.

When I sent a report of the above to my cousin Sigismund, one of Prince Heinrich's sons who now lives in Costa Rica, for checking, he made the following observations regarding his father's encounter with the King of England:

> 'As it turned out, family relationships—or friendship between the European Monarchs for that matter—proved quite useless. The secret groups who pulled the strings of global politics were so powerful that familial influences were quite incapable of stopping them, however hard they tried.'

There is little need to expand on this theme: quite clearly the First World War was a war of cabinets, not of Kings.

My father's conversations with me indicated his firm conviction that the war conducted by Russia, France and England was decidedly directed towards the annihilation of Germany, and the Austro-Serbian conflict was only a pretext. He believed that the strength of our people, and in particular that of the army, would overcome this alliance, though he knew it would be a difficult struggle. 'So many enemies!' How often did I hear these words from his lips—as did others! Our old Dr Zunker invariably countered with, 'We'll succeed, Your Majesty!' With this retort it was clear that Dr Zunker was quite aware of the worries besetting my father.

There was no room for any exuberance about the conflict. Nothing showed more clearly how my father felt about it than the fact that on the outbreak of war he changed his room in the castle. He wanted to shut out the noise of the people's jubilation in the streets and the clamorous enthusiasm of the outgoing troops. It was just too much for him.

I went back to Brunswick. Here, I hoped to have some news of my husband in the field, but I was disappointed. Day followed day without even a line from him. Finally, at the end of August, I received the first letter, or should I say, a scribbled note. In a sense, I had grown up among soldiers, but certainly I had no proper idea of the conditions in which they were advancing. In understandable anxiety about my husband, especially when I found out that by some miracle he had survived an artillery barrage, I asked Ernst August to send me more frequent letters. He replied:

> 'It's no better for other wives. You must be patient and be an example to others. At the moment it is a thousand times more important that munitions be moved around and there's a colossal struggle at the moment even to get them to the right place. If you don't get a letter for some time, then you can tell others "thank God at least something more important than the post, namely troops, munitions and provisions, is being dispatched." '

I was anxious about my husband, just as all the other war wives were, and had also the additional worry of being responsible for the Duchy. During my husband's absence, I had been installed as Regent and had to deal to the best of my ability with the running of the State. Naturally I immediately occupied myself with the care of the wounded, and set apart a large block of the castle for use as a hospital.

My husband had marched into Belgium and France with X Army Corps as an officer on the staff of its commander, General Otto von

Emmich. During the advance it had been his duty to liaise with Colonel-General von Bülow's General Headquarters, a task he did not relish. He wanted to be at the front. 'Our men are going forward as if they were on rails, and when one sees these chaps one feels downright ashamed that one cannot go with them. Hats off to each of these ordinary fellows,' he wrote to me.

Then came the first Christmas of the war and I was alone with my son, though not completely alone, for Brunswick, too, kept its vigil. My husband passed his Christmas at Neufchâtel. 'Today is Christmas Eve and we three are separated,' he wrote me. 'It is a severe sacrifice, but in these times it is the least we can do. The worse it is just now, the better it will be later. God bless you.'

Like my husband, all my brothers were in the field, too. Four of them found themselves on the Western Front. The Crown Prince, Wilhelm, commanded the Fifth Army and won one of the first great German victories at Longwy. Eitel-Fritz commanded the 1st Foot-guards Regiment and proved himself at once as an intrepid front line officer, and one knew that he suffered the same hardships as the men of this brave, élite regiment. August Wilhelm was a front-line staff officer and Oskar commanded the famous Liegnitz King's Grenadiers. An outstanding infantry officer, he had proved himself in the first months of the war, showing both prudence and cold-bloodedness. Adalbert was a serving officer on board the battleship *Luitpold*, while my youngest brother, Joachim, a cavalry officer, was wounded in the upper part of the thigh during the battle in the Masurian Lake District of East Prussia.

In the middle of August my father set himself up at the General Headquarters of the army. The turn of events, however, meant that during the war I did not see him very often. But it is worthy of note that once the war had begun, he sought only victory. He believed in the victory, only he never exulted in all the hurrahs despite all the mighty successes at the front.

Despite all the disappointments and extreme bitterness with which my father condemned the behaviour of the King of England and the Czar, he had no feelings of vengeance or hate. Today it may sound remarkable, but at that time it was thought almost a foregone conclusion that war hatred was a reaction which stemmed from the heads

of State and percolated right down to the man in the street. The
Kaiser believed otherwise. One of his orders, for instance, was that
air raids on London, which public opinion emphatically demanded,
should only be carried out if it was certain that Buckingham Palace,
Westminster Abbey and St Paul's Cathedral would not be damaged
and would above all not involve residential districts. Only the most
important military objectives were to be attacked.

It may still sound legendary today, how the Kaiser behaved
towards prisoners of war. In the same way that he visited our own
wounded, he went to see the enemy wounded in hospital without
even asking the officers in charge whether the visit of the German
Kaiser was agreeable to them or not. One characteristic action of my
father was when he one day passed a train carrying French prisoners
of war. He stopped his car and gave orders for the prisoner of war
train to be halted. Then he requested the French officers to step
forward and made a speech in French in which he praised the bravery
of the French army, offered them his sympathy as battle casualties and
promised them they would be honourably treated in the prisoner of
war camps. *That* was the attitude of the German Kaiser to the
conquered.

I publicly admit that whenever I look back and above all when I
consider what we experienced under a degenerate Second World War
leadership, I regain the pride I felt that this knightly, human and
thoughtful man was my father.

Karl Helfferich, at the time the director of the Deutsche Bank, told
me of a conversation he had had with my father when he visited him
at G.H.Q. at the end of August:

'The Kaiser spoke of the prodigious events of the past few weeks
with unreserved frankness. I had the impression of a man who,
despite his good fortune and successes at the front, was most
deeply moved and bore a heavy burden for the decisions he had
had to make. The Kaiser spoke of how he thought the future
would shape if victory were to be his, and considered that for
him the most important thing would be if out of the war there
came a healthy understanding and, in the eventual nature of
things, a happy alliance of the people of the European continent.

D

Of course, this had not been possible before owing to the antipathy between France and Germany. Peace must so be concluded
that this goal can be achieved. The French have always been a
chivalrous nation, with a high concept of honour, and previously
always had respect for, and wanted reconciliation with,
Germany. They understand that it has always been difficult for
their nation to submit to the decision of 1870 without new
recourse to the fortunes of war. So he hoped that after this war,
the French would feel that honour had been satisfied and that on
the conclusion of peace there would be a basis for honourable
and free co-operation both politically and economically between
the two great European civilisations.'

Those were my father's words on 23 August, 1914, as our armies
were winning triumphant victories and a successful end to the war
seemed to be in sight. My father's detailed reasoning demonstrates,
now that Franco-German understanding is an actuality, how he at
least predicted this grand reconciliation half a century before it
happened, and right in the midst of a war with France, too.

The Kaiser was not granted the privilege of bringing his great
ambitions to fruition. In September 1914, the fortunes of war turned.
After our troops' eminent, initial successes, their advance ground to
a halt on the Marne, the result of the failure of our military commanders. The Chief of the General Staff, Colonel-General Helmuth
von Moltke, collapsed, the ever-growing responsibility having been
too much for him.

8 The U-Boat Controversy

I had known von Moltke's predecessor, Field Marshal Alfred von Schlieffen, since 1906. He had drawn up the military plan for the West, which became renowned as the 'Schlieffen Plan'.[1] He was of imposing appearance and I can still visualise him, so very correct and quite unapproachable: there was something resembling the old Uhlans in him which was instantly recognisable. My father used to tell us about Schlieffen, referring mainly to his grand strategy, and when we met him, it was always with singular awe. He served as Chief of the General Staff for fifteen years, until he was seventy-three, but did not live to see the outbreak of war. He died in 1913.

Contrary to his predecessor Schlieffen, von Moltke lacked sureness of judgement. He was in sore need of a good dose of self-confidence, for he not only had to gauge but to execute his predecessor's plan, but he also had to transcend the reputation of his famous uncle, Field Marshal Count von Moltke—the victorious Commander-in-Chief of the wars of 1864, 1866, and 1870/1, Chief of the General Staff until 1888, and whose adjutant he had been for a long time. The younger von Moltke certainly had no easy task in always having to live and work in the shadow of the legendary talent of the great von Moltke and to endure the continual comparisons which were invariably made. My

[1] (The controversial 'Schlieffen Plan' is referred to in German as the 'Westaufmarsch', and many such westward manoeuvres were made between 1891 and 1905, when Schlieffen was Chief of Staff; during this time the plan was revised from the ground up, and was partly implemented in reaction against French manoeuvres. —Ed.)

experience of the younger von Moltke was that he was an earnest, perhaps too earnest, man. He lacked the verve and grandiose outlook of his predecessor, and he wore himself out with his own problems.

The subject of von Moltke preoccupied us incessantly during the war. Particularly affected by the failure of the General Staff was Crown Prince Rupprecht of Bavaria, the Commander-in-Chief of the Sixth Army and later of an Army Group. We esteemed him highly. Like many members of the Wittelsbach family, he was well educated and versatile. My husband suspected that Rupprecht's merits and skill, as well as the performance of his army, were not receiving the recognition which was their due simply because they were Bavarians, though we ourselves admired the bravery of the Bavarian regiments and the distinction of their General Staffs. Crown Prince Rupprecht was also one of those who had an unbounded admiration for Count Schlieffen—all the more reason, my husband said at the time, for his dismay at von Moltke's calamitous leadership. Rupprecht's prognosis for the outcome of the operations was portentously pessimistic, and in conversations with my husband he forecast the disastrous course of events.

My father picked General Erich von Falkenhayn, an experienced staff officer, to succeed von Moltke. To him fell the thankless task of finding new means of conducting the war following his predecessor's squandering of our chances of victory. A way also had to be found to clinch matters in the West. The successful offensives he had conducted in the East in 1915 served the purpose of allowing him further freedom to fight at his rear, and in the following year he began again in the West. As our forces were insufficient to bring France to her knees in a single, big offensive, Falkenhayn decided he would wear down the enemy by exploiting his own favourable front-line position and bleed the French to death in a war of attrition. The enterprise on the Meuse as Falkenhayn called it, began with one word: Verdun. The name of this fortress and the tremendous volume of blood which soaked the earth there still evokes shudders today. It is a name which arouses the deepest awe at the bravery with which both sides fought, even now. For six long months the ploughed earth reverberated to the thunder of guns. Sector after sector, fortress after fortress was captured by our troops. But Verdun did not fall. The French suffered grievous losses and so did we. My brother Wilhelm, whose army had to pursue this bloody battle, tried early on to convince the General Staff of the hopelessness of this offensive, but Falkenhayn was determined to carry his plan through to the end.

My husband followed the course of the battle for Verdun with the greatest anxiety. In May 1916, he wrote me of his fears. 'I am staggered,' Ernst August said, 'that F. is still there,' meaning Falkenhayn.

In August it became manifest that the onslaught on Verdun could not be maintained. Falkenhayn was relieved of his post. The last initiative resulted from the declaration of war by Rumania. 'F. just would not believe that it would happen,' Ernst August wrote from Pless where he was visiting the Headquarters. 'Our presumptions have proved correct.'

Falkenhayn had never been popular. He lacked every popularity trait, and furthermore had never sought one. He was a General Staff officer grown up in the conviction that he had to work in the background and not before the footlights.

From every quarter now there came demands for Hindenburg, and on 29 August the exalted Field Marshal, the national hero, assumed overall command of the armed forces. His closest collaborator, General Ludendorff, came with him to G.H.Q. and on 2 September the attack on Verdun was halted. Three days later my husband wrote from there, 'There's great joy here over H. Papa, of course, must first get thoroughly acquainted with him.' He had had an opportunity of speaking with Hindenburg while at Pless and saw new hopes for us in the Field Marshal's appointment.

In November 1916, we received news of the death of Emperor Franz Josef, aged eighty-six, after sixty-eight years on the throne. His accession had occurred in the year of revolution, 1848, when his uncle, Ferdinand I, had had to abdicate. When one realises that in the year when Franz Josef ascended the throne Prince Metternich still held sway, it gives one some notion of the length of his reign, and as at the beginning, so at the end of his administration, the Monarchy on the Danube was rent by severe storms. Anyway, we had a presentiment that this time Austro-Hungary was on the brink of catastrophe. For us, personally, the old Emperor's death meant the loss of a good, fatherly friend. Aside from our grief we feared for the future of the two allies in a war in which both Germany and Austro-Hungary faced hitherto inconceivable consequences. These were the thoughts that troubled us, as my husband went to Vienna to attend the Emperor's funeral.

Towards the end of that year the dreadful and pitiless distress of our people became apparent. Famine had broken out in the country as a result of England's blockade. Militarily, too, the situation was strained. By now Rumania had been crushed, thus weakening our forces, and in the East the Russian General Brussilov's brilliant offensive created a crisis which threatened the Austro-Hungarian front, where well over 100,000 Czech soldiers had deserted to the Russians. The Skagerrak sea engagement, however, in which our warships had inflicted grievous losses on the Royal Navy, was truly calculated to restore our confidence in victory, though the consequences of Verdun still weighed heavily on the feelings of people both at home and at the front. The ferocious French counter-attacks regained much of the territory for which we had fought in murderous battles earlier in the year.

As the pressure of this anxious situation mounted, came clamorous demands once more for unrestricted submarine warfare. It was believed that the destruction of England's freight carrying capacity, particularly that of food ships, would bring the island to its knees. Our Admiralty was convinced that this goal could be achieved, and possibly within the space of six months. Even Falkenhayn shared this opinion, but was unable to prevail upon the Reich Chancellor, Bethmann Hollweg, who not only had his doubts about the success of the Navy's scheme but was afraid that the ruthless U-Boat offensive would have disastrous consequences on the overall strategic situation. In his view, unrestricted U-Boat warfare which directly attacked neutral shipping heading for English ports would undoubtedly lead not only to momentous collisions with neutral states, and in particular with the United States of America, but would, by American entry into the war, further strengthen the enemy coalition against us. My father shared this view. He emphasised that '. . . the break with America must be avoided'.

Grand Admiral Alfred von Tirpitz, who had been Secretary of State for the Navy for about twenty years—Tirpitz the Eternal, they called him because he had seen Reich Chancellors and Secretaries of State come and go—was on the side of those who demanded unlimited submarine warfare. The Kaiser told me there had been many clashes of opinion between von Tirpitz and the Chancellor and von Tirpitz had requested Bethmann Hollweg's dismissal, but the Chancellor countered with a demand for that of the Grand Admiral with the haughty assertion that the Secretary of State was his subordinate and policy was the Chancellor's domain. 'It was with a heavy heart that I let this energetic but wilful man go,' my father said. 'He had previously carried out my plans cheerfully and been a tireless colleague of mine. Von Tirpitz will always be assured of my royal gratitude.'

There was another reason why my father was opposed to unrestricted submarine warfare, and it was reflected in an incident which occurred on 25 November 1914 when he was at our General Headquarters in Charleville. He was speaking at dinner regarding a report concerning the sinking of the English battleship H.M.S. *Audacious* after striking a German mine. One of those present remarked that one of the English ocean giants, the passenger ship *Oceanic*, had missed one of our mines only by a hair's-breadth. 'Thank God nothing happened!' my father answered. When he saw that his exclamation had aroused the astonishment of his guests, the Kaiser rose to his full height and declared passionately—'Gentlemen! Always think on this: our sword must remain pure. We are not engaged in a war against women and children. We want to conduct the war decently, regardless what the others may do. Mark my words!'

When the arguments for and against unrestricted U-Boat warfare were at their height, I was on a visit to the New Palace. Here I met Karl Helfferich who had taken over as head of the Treasury in 1915 and was now deputy to the Reich Chancellor. He had been summoned by my father, and I was with my mother as my father, accompanied by Helfferich, came into the room. My father asked him to express his views to the Kaiserin on the problem of the U-Boat war against England since he knew she was aware not only of the many sides of the question but of the attitude of Grand Admiral von Tirpitz.

Helfferich spoke clearly and calmly. His manner of expression as well as his arguments impressed us. 'Naturally there is the possibility of inflicting severe damage on England,' he went on. 'It could go so hard on them that they could scarcely recover from this blow. Still, before England is finished, so will we be. An unrestricted U-Boat onslaught would bring the United States of America into the conflict. And that, for us, is equivalent to the loss of the war.'

Both Hindenburg and Ludendorff held the opposite view. Both made progressive demands for unrestricted submarine warfare. Even in public the clamour for a ruthless offensive by U-Boats grew increasingly louder. In October 1916, the Principal Committee of the Reichstag renewed its discussion on this question. Helfferich, who had to put forward the Government's point of view, had a hard time of it. He had to concede the point to the members of the Reichstag that owing to the poor harvest of 1916 there had arisen the possibility of worsening England's food stocks, perhaps even endangering them, through an intensification of the U-Boat war. He went on: 'No one in the whole world can say with any certainty that England, in six or eight months, would no longer be in any position to carry on fighting because of her lack of cargo carrying capacity.' Helfferich then warned them against any underestimation of English tenacity and talent for organisation in times of emergency and for finding a way out of their difficulties.

He laid particular emphasis on the danger of a war with the U.S.A., and when one of the members of the Reichstag doubted the Americans would fight, he retorted: 'From all of the people I have seen and heard who have come over from America, I have never heard any view expressed other than that if you begin unrestricted U-Boat warfare, then you will have a breach and war with America.' Helfferich made plain the significance of any United States entry into the war—'Do you believe that our position would be improved,' he asked, 'if you throw a civilised country with a strong, vigorous race of more than a hundred million inhabitants on to the other side? . . . My optimism doesn't in any case go so far as to doubt that America in the event of war could send over here a considerable number of troops. If the cards for an unrestricted U-Boat war are dealt and they don't take a single trick, then we're lost!'

The warning went unheeded. In the Reichstag the scales of destiny weighed in favour of unrestricted U-Boat warfare, and it was the Centre Party which tipped them. Their faction declared:

'The Reichstag alone, not the Chancellor, is responsible for political decisions concerning the conduct of the war. Any decision of the Reich Chancellor will essentially have to be sustained by the resolution of the High Command, and should that resolution go in favour of an unrestricted U-Boat war, then the Chancellor can be certain of having the agreement of the Reichstag.'

There was no doubt whatever as to what the High Command resolution would be. On 9 January, 1917, came the day of decision. The High Command and the Chancellor together reported to my father. Hindenburg and Ludendorff stated that they could no longer take any responsibility for the further progress of military operations if unrestricted U-Boat warfare were not started by 1 February. On the other hand they were ready to take responsibility for the consequences of an extension of the U-Boat offensive.

On 31 January, unrestricted U-Boat war was declared. Our U-Boat crews fought like lions, and their bravery was beyond all praise. Despite the harshest winter weather, they sunk 750,000 gross registered tons of British shipping in February alone. This figure was exceeded in the following months and reached over a million tons in June, surpassing even the German Admiralty forecasts. England was on the verge of collapse. The First Lord of the Admiralty, Earl Jellicoe, described the situation with the words, 'We can go no further.' Winston Churchill, who had also once been First Lord, admitted: 'Only a little more and the U-Boat war, instead of bringing America on our side, would have forced us all to unconditional surrender through starvation.'

Two days after the start of the U-Boat onslaught, the United States broke off diplomatic relations with Germany; on 2 April, they declared war and many neutral States followed suit. By the summer of 1917 the first American troops were already in the West, eventually reaching a total of 1·7 million fighting against us.

Yet another forecast came true—England's tenacity and capability for successful improvisation in time of need. The English Prime Minister, Lloyd George, succeeded in establishing the convoy system to maintain supplies to the island, despite stubborn opposition from the British and American Admiralties, and doing away with the lone sea passages which had hitherto been the practice. The convoy procedure was invariably time-consuming since a whole fleet of ships travelled more slowly than a single one on its own, but at least more protection was offered against our U-Boats. 'It was the only way they could find to carry on the war,' Admiral Bauer, a First World War commander of our U-Boats, wrote. 'Only by the most keen and tenacious execution of the convoy system which had been rejected by their naval experts could England win the race, almost lost, for re-stocking supplies which they needed from month to month. By the end of 1917 the possibility of a German victory, which in the summer had seemed just round the corner, appeared scarcely credible.'

When we look back on the dramatic and drastic changes in the balance of power brought about by the entry of the United States into the First World War against us, and which determined the world's political configuration for decades, we can permit ourselves one observation. Not one of us could have forecast with any certainty whether the U.S.A. would actively have joined in the struggle against Germany even without the unrestricted U-Boat offensive. What no one else would have liked to prophesy either was whether the U-Boats would succeed in torpedoing England to the point of capitulation. The controversial opinions which were advocated by those responsible, both in Government and in the High Command, rested on the absolute conviction that they would lead the Fatherland along the only correct path. Mars decided who was in the right.

At the beginning of July 1917, the High Command demanded the dismissal of the Chancellor, as did the Centre Party leader, Matthias Erzberger, though for completely different reasons. My husband, who was staying with me at Bellevue during this present crisis, used his influence with the Kaiser to try and persuade him to retain Bethmann Hollweg as he felt he was the right man for the job and the right person to carry out the various internal political reforms, which had earlier been proclaimed by my father while the U-Boat offensive was at its height. My husband considered that if there had to be a change of Chancellors then it would be extremely important to find a better one rather than just have a change at any price. One of the Liberal members of the Reichstag, Friedrich von Payer, held the same view. He considered the proposed overthrow of Bethmann Hollweg as 'a leap in the dark'.

When Hindenburg and Ludendorff finally issued their ultimatum that the Chancellor had to go 'because they could no longer work with him', or they themselves would resign, Bethmann Hollweg told my father that the dismissal of these two very experienced men would lose the nation's faith in the military leadership. On 13 July he took the step himself and resigned. He was succeeded by Dr Georg Michaelis, previously Under-Secretary of State in the Prussion Finance Ministry and Prussian Commissar for Supply. His appointment was put to my father by the head of the Civil Cabinet, Rudolf von Valentini, but it was abundantly clear that Michaelis's nomination had originally been put forward by Ludendorff. My father doubted whether Michaelis had either the full qualifications to surmount the tense internal political situation or even if he had experience enough in the foreign field. The appointment, however, at least guaranteed the co-operation of the High Command with the Chancellor. Michaelis's Chancellorship lasted just three months. He did not solve the internal political crisis, and now nobody even wanted to admit any part in his original selection. It is worthy of note that during this time Prince Bülow was pulling strings so that he could become Chancellor. One of his most zealous supporters was Erzberger, the other Gustav Stresemann, but an Austrian intervention shattered this project, leaving my father holding the baby.

Bethmann Hollweg's resignation had been considerably influenced by the Reichstag's debate on the Centre Party's 'Peace Resolution' forced by their leader Matthias Erzberger. The resolution contained defeatist clauses, and the High Command rightly feared that it would have unfavourable effects on the fighting morale of our soldiers, would weaken the army's will to fight and its resistance, apart from strengthening that of the enemy. Hindenburg and Ludendorff asserted that the Chancellor did not want to hinder the resolution, though the opposite was the case. Bethmann Hollweg, Helfferich and Admiral von Capelle, head of the Reich Navy Department, had forcibly warned the committee against drafting the resolution at all. Bethmann Hollweg told them: 'Don't draft such a spineless resolution.' But it led to Erzberger's demand for the Chancellor's dismissal and on 19 July 1917, the majority parties in the Reichstag—the Centre, the Social Democrats and the Progressive People's Party—adopted the Peace Resolution. It immediately harmed the German war leadership considerably. My father had already undertaken steps towards peace in 1916, in consultation with Bethmann Hollweg and other responsible statesmen.

The next step towards peace was then discussed with the High Command. Hindenburg raised no objection and the terms were placed before the three Allied Governments. Finally—and it was eminently significant—a psychologically suitable time was chosen, that is, the peace proposal had to be put at a moment of victory, so that no misunderstanding would arise that it was being offered at a time of weakness. On 6 December, Bucharest was conquered after a successful campaign against Rumania, and a few days later, on 12 December, the Chancellor made his peace offer to the enemy powers through neutral intermediaries.

In the United States, which was still neutral at this time, the German peace overtures fell on fertile soil. President Wilson shortly afterward sent a Note to all the warring nations, in which he expressed his readiness to be of service during any peace negotiations, but the Allies turned down our peace bid and the French warned their people to be wary of 'this dirty manoeuvre which would poison public opinion'.

In their reply of 30 December 1916 to the Central Powers, the Entente declared:

> 'In full recognition of the severity and urgency of the hour the Allied Governments, in close unity and in complete agreement, reject and refuse to enter into an agreement which is without sincerity and significance.'

In their reply to President Wilson they expressed the view that 'it is impossible today to achieve a peace which guarantees reconciliation, reparations and the right of citizenship to which they have a claim as a consequence of the attack for which the Central Powers bear the responsibility . . . .'.

In the summer of 1917 the Pope sought to mediate between the warring nations. There was no doubt, bearing in mind the Vatican's notorious caution, that the Papal initiative had been painstakingly prepared. At the end of April Benedict XV had appointed one of the most gifted young diplomats in the Curia, Cardinal Pacelli, later Pope Pius XII, as Apostolic Delegate to the Bavarian Court. On 26 June, Pacelli called on Bethmann Hollweg in Berlin, and told him that he had a letter from the Pope to deliver to the Kaiser. Three days later the Nuncio met my father at General Headquarters in Bad Kreuznach. My father was immediately captivated by Pacelli's imposing personality—and so was I when I met him in Munich. My father described him with these words: 'Pacelli is a noble, sympathetic figure, highly intelligent, with polished manners, the epitome of a Prince of the Catholic Church.'

The conversation between Pacelli and my father was in French, as the Nuncio's German at that time was not as perfect as in later years. The Papal envoy immediately recognised that my father was striving for peace, and that every serious effort in this direction would be fully supported. My father told him of the Allies' unheard-of rejection, as he called it, of his December 1916 overtures, and in a spirited exposition, spoke of the exalted duty of the Holy Throne to intervene in the cause of peace. At the end of the audience, so my father told me, Pacelli grasped his hand and, deeply moved, said: '*Vous avez parfaitment raison! C'est le devoir du Pape, il faut qu'il agisse, c'est par lui que le monde doit être regagné à la paix. Je transmetterai vos paroles à Sa Sainteté.*'[1]

On 1 August the Pope signed a decree in which he invited the warring powers to put an end to their conflict. The contents of the Pope's proposals showed that the Vatican had worked for the good of both sides, but it was all in vain—Erzberger's defeatist 'Peace Resolution' knocked the wind out of the sails of those in the Allied camp who inclined to peace. And publicly, as the United States Ambassador in Berlin, Mr J. W. Gerard, was to say later, 'It would

---

[1] You are perfectly right. It is the Pope's task, he must act. It is through him that the world must win back peace. I will transmit your words to His Holiness.

have been easier for Germany to make peace with Bethmann Hollweg at the helm. The whole world knows him and honours him for his honesty.' Pacelli, too, said, though in confidence, that if Bethmann Hollweg had not resigned, the prospects for peace would have been good. Regarding Erzberger, the initiator of the 'Peace Resolution' and leader of the conspiracy against Bethmann Hollweg, the Nuncio added—'Now everything is lost, even your poor Fatherland.'

9 *The Fall of the Romanovs*

During 1917 there was a tiny, flickering flame of hope of a victorious end to the war as a result of the events in Russia, and public opinion had it that the overthrow of the Russian Monarchy would bring Germany a decisive step nearer to it. At first sight this glimmer of hope had some basis, but for those who could see beyond the background of the Russian Revolution there were gloomy perspectives.

My father had long recognised the precariousness of the Czar's situation, and recalled a conversation he had had with an old Russian General when he was on a visit to Russia while we were still at peace. The Russian had expressed his opinion of certain aspects of Russian foreign policy with the words—'And here we are together with this awful French Republic, which is full of hate of you and filled with subversive ideas which, should a war break out with you, will cost us our dynasty.' Perhaps it was just a feeling or maybe a realistic appraisal, but my father believed that revolutionary elements might be brewing in St Petersburg and considered it was now a matter of urgency to conclude peace in the interests of the Russian Monarchy. The steps he took to make known his views to the Czar are to a certain extent highly controversial.

There was a rumour going around in the 'twenties that in 1916 my father had sent the Grand Duke of Hesse on a very secret mission to the Russian Court in order to seek a separate peace between Germany and Czar Nicholas II. The source of this assertion was a certain Anastasia Tschaikovsky, who claimed she was the Czar's youngest daughter. Now known under the name of Anna Anderson, Anastasia

Tschaikovsky alleged that she had escaped the dreadful bloodbath which had overwhelmed the Czar and his family in Ekaterinburg in July 1918, and, after various adventures, had finally reached Germany. As proof of her identity as Princess Anastasia, she claimed that she knew of the Grand Duke of Hesse, the Czarina's brother's secret visit, and said that only the most intimate circles surrounding the Czar knew of it.

For their part the Hesse family maintained that this allegation only showed with certainty that Anna Anderson's assertion that she was Princess Anastasia was completely untrue. The Hesses maintained that as nothing was known of Grand Duke Ernst Ludwig's journey to Russia during the war, Anna Anderson's statement had to be an invention. My nephew Prince Friedrich Ernst of Saxony-Altenburg had a different opinion. For years he had been engaged in an intensive investigation into the case of Anastasia, and he gave me an exhaustive description of the result of his inquiries. He maintained that the Grand Duke of Hesse, with my father's consent, had personally sought out the Czar in order to get a separate peace, and had gone to Russia under the pseudonym of Thurn-und-Taxis. The Czar had given his brother-in-law an escort who had been sworn to absolute secrecy. At the transit point which the Grand Duke had to pass through the lines he was recognised by one of his escort's acquaintances and he, too, was sworn to complete silence. The mediation, however, failed as the military commanders abruptly forbade the Czar any thoughts of a separate peace. That was the essence of Prince Friedrich Ernst's report.

In 1961 the Hamburg County Court rejected the premise that the Grand Duke had been on a peace mission to the Czar 'because authentic witnesses to prove such a journey did not appear to be available'.

At an appeal before the Hamburg High Court in 1965, testimony was given by Prince Dimitri Galizin, who was living in Paris at the time, which could possibly have shed some light on the proceedings. Prince Galizin declared under oath:

'As assistant to the head of the Russian Red Cross organisation, Vladimir von Mekk, I was present at Tsarskoye Selo early in

1916. Von Mekk was there to make a report to the Czarina, who had founded the organisation, and while he was with the Czarina I sat in a chair in the Palace hall. Suddenly, a man in civilian clothes crossed over a little distance down the hall, leaving by one door and going through another. On his return von Mekk asked me if I had seen this man, and swore me to silence regarding the episode. That same evening, or maybe it was the next morning, von Mekk told me that the man in civilian clothes had been the Grand Duke of Hesse.'

I personally know of no one who has any evidence of the Grand Duke's journey to St Petersburg, neither did I hear anything from my father about it. But I do know that the proposal to send a Prince over there was discussed, and also with the military commanders, but Ludendorff was strictly against it. So, if such a step had been taken, it was taken without the knowledge of the High Command. That would explain why my father had wanted the strictest secrecy, and it would also explain the Grand Duke's absolute silence, too, particularly as regards his own family. They certainly never got the slightest indication from him.

My father had in any case told of the fact that he had expressed his readiness to the Czar to conclude a separate peace. He had suggested a return to the 1914 frontiers—and no claim for reparations—should peace be achieved. Alexander Kerensky, first Minister of Justice then Prime Minister of the Revolutionary Russian Government, revealed that a letter had been found in which my father had proposed a separate peace to the Czar in 1916, but the Czar had not answered it. Furthermore, he had ordered that my father should be told no answer would be forthcoming. It is manifest that there was also a letter written by the Grand Duke of Hesse to the Czar in which the subject of a conclusion of a separate peace was mentioned. It was brought over to the Czar by a Russian lady, according to Princess Xenia Alexandrovna, one of the Czar's sisters. Making such contacts was no problem, since they could be arranged via the Danish Court in Copenhagen.

However, the time drew near when the Czar had to entertain thoughts of a separate peace. Under pressure of the rapidly growing difficulties in all sections of the Russian military command, my father's efforts were beginning to have an effect, yet his moves had probably been perceived by Russia's allies. Already at the end of 1916, the English Press were publishing stories of tendencies in the Russian Court towards friendship with Germany, and they printed warnings against Russo-German understanding forced by reactionaries. *The Saturday Review* reported that there would be no end to the depressing rumour of Russia's impending crack-up, while *Nation* told its readers of the painful diplomatic situation in which England found herself. Accusations against the Czar appeared suddenly and grew in volume until the entire English Press finally followed suit.

While they criticised the Russian Court, they supported and encouraged the liberal forces. A summary of the report issued at the beginning of 1917 by the German Central Office which compiled and evaluated information they gleaned from the Foreign Press, said: 'From now on it will be clear that the English propaganda organisation in Russia has received instructions to create agitation against Germany and above all agitation against the Russian Government.' The French Secret Service also established its propaganda on the same lines both among the population and in the Russian army. Colonel Nicholai, head of the Intelligence Service of the German High Command, wrote in a report concerning this propaganda:

> 'The Czar and his advisers, who were united in their desire for peace, were made responsible for the length of the war, for the loss of battles, for all deprivations and for all the victims. The goal, however, was not to exact peace but to overthrow the peace-seeking and dangerous Czar's government which was jeopardising the Entente. The revolution was being prepared.'

My father maintained that Rasputin had been one of those at the Czar's Court who spoke in favour of a separate peace. 'Against him,' my father said, 'was the party of Princes, the nationalistic bourgeoisie organised by parliament and the English will for war incorporated in Ambassador Sir George Buchanan and the military commander, Colonel Knox. As these adversaries recognised Rasputin's influence,

they went to work. Rasputin was just murdered and the Czar's kingdom wiped out by the democratic revolution supported by England.'

By the end of January 1917, the Allies had sent special emissaries to
St Petersburg in order to encourage their allies to more strenuous
efforts in the war, and in particular to prevent the break-up of their
war coalition. England sent one of their gifted Ministers, Lord Milner,
and a few weeks later the Czar was overthrown. On 15 March,
Nicholas II abdicated and he and his family were imprisoned. Nicholas
and his Czarina, Alexandra Feodorovna, were accused of treason, and
under the term treason came the accusation that they had sought a
separate peace with Germany. The British Government congratulated
the revolutionaries, and President Wilson described the revolution
in a message to the United States Congress as a 'wonderful and
encouraging occurrence'. The new Russian rulers declared themselves totally against any thoughts of a separate peace, and their war
policy was made quite clear in the announcement that 'for us a
decisive victory is essential; the liquidation of the German Empire is
today more necessary and important than ever. Without it the ideals
for which we fight will be unattainable.'

News reaching us from various quarters indicated the direst fears
for the fate of the Czar, and the Danish Court put out feelers to find
out whether my father would be favourably inclined to take steps
for the rescue of the Czar's family. My father remarked: 'Why do
they turn to me?' and asked himself what behoved Copenhagen to
refer to him since he was at war with Russia. Nevertheless he ordered
Reich Chancellor Bethmann Hollweg to try and make contact with
the Russian Government through neutral channels, and to tell
Kerensky that the Kaiser himself would hold him personally responsible if just one hair of the Czar's family was out of place. The reply
which Bethmann Hollweg relayed to my father was that Kerensky
would only be too happy to see the Czar and his family leave Russia
altogether.

Bethmann Hollweg also told my father of suggestions that the Czar
and his family, who were interned at Tsarskoye Selo at the time,
would like to go to England. My father expressed his immediate
readiness to help. In a secret order to the Commander-in-Chief of
the northern sector of the Eastern front he instructed him to permit

the Czar and his family to pass through his lines without hindrance. The order further stipulated that a special train and a guard of honour should be placed at the Czar's disposal, and one of my father's aides and officers of the railway troops were personally to be responsible for the security of the Czar's family. The Czar had also to be permitted to reach the port from which he was to leave for England. In an order to the Commander-in-Chief of Naval Forces in the Baltic, Prince Heinrich, my father warned that the Czar would be leaving Russia by ship. My uncle Heinrich was also told to make sure that this ship, flying the Czar's personal standard, would pass unmolested and furthermore had to be conducted safely through the minefields and protected from torpedo boats.

My father could justly say afterwards: 'I have done everything humanly possible for the unhappy Czar and his family.' The Chancellor, who supported my father's measures in every respect, informed the Danish Court intermediary of the details and we waited for something to happen, but we heard nothing more.

Only very much later did we hear which way matters had gone. The British Government had telegraphed its Ambassador, Sir George Buchanan, to say they were unwilling to give the Czar asylum, and Sir George had accordingly informed the Russian Government.

Nicholas II had asked the Russian Revolutionary Government for permission to travel to England via Murmansk with his family. Some weeks before, while he was in Pskov, and relatives had advised him to go, he had refused, saying that he preferred to stay in Russia. Finally, he decided to put his wife and children first. Kerensky supported him and Foreign Minister Paul Miliukov approached the British Ambassador. He told the envoy, 'This is the last opportunity to save the freedom and perhaps the lives of these unhappy people.' He then asked that the matter should be dealt with as expeditiously as possible. Sir George informed London on 21 March. On the next day the British Cabinet decided to grant the Czar and his family asylum in England for the duration of the war, and Sir George then informed Miliukov. Both in St Petersburg and Tsarskoye Selo preparations were made for the journey. When it was believed that everything was in order, Sir George was asked when the British cruiser would take the Czar and his family aboard at Murmansk. The

Minister who asked this question of the British Ambassador, had difficulty in believing that the Ambassador was the same person he had known for so long. Sir George had tears in his eyes and was most deeply upset. He then said he had a disagreeable duty to perform and had to report that the Czar and his family were no longer welcome in England.

What, then, had happened? After the British Cabinet's decision to grant asylum, King George V himself intervened in the matter. Scarcely two weeks earlier he had telegraphed the Czar saying how worried he was about his fate. 'My thoughts are always with you,' the King's message read, 'and I will always remain the sincere and devoted friend which I, as you know, have always been.' George and Nicholas were cousins, their mothers sisters, and George and Nicholas resembled each other very closely. Only their uniforms told the difference between them. But when they came to Berlin to attend my wedding not in their own but in Prussian uniforms, it was extremely difficult to tell them apart. Only those experienced in uniforms could do so. They would say, 'the one with the white and green collar of the Cuirassiers is King George and the one in the blue of the Westphalian Hussars is the Czar'. Both cousins had always expressed friendship for each other, and a contributing factor was the fact that the Czarina was a cousin of King George's and her mother was his father's sister.

What had induced the King to prevent the flight of his relatives—who were also his allies—can be gathered from documents available today. After his Government's decision to grant asylum, he sent a message to the Cabinet through his Private Secretary in which he said:

> 'The King has thoroughly considered the Government's plan to allow the Czar and his family to come to England. As you undoubtedly know, the King cherishes the most friendly feelings for the Czar, and would on this account be only too pleased to do everything to help him in this critical situation. His Majesty doubts, however, whether it is advisable to receive the Czar and his family in England, not only because of the dangers of the journey, but also on the grounds of general expediency. . . .'

The Cabinet answered they felt it impossible to retract the invitation 'as long as there was no change in the situation'. They hoped, therefore 'that the King would agree to support the invitation issued on the advice of His Majesty's Ministers'. The King's Private Secretary replied to the Government giving George's opinion that the public might take offence if he were to meet the Czar and Czarina 'as His Majesty is not only related to them, but that the Czar, from the moment he had ascended the throne twenty-three years earlier, had been a close friend and ally of our country'. He added that he would agree only if the Government 'publicly declared that they would take the sole responsibility for the invitation to the Czar's family'.

The Prime Minister, Lloyd George, agreed with the King's contention and tried alternate solutions, in other words to find out if France, for instance, would take in the Czar and his family. King George thought Switzerland or Denmark might help, and the inquiry reached my father's ears as well as those of the German Government through Copenhagen. It indicated that the Czar, who was unacceptable in England because 'he had been a close friend and ally from the beginning' should be accepted by Germany, his enemy! They believed that my father would not shrink from making sacrifices in order to save the life of an enemy Monarch. I suppose one could think of no greater moral praise.

In fact, when my father was told by the Chancellor that the Czar and his family were possibly wanting to go to England from Tsarskoye Selo, he declared himself ready to help, as I have already shown. Yet for years the British Government maintained that their grant of asylum to the Czar had been thwarted by the events of the Revolution in Russia. Sir George Buchanan, who published his memoirs and in them wanted to reveal the truth, was, however, prevented by the Foreign Office from doing so. His daughter later revealed the background to this macabre affair, and told of the moment when her father received the fateful news in St Petersburg. She said:

'After my father had read the telegram, he paled.
' "What's the matter?" I asked.
' "They're refusing to allow the Czar into England. They say

it would be more prudent to dissuade the Imperial Family from coming to England."

' "Why?"

' "They're worried."

' "What about?"

' "Of unrest in England. There could be strikes in the docks, in the munition factories and in the mines. Even a revolt may be possible if the Czar came to England. . . ." '

We ought to mention the additional fact that in 1919, after the murder of the Czar and his family, the British Government also denied asylum in England to the Czar's brother-in-law, Prince Alexander Mikhailovitch. Here, I would like to cite a remark made by an English Brigadier-General, W. H-H. Waters, which matches my own opinion. The Brigadier, a reliable observer of Russian affairs and who had had no knowledge of my father's endeavours or those of the Danish Court, had himself advised the British War Office to free the Czar. He later said: 'If the British people openly had been put into the picture both on the question of granting asylum to the Czar and his family, and on the German Kaiser's willingness to help, it would have been certain to have spurred their Government on to rescue the Czar and his family.'

After the failure of the England Project, as it might be called, the Russian authorities wanted to keep the Czar away from the area of St Petersburg. The Czar wanted to be brought to the Crimea but Kerensky, now the Prime Minister, decided on Siberia, so the unhappy family were left in the dark as to where exactly they would be taken. Kerensky, however, advised them to provide themselves with winter clothing, while he busily occupied himself with all the transportation details. Only five or six people were in the know and he kept everything secret. Later, he boasted of the 'ease and smoothness' with which everything had gone. For us it was an indication of how easily and smoothly their deportation of the Czar could have been, too.

Kerensky had chosen the remote west Siberian town of Tobolsk, which had no railway connections, as the Czar's place of internment. The departure was fixed for 1 August at one o'clock in the morning, but it was delayed for a few hours while the Prime Minister kept going in and out of the Palace giving fresh orders. Prince Michael Alexandrovich then appeared in order to bid farewell to his brother and also to see the Czarina and the children, but Kerensky refused him permission.

At 6 a.m. the lorry with the Czar and his family, accompanied by a few of their faithful retainers, set out for the station. A few hundred soldiers were guarding the route, and on arrival at the station building the Czar handed over a sum of money to be distributed to the soldiers who had guarded him during the night.

The journey to Tobolsk lasted thirteen days and on the last stretch they had to go along the River Irtysh in a boat. For their stay in Tobolsk the Czar and his family were given the house of the former governor. It stood in the middle of the town, was fenced in and was guarded by soldiers. Today, it's named 'the House of Freedom'.

At first, everything went relatively well. A town official reported to the Czar and promised him newspapers and that his mail would be forwarded. The Czar asked him: 'Would you not allow me to saw wood? I love the work.'

The alderman replied: 'Perhaps you would prefer a carpenter's shop? That work is more interesting.'

'It would be better if you had wood brought to our yard and gave me a saw,' the Czar rejoined.

Soon, the troubles started. Their food supplies were endangered for the town commandant received nothing from St Petersburg and the shopkeepers would only deliver if they were paid. Two of the retainers who had accompanied the Czar helped out. Then the soldiers on guard refused to obey their superiors any more, and the commandant, feeling himself powerless, lost his nerve. He sought out the Czar and asked for his understanding, saying he wanted to go away. 'I cannot go on,' he cried despairingly.

The Czar put his hands on the commandant's shoulders and said: 'Stay, for the love of me, my wife and children. I implore you, stay. You can see that we are all suffering. You must just have patience.'

The Colonel stayed.

As the Bolshevists' grip on St Petersburg strengthened, the effect became even more apparent to the Royal prisoners. Their treatment became stricter and their rations smaller. Finally the family was transferred to Ekaterinburg in the Urals. One of the Czarevitch's companions, a Swiss named Pierre Gilliard, told of their experiences on the way:

> 'One of the sailors attached to Alexei, Nagorny, carried the little sick child in his arms. Behind him came the Princesses carrying their cases and little effects. I wanted to go out and help but was brutally thrown out of the lorry by the guards, so I went back to look out of the window. Tatiana was the last to leave, carrying her little dog and laboriously dragging her heavy case. She was weeping and I watched as her every step sank into the mire. Nagorny wanted to come to her aid, but he was held back by one of the commissars. . . .'

The new lodging was an engineer's house surrounded by high wooden partitions, and as it had to accommodate both the prisoners and their guards, there was not much room. The young Princesses slept on the floor. The food was bad, their treatment spiteful, the commissar a drunk and a sadist. The soldiers behaved with obscene vulgarity towards the Czar's daughters. They sang dirty songs and there were indecent scribbles on the walls which the children could see as they passed by. The humiliations were deep and unbearable. Even the Czar's sawing was forbidden. To console themselves, the Czar, his wife and children sang hymns frequently, and the Mass which was allowed to be said by a priest every Sunday gave them comfort.

The Czarevitch's Swiss teacher, who tried to help them from the outside, sought out the British and Swedish Consuls and urgently requested their aid. According to his report they answered: 'Steps have already been taken. We do not believe there is any immediate danger.'

On the Bolshevist side it was decided to put on a show trial for the Czar and Czarina. Then, at the beginning of July 1918, the White Forces of Admiral Koltshak reached Ekaterinburg and the Reds asked themselves what they should do. During the night of 16/17 July, the Czar's family were awakened. One of the witnesses gave the following description of what happened then:

'Everybody got up, dressed, and finally came out of their rooms about an hour afterwards. They were quiet and suspected no danger. Then they went downstairs, Nicholas himself carrying Alexei.'

They were led into a room on the ground floor. The Czar, the Czarina and Alexei sat on chairs while the Princesses, the doctor, Dr Botkin, the cook, Charitonov, the ladies' maid, Dmidova, and Trupp, the servant, remained standing.

Then Chekists and soldiers stormed in. The massacre began.

The Reds did everything to remove all traces of bloodshed in the house, and buried the lifeless bodies secretly in a wood.

Regarding the responsibility for the murder, Leon Trotsky, then Commissar for War, described a conversation he had had with the Chairman of the Central Committee, Jacov Sverdlov, after the conquest of Ekaterinburg by Admiral Koltshak. Trotsky said:

'I asked him casually, "where, then, is the Czar?"
' "It's all over," he said. "He's been shot."
' "And where are his family?"
' "The family, too."
' "All of them?" I asked, somewhat surprised.
' "All," said Sverdlov. "What did you expect?"
'He wanted some reaction from me, but I didn't answer. "Who decided it?" I asked.
' "We decided it here. Ilych (Lenin) was of the opinion that we couldn't allow the Whites to have a living symbol around whom they could assemble. . . ." '

Only four of the Grand Dukes escaped death—Demetrius, who had been banished by the Czar, penetrated through the lines to the English forces, and the brothers Andreas and Boris who were rescued by the man who had been designated to execute them. That man was an artist who had lived overseas for years and, as things turned out, it was Boris who had been interested in his work and supported him. The functionary followed the dictates of his heart and let the two Princes go. Kyrill reached freedom via Finland. The other Romanovs who survived the catastrophe had to thank German troops for their rescue. Early in 1918, Field Marshal von Eichhorn's Army Group was thrusting through the Ukraine in the direction of the Sea of Azov, and in doing so succeeded in freeing a group of members of the Romanov family in the Crimea. I obtained knowledge of this through a secret report my mother showed me—'Regarding the Russian Imperial Personages. . . .'—those were the first words, handwritten by my mother, which I saw on the document. From this report my mother-in-law was able to learn that her sister, the Dowager Czarina, was still alive. It listed these names:

'Living at Dzubga near Cape Aitodor (south coast) are Empress Maria Feodorovna; Grand Duke Nikolai Nikolaevich with wife and son; Peter Nikolaevich with wife, son and daughter; Grand Duke Alexander Mikhailovich with wife and six children. At Charak, east of Dzubga, Grand Duchess Olga and her husband, Colonel Kulikovsky. . . .

'A couple of days ago their guard was taken over by Germans. The living conditions of the Imperial Personages are, considering the conditions, good. A change of dwelling is not at present envisaged. At the most they will be more dislocated, but for the moment there is no danger. . . .'

My father invited the Dowager Czarina to make the journey to Denmark through Germany, but despite all the blows fate had dealt her, she was too proud to accept. November 1918 saw the defeat of Germany, our troops had to evacuate the occupied Russian territories, and Allied troops took over the protection of the Dowager Czarina from the Germans who had freed her. Finally, she left by sea. Thus, the Romanovs were thrown to the four winds.

On an October day in 1928, I stood by Maria Feodorovna's grave in the solemnly lit Roskilde Cathedral on Zealand, the burial place of so many Danish kings. After a severe illness, she had at last been relieved of her sufferings. She had spent her last years at Hvidoere in Denmark. In her hour of death, she had clasped the old Bible which had earlier been stolen from her by Red sailors, but a Danish diplomat who had accidentally come across it in a Moscow antique shop, purchased it and brought it back to the Czarina.

The Danes crowded her funeral route, their bare heads silently bowed in a last tribute to their own Princess who, though she had achieved the radiant heights of one of the mightiest Thrones on Earth, had never forgotten her own country. But neither had she been able to grasp the sudden collapse of the great dynasty to which, for so many decades, she had dedicated her entire energies.

Her daughters Xenia and Olga were there. So, too, was Grand Duke Kyrill, who had become the head of the House of Romanov, who then lived in France. At this farewell to the Dowager Czarina, it came into my mind that even here in exile she was still the dominant personality that she had been in her family during her lifetime.

I wrote to my father in Doorn: 'For the poor Russians, it means the end of an era; Aunt Maria held them all together. Now it is Kyrill who is in charge. . . .'

10   The Beginning of the End

The end of German war operations in the East meant we were able to switch forces for a great offensive on the Western Front. On 21 March 1918, the big offensive in France began, followed by two further ones in April and May. All available troops were thrown in, including our last reserves, and our soldiers achieved tremendous results even in this, the fifth year of the war. The enemy armies sustained heavy losses, large territorial gains were made by our men and their booty, both in arms and other war equipment, was immense. As in 1914, the front once again neared Paris and, as then, German cavalry galloped once more across the battlefields. Once more, the thought that victory was perhaps in sight was uppermost in our minds and we were thrilled at the developments in the West.

The fourth offensive which began in the vicinity of Rheims in July failed. The attack was abortive, for a deserter had betrayed our plans and the High Command had to break off operations after only a couple of days. On the following day the enemy launched a powerful counter-attack with huge masses of infantry, supported by tanks and aircraft, and pressed our troops back. The fresh United States divisions which had been pushed into the fray gave to the onslaught enormous amounts of war material.

The heavy losses sustained by England and France in the spring had forced them to turn to the U.S.A. for urgent help. Lloyd George told the Americans: 'In this war, time is everything. It is impossible to overestimate the importance of conveying American reinforcements across the Atlantic in the quickest possible time.' In the West, it was recognised that the hour had struck. Between March and June, 1918, the American contingent on the Western Front was strengthened by 600,000 men. In August alone another 350,000 men were sent over, and in a continuous series of attacks they were now able to overrun the German lines. Our troops were no longer able to resist the wave after wave of assaults; they were exhausted, and reserves as good as non-existent. Retreat followed retreat and the Allies attacked the entire front from Verdun to the sea in one general offensive.

At the beginning of August, on the so-called Black Friday as Ludendorff confirmed in his memoirs, came 'the downfall of our military strength'. He lost all hope of 'finding a strategic way out which would restore the position in our favour'. Verbally, he said: 'On the contrary, I came to the conclusion that the measures taken by the High Command which I—insofar as it is possible in war— could build upon securely, were now without foundation. The conduct of the war, as I told myself, had taken on the aspect of an unjustifiable game of chance. And that I have always considered fatal. For the fate of the German people, that was too high a hazard. The war had to be ended.'

On 25 September Ludendorff ordered the representative of the Foreign Office at the High Command, Baron Kurt von Lersner, to report to Berlin and to tell them of the news that pulmonary disease had broken out in the French army. When Lersner told him that he doubted the veracity of this information, the General retorted: 'Just communicate this news to the Secretary of State. As a drowning man clutches at a straw, so do I clutch at this report.'

Lersner's reply to this disclosure was direct: 'Today,' he said, 'your Excellency has for the first time given me a clear picture of the war situation.' In his description of this incident Lersner went on to say that Ludendorff had been openly thankful that the meaning of his statement had so quickly been appreciated.

On the evening of the same day the General in charge of the medical services, Otto von Schjerning, told General Ludendorff why, according to his experience and inquiries, the news of the outbreak of lung disease in the French army could not be true. According to Colonel Mertz von Quirnheim, a divisional leader at the High Command who was present at this meeting, Ludendorff answered formally and hopelessly: 'I am clutching at this news just as a drowning man clutches at a straw.' Colonel von Quirnheim noted in his diary: 'The effect of these words on us all was frightful.'

During the following day many of Ludendorff's associates deliberated on what inferences were to be drawn from the General's statement, among them the Chief of the Political Division, General Paul von Bartenwerffer. Finally they decided to call on Counsellor von Lersner to telephone the Secretary of State at the Foreign Office, Paul von Hintze, and ask him to come to Spa immediately for a conference with the High Command. When he was informed of this move, Ludendorff agreed.

On 28 September, two days later, Ludendorff sought out Field Marshal von Hindenburg. Ludendorff noted what transpired:

'At 6 p.m. I went to see the General Field Marshal whose office lay on the floor below and informed him of my thoughts concerning peace and an armistice. It told him that due to the state of affairs in the Balkans our position could only worsen and that also applied if we held out on the Western Front. We had but one duty—to act clearly and without delay. The General Field Marshal listened to me deeply moved. He answered that he had wanted to tell me the same thing that evening, that he had long deliberated on the situation and had come to the conclusion that we had to take just such a step.'

In his own notes Hindenburg described his side of the conversation with Ludendorff:

'I respected what had made him come to me. So often since 23 August 1914, had our thoughts, like today, been identical—before they were even expressed in words. Our most difficult decision will be made from identical convictions.'

Ludendorff commented in conclusion:

'The General Field Marshal and I parted with firm handshake, like men who had not only borne their love to the grave but who had also wanted to stand together through the worst hours of their human existence.'

On the next day my father, Reich Chancellor Count Georg von Hertling and the Secretary of State von Hintze, met at Spa. Von Hintze, who had left Berlin before the Chancellor, was the first to meet Hindenburg and Ludendorff. He simply did not believe his ears when Ludendorff confronted him with the proposition to sue for an immediate armistice. He stood there uncomprehendingly, as he said later, 'in view of the alternation from victory fanfares to graveside dirges of defeat'. After he had absorbed Ludendorff's proposition he expressed his fears that the rapidity of the High Command's changes of opinion would have the most severe consequences on the army, the people, the State, and the Monarchy.

When the Chancellor arrived at midday, von Hintze appraised him of everything that had gone on. Count von Hertling, too, was quite unprepared for the news. Shocked to his foundations, he told his son, who had accompanied him: 'That really is dreadful. The High Command is demanding that the Entente should be asked for an armistice as soon as possible!'

My father arrived from Schleswig-Holstein where he had been visiting the shipyards in Kiel and the torpedo and mine establishment at Eckernförde at Admiral Scheer's suggestion. He had also taken part in the U-Boat School submarine exercises in Kiel Bight. On the way, he had broken his journey to Spa at Kassel in order to see my mother at Wilhelmshöhe where she was recovering from a stroke she had sustained in the middle of August.

My father was accompanied on his journey by Lieutenant-Colonel Alfred Niemann, his Liaison Officer at the High Command. Both had no inkling, as they arrived at Spa, of what was in store for them there. Immediately on arrival Niemann made his way to the Operations Division so as to acquaint himself with the situation. On the way, he met General Bartenwerffer who greeted him with the words: 'The die is cast. We're going to ask our enemies for an armistice and peace.'

Niemann thought he had not heard aright. 'Armistice?' he asked.

'Yes, armistice,' answered the General. 'Our situation brooks no delay. The Field Marshal and General Ludendorff have independently come to the conclusion that we must not lose another hour.'

It was at 9 a.m. that Hindenburg's Liaison Officer, officially called the Deputy Chief of the General Staff, learned of the change of official opinion of the two leaders Hindenburg and Ludendorff. Two hours later, in a conference with Hindenburg, Ludendorff and von Hintze, the Field Marshal informed my father that the military situation made an immediate armistice imperative. Ludendorff supported Hindenburg. It was a crushing revelation just the same, a sudden, severe blow for my father. He felt the ground had been torn from under his feet.

When Lieutenant-Colonel Niemann met my father again that day, he found him 'quietly resigned but unmistakably ill-humoured towards Ludendorff'. He learned, too, that 'the High Command had suggested an armistice which was akin to capitulation and the Kaiser had been told during the exposition of the military situation that it was merely a matter of hours'.

In Hindenburg's and Ludendorff's notes one can find only two or three sentences regarding their fateful conference. The Field Marshal wrote: 'On the basis of our deliberations we laid our proposal for peace before His Majesty the Kaiser. It was incumbent upon me, owing to this political step, to describe to the Supreme Commander-in-Chief the seriousness of the situation, of which the Kaiser was not unaware. His Majesty approved of what we had proposed with a firm and strong heart.'

General Ludendorff said: 'The Field Marshal outlined the picture of the military situation which, briefly, I corroborated. His Majesty was extraordinarily quiet.'

The catastrophic suddenness of the two leaders' demand for an armistice was not mentioned, although in transcribing this meeting my father's 'reaction' came out indirectly. The Field Marshal remarked on 'the *present* seriousness of the military situation of which the Kaiser was not unaware'. By *present*, that also meant the final situation which the Field Marshal and his chief adviser had previously not allowed to be divulged.

Ludendorff published his account in 1919, Hindenburg in 1920. These publications were produced before my father expressed his opinion from exile in a paper published in 1922 in which he confined himself to the allusion that Ludendorff had suggested on 29 September they should merely prepare for an armistice in place of peace negotiations. In that statement lay a conscious reticence on my father's

E

part for which there were several reasons. My father stood by his two closest military collaborators and their assessments, which he felt could not be made public.

I think I have a duty to relate today the way events ran their course, above all the events of 9 November 1918, as well as the way in which Imperial Germany collapsed, and the proceedings of 29 September and its consequences, all of which are closely connected. If I quote hitherto unpublished documents of my father's statements relating to the collapse, I do so with the observation that my father expressly approved of posthumous publication. 29 September 1918 was the beginning of the end:

'What I learned during this day of the negotiations signified utter confusion,' Niemann reported. 'The military crisis had also created an acute political one and both had to be solved simultaneously.'

The first sign of a change in the political views of the High Command was perceived by the Chancellor in Berlin on the day of his departure for Spa. Colonel Detlev von Winterfeldt, the High Command's representative at the Foreign Office, summoned to Count von Hertling, brought him a communication which stated that 'the High Command had formed the opinion that a reform of the Government or its extension on a broader basis had become necessary'.

It was not easy for the Chancellor to grasp this complete change of front. It came as too much of a surprise 'that the High Command should suddenly turn in favour of parliamentary democracy'. The seventy-five-year-old Count, a Catholic Conservative with a long, rich and honourable career in the service of the Kingdom of Bavaria and who had become its Prime Minister, was a man of firm principles. When he was offered the post of Reich Chancellor after Bethmann Hollweg's fall, he refused, saying that he did not feel strong enough to 'carry on a battle with the High Command, i.e., Ludendorff, who meddled incessantly with the conduct of political affairs'. After Michaelis's departure, he was offered the post anew. After receiving assurances in black and white that 'the High Command will no longer interfere in politics', he accepted. Now, he considered Colonel Winterfeldt's dispatch from the High Command demanding governmental reforms as inadmissible interference in politics. For him, however, the decisive sign 'was the change in the High Command's own political views'. He declared: 'When the development of affairs reaches such a state as to initiate parliamentary reforms, then I deplore it. Naturally, considering my whole past, it goes against all my principles.' True to his convictions, the Reich Chancellor requested on 29 September at Spa that he be relieved.

My father discussed the question of his successor with him. Next day, during the course of these talks, Ludendorff marched into the room unannounced. He was obviously excited and turned immediately to my father and the following dialogue took place:

Ludendorff: 'Hasn't the new government been formed yet?'

My father (somewhat angry): 'I can't just conjure one up!'

Ludendorff: 'The government must be formed at once because the peace offer must go out today.'

My father: 'You should have told me that fourteen days ago!'

The conferences at G.H.Q., on 29 September 1918, resulted in the following demands: changes in the parliamentary system providing openings for the Left, an immediate cessation of hostilities, and an immediate offer of peace to the Entente. That was the material result. From a psychological viewpoint the proceedings at Spa were to lead to important, far-reaching consequences: it would have been the equivalent of a miracle if so abrupt an admission of military defeat had not produced panic.

In addition to the cares of State and the people, my father had the worry over his wife to contend with. How could she be prepared for the news of the impending catastrophe in her state of health? Someone in the Kaiser's entourage said he seemed to have aged years in one day and that he was tormented by the thoughts of the pain his wife would have to undergo. On the evening of 29 September he wrote her a few lines which would prepare her as carefully as possible:

'We are approaching grave days and important measures will have to be sought to find internal rest and unity as well as external peace. God help us in this work and our heroes, too.'

Then my father instructed his Adjutant, General von Gontard, verbally to inform the Kaiserin in Wilhelmshöhe of the military and political developments. Ever since the time he had been private tutor to my brothers, Gontard had been a very close confidant of our family and we esteemed him very highly, particularly for his knightly character and his readiness to help or smooth over any difficulties which might arise. My husband and I often sought him out and obtained his advice. The High Command had placed a special train at Secretary of State von Hintze's disposal so that he could go to Berlin as speedily as possible and Gontard used this train for his journey to Kassel to see my mother.

Gontard began his report to her with the words: 'Your Majesty must be strong, for I bring no good news.' Like my father on the previous day, my mother kept her self-control when she heard the fateful tidings. Countess Keller, who had met the General on his arrival at Wilhelmshöhe and had been briefly informed of the situation, expressed her concern for my mother: 'I shall only live through this next hour with the greatest anxiety,' she told him. 'How can the Kaiserin bear this blow when she's in need of such care? Minutes turned into hours before I was finally summoned to her. She stood like a heroine before me, terribly sad, fully aware of the gravity of the situation, but there was no wailing and moaning. Her composure was remarkable!'

That day my father wrote my mother from Spa:

'Gontard will already have told you how serious it is for us. Our brave army, in glorious defiance, is daily smashing back the overwhelming attacks by the enemy masses. But we, too, are suffering losses and our troops are steadily being reduced. Domestically, there's nothing but discord, wrangles and vexation! So it was decided at yesterday's conference, 1: In order to restore domestic peace, there will be an enlargement of the government by some men from the different parties who will assume responsibility, 2: To sue for peace and an armistice. Old Count Hertling has asked to be relieved. Berg and I are once again looking for a successor.

'God has not allowed us to achieve the goal we had hoped for; He has decided on a path of pain and sorrow. We yield to His Holy Will and go to Him with the hope and prayer that He will be willing to give us the strength of His Spirit to pass through this difficult time in the belief that He will lead us to our best way even if His way is also difficult and appears to us to be obscure. May He strengthen our faith, all of us, and not abandon my poor people and the Fatherland, but be a Saviour in need. Without His help it would have been worse for us. I will continue to do my duty to Him and to the Fatherland, with all my strength, as long as God allows me!'

In a postscript, he bade my mother to remain in Wilhelmshöhe and returned to the subject of the change of Chancellors:

'The Chancellor has gone in order to make room for new men: noble, distinguished and quite without personal consideration for himself. It will be bitterly hard for me to part from this admirable man. Who could follow him? God help us!'

The task of the new Chancellor was the liquidation of the war. Ludendorff had demanded that the latest date by which the new government should sue for an armistice was 1 October. This short period left the new Chancellor neither the time either to make his own estimate of the military situation nor the time to make a scrupulous choice of cabinet. Only later, when the disastrous consequences of his pressures became apparent, did Ludendorff recognise his error. 'Had I foreseen the situation more clearly,' he admitted, 'then I would have allowed the date for the dispatch of the Note to lapse.' But this recognition came too late.

Without cease, Ludendorff bombarded government circles in Berlin with his demands for an immediate armistice. He ordered the representative he sent from the Operations Division to the capital, Major the Baron von dem Bussche, 'to pressurise Vice Chancellor von Payer on my (Ludendorff's) behalf so that the peace offer would be speeded up'. Ludendorff made Counsellor von Lersner telegraph the Head of the Foreign Office:

'General Ludendorff requested Baron von Grünau and me, in the presence of Colonel Heye, to transmit to Your Excellency his urgent request that our peace offer goes out immediately.

Today the troops are holding out; no one can say what will transpire tomorrow.'

On the same day Ludendorff once again demanded the immediate dispatch of his petition. Lersner telegraphed:

'General Ludendorff told me that our offer must be issued from Berne to Washington immediately. The army cannot wait another forty-eight hours. He urgently requested Your Excellency to do everything to ensure that the offer is dispatched by the fastest possible means. . . . The General said that everything depends on the offer being in the hands of the Entente by Wednesday or earliest Thursday and requests Your Excellency to use every means to set this in motion.'

The unhappy man who had to take up the post of Reich Chancellor in such circumstances was my brother-in-law, Prince Max of Baden. He seemed predestined to take up the task of talking to the enemy through his successful occupation with the Red Cross and provision for prisoners of war. In addition, he was well known abroad as a champion of conciliation. He was proposed as Chancellor by the Liberal, Friedrich von Payer.

When Max set out on his journey to Berlin at the invitation of Friedrich von Berg, Chief of the Civil Cabinet, he had no idea of the radical changes of opinion which had taken place in the High Command, but was put into the picture immediately on arrival by Colonel Hans von Haeften, Head of the Military Division of the Foreign Office. My brother-in-law was particularly confounded by the demand for an immediate armistice which had been formulated in Spa since he had no idea of the dreadful gravity of the military situation. It seemed of special importance to him, however, that even abroad they were uncertain of the gloomy prognostications of the German military leaders. He came to the pertinent conclusion that a precipitate armistice would not only enlighten the enemy Powers of an impending collapse and weakening resistance but that it would also induce them to stipulate the harshest terms. The programme that my brother-in-law determined upon should he take over the government was simply to 'clear the way for peace'. But he had also learned the necessary lessons of the frustrated peace bids of earlier years and arrived at the conclusion: 'No peace offer—better the distinct proclamation of our aims, a declaration that we can contain concessions to the enemy, with the emphasis on our absolute determination to fight to the death if dishonourable terms were to be proposed.'

Max asked Colonel Haeften: 'Don't they even give me until November?'

'No,' he replied.

Max rejoined that he would then have to decline the Chancellorship and both went to see von Payer and they all went along once more to the representative of the High Command, Major von dem Bussche. Prince Max again heard from the Major as to why the High Command were requiring an immediate armistice and was given the brief additional summary that 'the situation can worsen every twenty-four hours'. Bussche then read out a text that had already been given him from Spa:

> 'If it is absolutely certain by 7 or 8 this evening that Prince Max of Baden is forming a government, then I am agreed to a postponement until tomorrow morning. Should, on the contrary, the formation of a government be in any doubt whatever, then I shall consider putting the Declaration to the foreign governments tonight as imperative.'
> —von Hindenburg

Max continued to resist the High Command's pressures. 'If the situation were really so grave,' he said, 'then there would be no more to save through an offer of an armistice and therefore one must never let this happen, if a catastrophe follow or not; the precipitation of a peace or armistice offer can only have fearful political consequences. I refuse to give my name to it.'

He then sought out the Civil Cabinet Chief, Berg, having decided not to accept the Chancellorship. Berg told him: 'You were certainly not my candidate, but I have no one else.' Now Max knew exactly how things stood. When he met Haeften later he told him that his signature on an armistice offer would be intolerable in view of his position as heir to the Baden throne, whereupon the representative of the High Command retorted: 'Your Highness is not only the Baden heir, but also a General in the Prussian army whose fate it concerns.'

My father, who meanwhile had given much thought to the call for Max's appointment, was asked by the High Command to intervene. A special train which had been put at his disposal to go to Berlin was halted at Cologne and he was requested to send a telegram to the Grand Duke of Baden to obtain his sanction in order to speed up Max's appointment.

As soon as Ludendorff had received what was tantamount to the Grand Duke's approval he told Colonel Haeften—it was shortly after midnight—to go and wake Prince Max up immediately and induce him to sign. But the Colonel waited until morning and in forcible words implored him not to fail in his duty as an officer and do what the army demanded.

Prince Max saw clearly what was expected of him. He telephoned Grand Duke Friedrich and reported afterwards:

> 'I had to listen to some sorrowful words; the Grand Duke hated the thought that a Prince of Baden had been charged with the liquidation of a lost war. He warned me of the awful conse- quences for me and our House. I could only repeat that accord- ing to my convictions the sacrifice had to be made.'

Before Max decided to take the fateful step demanded of him to seek an armistice, he tried everything once more to convince Hindenburg and the High Command that there were better, more realistic ways. The Field Marshal told him: 'We have managed to contain this latest attack; within eight days I expect a new, big offensive and I cannot take the responsibility for any catastrophe which overtakes us or at least any other severe consequences.'

The following day Max made his final attempt, outlining the conse- quences of an immediate demand for an armistice and peace for Germany in defeat, and the High Command refused to budge from its decision of 29 September.

On the evening of 3 October, the Note asking for an armistice was written and Max signed. Thereupon, he was appointed Chancellor.

Later, he wrote: 'When I awoke on the morning of the fourth, I felt like a man who had been condemned to death and had forgotten it in his sleep.'

11   *Abdication*

It was with considerable anxiety that we followed Prince Max's tribulations, and the news which reached us from Berlin confirmed our worst fears.

The High Command's sudden realisation that the war was lost, and which produced such a shock in Spa on 29 September, produced panic in Berlin. Party leaders who had been informed by Ludendorff's liaison officer, Major von dem Bussche, that the continuation of the war was impossible, felt as if they had been hit by a bomb. Prince Max reported: 'The deputies were completely broken. Ebert [Friedrich Ebert, the Social Democrat, later President; Ed.] grew deathly pale and could not utter a word while Stresemann [Gustav Stresemann, a Liberal politician, later Chancellor and Minister of Foreign Affairs; Ed.] looked absolutely crushed.'

Our people themselves felt they had been robbed of their last hopes of a good end to the war. They grew bitter at not having been prepared for Ludendorff's proclamations of danger the previous August, for he had known then how utterly dangerous the situation had become. The deaths of millions of German men, the years-long hunger and many deprivations suddenly seemed to have been senseless and in vain. Their powers of resistance received a deadly blow particularly when they lost all their faith in the military leadership. One day they would read all the official announcements proclaiming confidence in victory, the next that we were militarily finished. That was too much to bear.

Prince Max wrote in a letter:

> 'We are in the middle of a revolution. If I can contain it peaceably, then we can come through as a nation after peace has been achieved. If not, it will be the revolution, violence, and then ruin. Even now I hope to be able to save the Kaiser and the Hohenzollern dynasty; but this alone requires extraordinary courage and spiritual strength. The Conservatives are openly speaking of abdication . . . with the help of the Social Democrats I will hopefully be in a position to save the Kaiser. . . .'

The general despair and war weariness, mistrust of the nation's leaders, enhanced the chances of subversive propaganda—which previously had been devastatingly put into effect by the Entente and by us in Russia. Imperial Germany was the next victim.

The offer of an armistice put forward on 3 October was deliberately handled dilatorily by the Allies. They wanted to gain time. They saw in Germany's desire for an immediate cessation of hostilities only an admission of complete exhaustion. Every delay could only improve their position. Those who, in their euphoria or credulity, thought they saw a kind of angel of peace in President Wilson soon learned better. Matters simply developed into weeks-long exchanges of Notes—an extensive exchange of letters, as Churchill said, which particularly suited Wilson.

In his first Note, Wilson demanded the acceptance of his Fourteen Points as a precondition for armistice negotiations and the immediate evacuation of all occupied territories. In his second Note, he went a step further. He turned on our U-Boat units and demanded security for the future military superiority of the Allies. In a third Note the President intimated that after the Reich Government's acceptance of his conditions, the correspondence was to be communicated to his allies with the proposal that 'if these governments are inclined to bring about peace on the conditions and principles offered', they would invite the Allies' military advisers for discussions of all conditions for an armistice. In his fourth Note, Wilson demanded reparation payments.

Wilson's new points additionally demanded the abdication of the Kaiser. In his first Note he had already asked the oft-put question:

'Does the Chancellor speak for those forces which had so far conducted the war?' He laid stress on the fact that he attached the greatest importance on the answer to this question. In the following Note, Wilson said quite clearly that for him the German Monarchy represented a tyranny whose destruction was one of his aims. 'The German nation has the choice of changing this,' he added. 'The removal of the Kaiser constitutes one of the conditions under which peace can be achieved.' The President said he was duty bound to declare that in his opinion the whole accomplishment of peace was subject to the positive and satisfactory character of the security offered and which was inherent in this basic question. What it all meant was removal of the Monarchy or capitulation.

The Monarchy fell, but nevertheless they still demanded capitulation, and the youthful German democracy was forced to submit in disgrace at Compiègne and Versailles.

Later, in 1933, when my nephew Louis Ferdinand met the English wartime Premier Lloyd George, he was told: 'You know, Prince Louis, we neither expected nor intended the overthrow of your dynasty. . . . Had your House in Germany remained in government, then we wouldn't need to give ourselves such headaches now about Herr Hitler.'

And Sir Winston Churchill said: 'American prejudice against monarchies which Lloyd George in no way sought to counteract, made known to defeated Imperial Germany that negotiations could better be conducted with a republic than with a monarchy. A wise policy,' he added, 'would have been for the Weimar Republic to have established and crowned in the person of one of the Kaiser's grandchildren a constitutional sovereign under a Regency Council. Instead of this, a yawning gap was revealed in the national life of the German people. It was into this gap that Hitler stepped.'

The question has often been asked why my father did not campaign vigorously against his overthrow or, for that matter, why he had not set himself up as a dictator. That I can easily answer.

My father had never wanted a dictatorship. He who had ascended the throne in 1888 had not been very fond of parliamentary government during the early years of his reign—which was quite normal since his ideas coincided with those of the German people. But he had never approved of dictatorship. His high conception of duty, to which he held, in the most true and noble way, as if by the very Grace of God, would have prohibited him. Certainly my father reigned very energetically, but always within the Constitution.

After 'the *Daily Telegraph* Affair' of November 1908, when the Reichstag had set itself against him, he had kept himself in check. He did not succeed in mastering the deep psychological shock of that time. On the contrary, the succeeding years of his reign—almost ten years to the day—were influenced by this. The shadow of the mounting clouds of which my father had spoken at the time ruled his way of life and his commissions and omissions were determined for him from then on.

However, he never let us know he was going to resign, but from some of his remarks regarding his relationship with Hindenburg and Ludendorff we can gather he had a clear conception of his restraint. When my father was approached on the question of a dictatorship, he declined and was severely criticised for it by the extreme Right though his critics perceived that Ludendorff, too, had categorically rejected the Secretary of State, von Hintze's, suggestion of a dictatorship. It must be made clear that when the question of for or against a dictatorship arose, my father's views were not be be mistaken and could be put in one phrase of his: 'Dictatorship is nonsense.'

The Kaiser recognised the sign of the times when he acknowledged parliamentary democracy and accepted the reforms which came about as a natural development. That was confirmed not only by Lieutenant-Colonel Niemann, who talked to my father in that autumn of 1918, but by Prince Max who was convinced the Kaiser wanted to work absolutely loyally with the new government. And my father actually said so at a reception he held for the new administration at Bellevue Castle on 21 October.

> '. . . Gentlemen,' he said, 'with regard to my Decree of 30 September, from which your appointment follows, it is your task to lead Germany in its new situation. I know there is none among you who is not aware of the immensity of this task and its vast responsibilities. I have it at heart to express to you at this time my firm determination to do everything I can to help you

and the representatives of the people reach the goals set out in the Decree. . . .'

Yet the Entente propaganda screamed 'Hang the Kaiser!' And in Germany the broad masses, as well as many members of Parliament, saw in my father not just one of the hindrances to peace but *the* hindrance. A few days after President Wilson had proposed the Kaiser's removal, the mood of the people turned against my father. Friedrich Ebert said at the time:

'The people considered Ludendorff as the guilty one, but all the hate was directed against Wilhelm II.'

His Party associate, Philipp Scheidemann, signified the signs of the times with the acknowledgement that:

'If the war had ended in a German victory, then the Kaiser would have been rapturously acclaimed, probably would even have been raised to the status of demi-god. As things turned out they wanted a scapegoat and they found the Kaiser right in front.'

Prince Max did everything in his power to oppose the abdication and occupied himself fully in trying to reconcile the Kaiser with the people. But my brother-in-law's efforts to swim against the tide were condemned to failure. When he realised this, he felt the only hope lay in my father's voluntary abdication. In the Monarch's sacrifice for his people, he held out great hopes for a successful path to a tolerable peace and the retention of our dynasty. Prince Max considered it as his aim, once my father and my brother Crown Prince Wilhelm had renounced the throne, to set up a Regency of Prussian Princes during the minority of the eldest of the Kaiser's grandsons. By this means he hoped to eradicate the dreadful nightmare of the German Kaiser and the House of Hohenzollern being set upon by the mobs.

The Chancellor restrained himself from doing anything in order to give my father the opportunity of arriving at his own decision regarding the renunciation of the Throne, though he endeavoured to find men who were regarded by the Kaiser not only as personal friends but as pillars of the throne, so that these men might be able to see an honourable way out. Pastor Dryander, the Court Chaplain, whom Prince Max considered as particularly close to my father as his spiritual adviser, refused to advise him on the question of abdication. The Court Marshal, Count Eulenburg, and General von Chelius, for years one of my father's aides, also refused the task.

Prince Max told me how he despaired of these failures and I decided to go to Potsdam to see my father myself. I had the feeling he had to know what I had to say to my sorely tried parent, that the only way out was to renounce the Throne, for it was the sacrifice the Kaiser had to make to save his people. I spoke to my husband about it all, as always, and he was of the same opinion. He said that perhaps I was the only one who could carry out this task. So, I notified Potsdam; but my father's entourage practically forbade the visit. Nevertheless, I decided to go there. Suddenly, I was laid low by the Spanish 'flu, which was rampant at the time. I could hardly stand, let alone travel, so Max decided he himself would go to my father. That was on 29 October.

Prince Max could not carry out his project. In the afternoon my father informed him that he was going to General Headquarters at Spa—a decision that completely surprised us all.

The apparent motive for my father's trip to the army was due to Hindenburg's express wish that he should do so. The Chancellor tried to change my father's opinion round into staying, and asked Count Eulenburg and the Chief of the Civil Cabinet to get him to defer his journey. Then Prince Max personally telephoned the Kaiser and requested an immediate audience. 'We are presently going through our worst days,' he said, 'and Your Majesty cannot possibly be absent at this time.' But he got no further and did not succeed in obtaining an audience. That evening, my father left, and my mother went with him to Wildpark Station. As the train drew away, no one present realised the German Kaiser would never see his capital again.

It was in every respect ominous that my father left Berlin, and we kept asking ourselves what made him do it. Later we realised why. Some people in my father's immediate entourage had recognised that it had become a mere matter of hours until the question of abdication would have been put to the Kaiser. They were men who had served my father for years, who had been loyal to him and had endeavoured to do the best for him and the Monarchy. An abdication was not, in their minds, to be contemplated. Already at the beginning of October the Chief of the Civil Cabinet had told Prince Max: 'The Kaiser is toying with the idea of abdication,' and recommended that he be warned of its dire consequences. In the present critical situation they could see only one way out—the Kaiser had to go as quickly as possible to the army and right out of Berlin.

It was a view they shared with some in the High Command, so it was not difficult to convince my father that it was imperative he should respond to the Field Marshal's urgent request. Besides, there was also mistrust of Max of Baden and his government which, in the Kaiser's entourage, was considered to be illusory and opportunistic in its policies.

Before he left Potsdam my father had, as I know, come to terms with the question of abdication. It was not merely like renouncing a Ministry. The Kaiser was deeply convinced that he ruled by God's Grace over a people entrusted to him. His conceptions were based not only on political but religious grounds, and this conviction permeated his thoughts. There was also his Prussian interpretation of duty, in which he saw abdication as a form of desertion. Very seriously, he said once: 'A successor of Frederick the Great does not abdicate.'

Nevertheless, even considering the duty he felt towards his people, the Kaiser reached the conclusion that he had to offer himself as a sacrifice for the German people and his brave armed forces. The prerequisite for him was that our enemies were ready to pay 'the price of an equitable and honourable peace' for it. Max of Baden thought likewise. He, too, wanted 'no obscure foreign reports' to pass as a reason for abdication. It is a deep tragedy that my father and brother-in-law, who were so near to each other on this decisive question, never got together.

My father's departure showed that Max of Baden did not have his confidence but that Field Marshal von Hindenburg did, and it was to him that he entrusted himself at Imperial Germany's hour of destiny.

To the public, the fact that the Kaiser had gone over to the army indicated that he was not considering abdication and the demands for his renouncement of the Throne became more clamorous. In the

Cabinet, there were long discussions of the subject and the Chancellor declared:

> 'I have pondered for days without cease on the question of the Kaiser's abdication and discussed the matter with men in His Majesty's confidence. I have given them material to enable them to explain to His Majesty what the situation would entail both at home and abroad and I will see to it that these explanations to him will go on uninterrupted. I must positively declare, however, that the abdication of His Majesty the Kaiser can only be voluntary and must be done in such a way as to protect both the Kingdom and the forces from harm and retain the honour of Germany. In any case, the basis for my own handling of the affair must be freedom of action, unprejudiced and without pressure.'

Prince Max endeavoured to win over some German Princes who were going to the Kaiser at Spa, so that they could explain the question of abdication. At his request, Grand Duke Ernst Ludwig of Hesse, and Prince Friedrich Karl of Hesse, came to see him in Berlin. The Grand Duke refused the task of speaking to the Kaiser, but Prince Friedrich Karl asked for time to think it over before finally agreeing. The Chancellor was convinced he had found in him the best intermediary he could, for the Prince was married to my father's sister, Margarethe, and two of his sons, the Princes Friedrich Wilhelm and Maximilian, had been killed in action. The Prince was also a Prussian General, had fought splendidly at the front, and had also been wounded.

A special train for Spa was speedily ordered, documents and other evidence prepared which the Prince was to place before my father. Among them was the draft of a proclamation by the Kaiser to the people and the armed forces. The text read:

> 'For more than twenty-five years I have been able to maintain peace in Germany. Finally, war was forced upon us which our People's Army fought defensively in our own as well as in enemy country. The war has been decided against us, and misguided enemy public opinion has laid the blame, and all the suffering which they have caused, on us. The deeds and the sufferings of the German people, particularly my Prussians, have

not given them the rewards of victory, but they have earned immortal glory in heroic battles and performances, endurance and suffering. This glory, insofar as it lies in my power, will not be dimmed by armistice or peace terms which are incompatible with our honour. The enemy's hate for me could render those terms more severe. I therefore consider that at this moment it is more my duty to renounce the Crown of Prussia, and with it the Imperial Crown, than to prolong your burden any further.'

On the evening of 1 November, Prince Friedrich Karl went to the Reich Chancellery to get a final briefing. While he was speaking with Prince Max, the gentlemen of the Chancellery and of the Foreign Office, there came futher news from the High Command and the Foreign Office itself. The Prince got the impression that there now seemed to be a lack of clarity regarding the political and military situation, but that there also appeared to be a slight improvement in the situation at the front. And doubts appeared to have arisen in the minds of the Chancellor's advisers regarding the Kaiser's abdication, brought about by an energetic rejection of it by the High Command. As to the precise question whether there was an alternative to abdication, Prince Friedrich Karl found there was no information. After a long discussion he finally declared that under these given circumstances, should he have to go to the Kaiser to announce such a weighty irrevocable act, he would only do so if this were in accordance with his innermost conviction. However, he said he would remain at the Chancellor's disposal if it could be confirmed that there was no way other than abdication.

The High Command's watchword was: 'For the army there can be no question of the Kaiser's abdication.' Their interpretation was that of General Groener, who had succeeded Ludendorff at the end of October. He said:

'The General Field Marshal has authorised me to declare, insofar as the question of the Kaiser's abdication is concerned, to say that he would consider himself a scoundrel if the Kaiser were to leave; and so, gentlemen, do I and all honour-loving soldiers think.'

In a conversation alone with General Groener, Prince Max tried to convince him of the necessity of the Kaiser's abdication. 'Groener felt this discussion showed a complete disregard for the men at the front and refused to see reason,' my brother-in-law reported. Groener had been empowered to pledge the Kaiser's return to Berlin within twenty four hours, but on his arrival in Berlin received a telegraphic recall from the High Command.

This happened on 5th November 1918 the day the German Fleet mutinied at Kiel. On the following day the revolt had spread to Rensburg, Lübeck, Altona, Hamburg, Bremen, and Cuxhaven and on this day, 6 November, General Groener had a meeting with the leaders of the Social Democratic Party and the Trades Unions in the Reich Chancellery. Ebert declared:

> 'It is not yet time to seek those guilty for the general collapse. The voice of the people puts the blame on the Kaiser, whether correctly or incorrectly is a matter of indifference. The main thing is that the people want to see those presumed guilty removed. The abdication of the Kaiser is therefore necessary if we wish to prevent the move of the masses into the revolutionary camp. The Kaiser must announce his abdication at the latest by tomorrow morning and authorise one of his sons, Oskar or Eitel Friedrich, to take his place. It is impossible to have the Crown Prince, as he is hated by the masses.'

General Groener replied:

> 'There can be no question of an abdication. At this time, when the army is heavily attacked by the enemy, it is impossible to take away its Commander-in-Chief. The interests of the army must surmount all others.'

Ebert turned to Groener:

> 'I advise you, General, to take this last opportunity to save the Monarchy, and speedily entrust one of the Royal Princes with Regency.'

Groener answered that for him, it was not a matter for discussion, whereupon Ebert told him: 'Then things must take their course.'

Silent and serious, the Social Democrats then left the room. Even those who remained were silent. Colonel von Haeften, who took notes of the meeting, turned to Groener. 'That means revolution,' he said. 'These leaders can no longer control the masses.'

While these events were taking place my father was with the army, both at Spa and at the front. What Max had feared and had wanted to prevent at all costs, had happened. My father, in the hour in which he had to decide the fate of the nation and the Monarchy, was in the wrong place. It was in Berlin, not in Spa, where the decision had to be made, for it was in the capital that other prospects and other views were recognisable. His views of the situation and its development were now extensively influenced by the opinions of his military entourage, and the rôle the Kaiser had to play now was merely that of a spectator. The letters he wrote to my mother at the time made this quite clear. On 7 November, he wrote:

'This is truly a ghastly state of affairs! My Fleet has mutinied. . . . The Commission to receive the armistice terms has arrived here and has been with the Field Marshal. It has been laid down that two civilians have been authorised by Max to handle the negotiations—Erzberger and Count Oberndorff—formerly in Sofia— Max has presumed to give himself the sole right to decide the armistice. The army, above all the High Command and I, have been totally passed over and excluded. . . . If the people, and above all, the army, are agreed—good. If not, then the storm will intensify. . . . We're concentrating on getting the troops I consider necessary ready for the security of the country, for the repression of rebellion and conquest of Berlin. 2nd Guards Division is in Altengrabow; the Rohr Assault Battalion— 1000 men—would go with me to Potsdam; as soon as there's a suspension of hostilities then the trustworthy part of the army will return and the Corps of Guards will be concentrated around Berlin. . . .'

In a letter dated 8 November, he wrote:

'My letter of yesterday did not come through as there is insurrection in Cologne and the station is occupied. The people have all gone insane! They have proclaimed a republic in Munich, as the King is supposed to have abdicated. I don't know if this letter will reach you. God be with you and us. I am gathering all the troops from the front together, so as to march on Berlin with them as soon as an armistice has been declared. Our sons must take over your defence until we can come to your help from here. If it's no longer safe for you in Potsdam, then you must go with the children to Königsberg or Rominten if necessary. I cannot judge matters from here. All connections are so uncertain . . . The War Minister has been appointed Commander-in-Chief, Home Forces, Mackensen's army is being posted to Silesia, 2nd Guards Division is on the march to Cologne, 52nd Division, Fusilier Division are on their way home. The Field Marshal will be advising me on further measures.'

What my father did not know as he penned those few lines was that the High Command had changed their minds regarding military operations at home. On 8 November, Hindenburg and Groener decided that action against the revolution would be hopeless.

On the following day, that tragic 9th of November 1918, my father was told of the new estimates of the situation by Hindenburg and Groener. The Field Marshal began by asking that he be relieved of his post. He stated: 'Before reporting on the latest military situation I asked His Majesty if I could be relieved because it was unbearably painful for me to dissuade him as my Commander in Chief from operations to be directed against our own country.' My father withheld his decision on the Field Marshal's plea and Hindenburg and Groener then outlined why they should refuse to let the army march against the revolt at home, saying: 'The army will march back home under their leaders and commanding Generals in peace and with discipline, but not on Your Majesty's orders, for the army no longer stands behind Your Majesty!'

The talks had begun at ten o'clock in the morning. Towards 1300 hours, Colonel Heye appeared. He reported the result of a series of questions which had been put to thirty-nine Generals and Regimental Commanders of the various Army Groups who had been

summoned to Spa by Groener. They had been asked what the attitude
of the troops was towards the Kaiser, and if they considered it possible
they would march against the revolutionaries under the Kaiser's
leadership. Only one of those asked answered in the affirmative,
fifteen left the questions unanswered, and twenty-three said no. In the
report submitted by Heye to his Commander-in-Chief he said:

> 'The troops are tired and apathetic and only want peace and
> quiet. They will not now march against their homeland even
> with Your Majesty at their head. Neither will they march against
> the Bolshevists; they purely and simply want an armistice soon
> and the quicker the better.'

That, then, was the end, my father thought. Only the previous
evening he had refused to abdicate following the Chancellor's urgent
recommendation that he do so, considering it as a foregone conclusion
of the High Command that he should remain as Kaiser. Now, a few
hours later, this devastating transformation. And also this same
morning—the sounds of the army's defection had hardly faded away—
they were asking at General Headquarters, 'Where should His
Majesty go?' Officers who were present at the meetings stated
afterwards: 'Some gentlemen recommended Switzerland, while the
Field Marshal preferred Holland.'
Hindenburg explained this as follows:

> 'I suggested Holland because the Kaiser would encounter more
> sympathy in this monarchical State than in half-French, republi-
> can Switzerland and because Spa was only fifty kilometres from
> the Dutch frontier.'

Early that afternoon the Field Marshal ordered Admiral von Hintze
to make the necessary preparations for my father's journey to
Holland, 'at a time', as General Baron von Marschall, who was
present, testified, 'when His Majesty knew absolutely nothing about
these proposals'.
A little later there was a conversation between my father and
Hindenburg at the Villa Fraineuse. Hindenburg, obviously deeply
moved, said: '. . . Therefore I advise Your Majesty to renounce the
Crown and go to Holland. . . .'

My father now faced the end of a glorious Monarchy, the end of the 500-year-old dominion of the House of Hohenzollern, and he was burdened with the weight of Germany's collapse. Even more burdensome at this moment was the decision as to whether or not he should leave the army as advised by his military commanders. As an old soldier, he was against such a step.

'I will hold out with my army to the very end and pledge my life,' he told his entourage. 'They're trying to induce me to desert my army. That is a scandalous demand—it would look as if I were afraid. My wife remains bravely in the middle of all the disturbances in Potsdam. I, too, will stay where I am.'

When the Kaiser's hesitation over leaving the army became known, Baron von Grünau was told to inform him that his departure was now most urgent. 'The Field Marshal and Secretary of State von Hintze earnestly beseech you not to lose another hour,' the Baron said. 'Going over to Holland is the only solution in this confusion.' It was only now that my father bowed to the inevitable—to go abroad.

Late that afternoon he wrote my mother:

'We are organising a defence here, towards Aachen and Cologne. If the troops refuse to halt, then I must cross over into Holland. God grant that it won't be necessary! But since the troops have become weary and not in favour of fighting, it is becoming more and more doubtful whom I can trust. If I am not allowed to stay in the midst of the remaining faithful, then I must go with you to a neutral State, Holland or elsewhere, where merciful heaven may permit us to eat our bread—in exile. God's hand lies heavily upon us! His Will be done! So, on Hindenburg's advice, I am leaving the army, after fearful mental struggles. As God wills, *auf Wiedersehen*. My lasting gratitude for your faithful love—
Your deeply mortified husband.'

Prince Max of Baden made the announcement of the Kaiser's abdication known from the Reich Chancellery in Berlin. He had been under pressure to give notice of the Kaiser's abdication, since it had already been decided upon at Headquarters. 'The Kaiser and King has decided to renounce the Throne. The Reich Chancellor will remain in office only until the questions regarding the Kaiser's abdication, the renouncement of the Throne by the Crown Prince of the German Reich and Prussia, and the installation of a Regency have been resolved. . . .'

Prince Max was severely reproached for this proclamation, and the odium of the betrayal followed him to the grave. However, the Chancellor's Press release was, in the final analysis, not correct, for the Kaiser had never authorised it. The decision regarding the Monarchy had been that of the High Command and even before it was announced, Hindenburg had made all the preparations for the Kaiser's exile. The Chancellor's step was a last, desperate attempt to save what could be saved.

On 10 November 1918, my father crossed the Dutch frontier at Eysden where, in a symbolic gesture, he gave up his sword to the guard. Then he waited for permission from the capital, The Hague, to go there. On the following day he was told he could stay temporarily at Amerongen, the seat of Godard, Count Bentinck.

On the way there, my father scarcely spoke a single word. 'It was easy to see,' Count Bentinck said, 'that he had been stunned beyond comprehension by the rapidity of the catastrophe.'

Next day my father wrote to my mother:

' . . . My reign is ended, my dog's life is over, and has been rewarded only with betrayal and ingratitude.'

12   *Death of an Empress*

Revolution had spread to Brunswick with the Spartacists [a left-wing splinter group of the Communist Party which originated in Berlin; Ed.] well to the forefront. It was 7 November, and thousands of armed demonstrators, many soldiers among them, rampaged through the town. The prison was forced open, prisoners released, and public buildings were occupied. Then they formed a Worker's Council with the Spartacist August Merges at its head.

I lay seriously ill with Spanish 'flu, and from time to time my husband came to tell me what was happening. That evening, I learned that some convicts had entered the castle guardroom and as the guard itself fled into the castle, my husband slammed the doors behind them, though it really provided no security. Then we waited to see what would happen. Nothing did, at first, if one discounts the fact that our Standard was shot down. Early next morning mutinying soldiers burst into the castle and demanded to see the Duke. My husband went down to see them and was greeted with wild shouts. The men were grumbling vociferously about the food, those in authority, and about everything else. My husband demanded quiet and then asked if any of them came from Brunswick. Only one said he did and my husband told him: 'You speak up, then—and no one else!' Finally the Duke made it clear that, since the beginning of the war, he had had no military authority at all, so he could not redress their grievances. The men were astounded: they had not known the fact. However, they then asked if they could in future come to him if there were any further grievances, and left. My husband saw that one of the men had taken a cigarette box, but that another had hit him on the hand, telling him to leave it alone as one didn't do that sort of thing. After that, none of our effects was touched.

On 8 November, a Soldiers' Council was formed and was immediately taken under the wing of the Merges-led Spartacists. Their slogan, 'Long live the dictatorship of the proletariat', was everywhere, together with red flags, red armbands, red cockades. Workers, soldiers, and sailors ganged up to become the 'Brunswick Red Guards' and terror reigned. Ministers and leading officials were arrested and Merges appeared before my husband, accompanied by some other men. When I heard about this I hastily got up from my sick-bed in order to look after my husband. I thought they would take him away, seeing that the Russians had set such an example. I could not even stand up straight and crawled rather than walked. However, I found my husband in his room and he told me the men had just left, having told him the Workers' and Soldiers' Councils had taken over the government and the Duke had been deposed. My husband had told them: 'If you want to do all that, believe me, it's a great relief to be absolved of the responsibility.'

The revolutionaries then ordered us to leave the State, so we travelled to Blankenburg to fetch our children, Ernst August, Georg Wilhelm, and Friederike [later, Queen of Greece; Ed.] who had been born in 1917. We had taken them there to safeguard them from the 'flu epidemic. We were only there a few hours, but here, too, the Reds were in control, so we went on to Aschersleben where, with our Baden relatives, we were to meet Prince Max and where Social Democrat President-Elect Ebert had laid on a special train for him. 'Get your relatives out of Brunswick,' he had told Max. 'It's a windy corner.' Then, accompanied by Max and his family, we all left for Karlsruhe.

We were scarcely aboard the train, the greetings between us scarcely over, than Prince Max von Baden told us of the recent events in Berlin and described in detail the pressures which had been put upon him regarding his decision in Spa on the Kaiser's abdication. He spoke with bitter disappointment of the High Command. 'I know,' he told me, 'that I will be tainted with it, but I could not let the Kaiser be deposed by the mob. I had no other choice—there was no other way.'

The journey itself was gruesome. We got the impression that the revolution had even broken out at the railway stations. There was fighting at various stations we passed through, while others were already occupied by the Reds. Often we had to wait until after the station had been stormed, then the train would proceed under a barrage of artillery, machine-gun and rifle fire. The worst of it was that our children had to be exposed to this inferno. However, the train eventually moved on. We approached Karlsruhe and hoped to find quiet there, but we jumped straight from the frying pan into the fire. The Devil himself was on the loose. At the station my brother-in-law and ourselves were arrested by members of the Soldiers' Council and taken away. Prince Max asked the Reds: 'Am I your prisoner or what?' but an answer seemed superfluous. We went through a frightful night, believing we would all be killed, for the expressions on the faces of the Red guards indicated that we could expect nothing else.

Our rescue was effected by thoughtful Karlsruhe citizens. During darkness, a man sought out my brother-in-law and told him that he had to get out, or all would be lost. I can still hear how Max told us about him: 'He's a genuine democrat, but just now a supporter of the Throne.' As it turned out, we were soon able to escape to Bavaria. Our old manservant, Haupt, managed to find a horse and carriage in which he took us to the station, but it was swarming with Reds and the railway officials were concerned for our safety. Finally, the inspector dragged us into a small room and told us to wait there as all trains had been completely filled by the soldiers behind the lines. I held Friederike firmly in my arms as she could hardly walk yet, until finally, after endlessly anxious waiting, the railway inspector fetched us and brought us to a carriage. We got in and the journey began, but was stopped again as fighting in the stations broke out continually. From time to time we stopped there for hours before the train eventually moved again. Then we noticed a man who appeared to be watching us closely. Naturally, we were suspicious and thought he had designs on us, but years later we met him accidentally and discovered he had been ordered by the railway administration to see we got out safe and sound.

Haupt and my lady's maid, Louise Holzheuer, accompanied us the whole journey. They took it as a matter of course that they should share in all our difficulties and dangers. It was old Haupt who managed to find us a place to stay in Augsburg—with acquaintances of his, relatives of a Brunswick hairdresser. We found refuge there in their small house and it was a strange feeling as the door closed behind us. We had lost everything—Crown and State. We did not know what had happened to our parents and brothers and sisters, but at least we felt safe and out of danger, and thanked God for letting us have our children with us.

We could not stay long in Augsburg for the town fell into the hands of the Spartacists, so we started off for Gmunden. In Munich there was fighting and more waiting. When we finally found a train, there was no room. Once we were helped by a railway official. As we were waiting to board, he climbed into one of the carriages and—we could hardly believe our ears—shouted: 'This carriage is infected! This is an infected carriage!' In a trice, everyone had jumped out and the carriage was empty. We boarded and soon were on our way to the Austrian frontier.

The railway stations in Austria bore the same aspects as in Germany: Red soldiers had control. And in Salzburg the station inspector, who was well known to us, was extremely puzzled, for the revolutionaries had repeatedly shot at him. They had taken him for a high ranking military man because of the gold braid on his collar. When the shooting broke out, the only way the officials could save themselves was to jump on the train and travel with us.

Finally, we reached Gmunden and were met by my parents-in-law and brought to their home on sleighs. We could hardly believe that the countryside, this beautiful corner of the Earth, was real. It seemed strange to us that nothing here had changed. Everything was as we had known it, and everything that had happened was like a bad dream. One world had been shattered, but one still remained to us— that of the mountains.

We lived with my parents-in-law, the Duke and Duchess of Cumberland, until the Villa Weinberg, which had served as a hospital, was ready for us to move into. For my husband, whose pronounced sense of duty had made him bear all the responsibilities of ruling his State, the burden had fallen from his shoulders and we could now live just for our families. But they were far from trouble-free years and we also ran into financial difficulties.

Above all, however, our worries centred on my parents and my brothers. Despite all warnings about the revolution my mother had stayed defiantly in Potsdam even though she was seriously ill. They had advised her to leave the New Palace, but she answered: 'I will *not* leave this house. It would be cowardice to leave this house, my husband's!' When she wrote to us on November 11—a letter which reached me by a circuitous route, she said:

> '. . . I'm still here in our old home, but for how long? With me I have some of my boys, some daughters-in-law and grandchildren and their love does me good. I worry so much about beloved Papa! He is so alone in his misfortune and I am not with him to help him bear it, he who has always wanted and done his best for the Fatherland. May God grant that I should be reunited with him once more. . . . God grant that we shall see each other again.'

My father's bodyguard took over the security of the New Palace during the days of the revolution, but the task proved too difficult and my brother Eitell-Fritz persuaded her to transfer to his home at the Villa Ingenheim. It was here that the revolutionaries made a raid in an effort to rob my mother of various documents and correspondence. When she was being questioned by the interrogator, a former Naval officer who had been dismissed from the Navy, he suggested the Kaiserin should sit down. '*I* am accustomed to sit down only when I feel like it,' she retorted. The Reds left without accomplishing their purpose and on 27 November my mother went to join my father in Holland. She was escorted to the frontier by soldiers of the 1st Guards Regiment—in civilian clothes.

The first news I received from my mother in Amerongen, Holland, merely said: 'Reunited with Papa eight days ago, praise God!' My parents' reunion was moving. The Kaiser had waited alone in front of the bridge which spanned the moat which encircled Amerongen Castle to await his wife—a lonely old man. And there came the woman who had given up everything to share his fate in exile. He wrapped her in his arms, completely unable to utter a word.

Despite her worries and her illness, my mother wrote me often, always pleasantly, but I could read between the lines the pressures she was under. The worst agony for my mother was when the Allies demanded the Kaiser's delivery into their hands. In June 1919, the Treaty of Versailles was signed in which Article 227 stated: 'The Allies and associated Powers publicly indict Wilhelm II von Hohen-zollern, former Emperor of Germany, for the gravest violation of the international moral code and the sanctity of treaties.'

A special court was to be set up and five judges were to be nomi-nated from the U.S.A., Great Britain, France, Italy and Japan to form the court. It was further stated: 'The Allies and associated Powers will address a request to the Government of the Netherlands to deliver the former Emperor for the purpose of his judgement.'

The hate campaign which had been pursued in the countries of the Entente with the catchphrase 'Hang the Kaiser!', demanded a victim. So, too, did the Treaty of Versailles demand other 'war criminals' among whom were included my brother Crown Prince Wilhelm, Rupprecht the son of the King of Bavaria, Hindenburg, Mackensen, and Bethmann Hollweg, though the prime interest was concentrated on the person of the Kaiser. In the English House of Commons Lloyd George announced: 'The ruler who, for thirty years spoke only of his pride, his dignity and his power, is now a refugee who will soon be arraigned before the Court.'

The Entente requested the extradition of my father from Holland, though it was uncertain which way the Government at The Hague would decide and public opinion in the country was divided. In any case, the situation was serious. We thought perhaps my father should flee rather than fall into the hands of the Entente and in certain quarters preparations were put in hand to enable him to do so. But my father refused, though he wondered whether he should give himself up, the main consideration being whether by doing so he would be rendering his Fatherland a service. However, he had to consider the fact that he could hardly expect a fair judgement from a court which was composed of men, his antagonists, who were to be both accusers and judges and the end result would have great historical and political consequences. Finally, my father gave up the idea of surrendering himself. 'If there were the slightest prospect of obtaining an improvement of the situation in Germany through such a step,' he wrote, 'then there would be no possibility of doubt regarding my surrender. I do not wish to play the rôle of a Vercingetorix who deliberately delivered his person into the hands of his enemies, relying on their magnanimity and trust, in order to obtain an improvement in the lot of his people. Considering the behaviour of our enemies during the war and the peace negotiations, it is unlikely that the Entente will show themselves any more magnanimous than Caesar, who put the noble Gaul in chains and later executed him but still did not spare his people slavery.'

At the beginning of 1919 a group of American officers, led by a Colonel, made an attempt from Luxembourg to kidnap my father. They succeeded in penetrating Amerongen Castle, but thanks to the courage and determination of Count Bentinck, the Kaiser's host, and the local Mayor, the attack was thwarted.

In understandable anxiety, we did everything in our power to obtain clarification from the Dutch Government as to exactly what their views were concerning my father. One of the bits of information we received through an intermediary and which I can reveal today in the conviction that it would no longer be indiscreet to do so, was as follows:

'Most gracious Baroness,

The contents of this letter are intended for Her Royal Highness the Duchess of Brunswick, but I prefer to send it to your address because the danger of it being opened by unauthorised persons is not so great. I was with Herr von W. today and although he considers the matter in question as very serious, he does not think it altogether hopeless. He said he is being careful not to arouse any hopes which might lead to disappointment. W., who was himself a former Foreign Minister, is presently exchanging letters with the present Minister on the subject. He is of the opinion that under no circumstances should Holland give in, not even under the threat of war with the Entente. He is convinced that the Entente would not risk it if the Dutch stand firm. A blockade is possible and if it lasts Holland would have to submit, but if Dutch stubbornness is aroused, Holland will not so easily be made to yield. The question is whether the Entente would not have come round if they are faced with dissension and disunity amongst themselves. . . . Yesterday W. spoke with Princess F. who has connections with English people and she told him that there were wide circles who were indignant at the infamy of Lloyd George and his associates and opposition is increasing. . . . One need therefore not give up hope, but one must not underestimate the danger.'

So we hovered between hope and fear. It was horrible, especially as the Entente put increasing pressure on Holland to surrender the Kaiser. Notes were sent hither and thither. Then, The Hague decided to reject the demand and remained obdurate despite further pressures. Numerous expressions of sympathy and compassion from Dutchmen reached the refugee himself.

My mother's health deteriorated throughout this time. Like the Sword of Damocles, the threat to my father hung over her and my father wrote me: 'She suffers dreadfully and her condition often makes me despair, especially when the pain overcomes her.' Every week Countess Keller sent me a detailed report of my mother's condition. Occasionally, there was a glimmer of hope, but the seriousness of her illness was a sad certainty.

In March 1920, I was allowed to go to Amerongen to see my parents and we took the opportunity of visiting my brothers and other relatives in Germany on the way. It was a moving reunion with my beloved homeland and my father's house which now no longer belonged to us. I shall never forget the moment when my sister-in-law, Crown Prince Wilhelm's wife, Cecilie, drove me past the New Palace. I wept. Everything looked as it had been, but it was lost to us and we could now only enter my favourite rooms as visitors. For me, such a world had ended, though for my brothers it went on gently in their Potsdam houses. But in 1945 that, too, had come to an end and in the Cecilienhof, my brother Wilhelm's house, the men of power of the time—Stalin, Truman, Churchill and Attlee—sat discussing the fate of our Fatherland.

The Kapp *putsch* [after Wolfgang Kapp, 1858-1922, born in New York, founder of the German *Vaterland Partei*, an ultra right wing precursor of the Nazis; Ed.] occurred in Munich on the day we left Berlin and when we reached Gelbensande, the home of the Grand Duke and Duchess of Mecklenburg, we were beset with questions as to what had happened, but we knew nothing. Soon afterwards, however, we received a report of the *putsch* and its frustration. It showed that the unrest was in no way at an end. Instead, it was spreading and was rapidly taking on the aspect of civil war. We ourselves were once more on the move, this time to Stralsund and Rügen, and once more came face to face with fighting at the railway stations. Before Rostock we were surprised by the Reds at a small station, and had to take cover behind a wall and next to some Rostock professors who had fled from the terror. Passing backwards and forwards in trucks and armed with machine-guns, they were really in search of the professors and were checking from station to station. The situation was anything but pleasant. In Stralsund we encountered more street fighting and had to lie flat on the floor of our hotel room while the fighting was going on in the station opposite.

As the unrest quietened down, we travelled back to Berlin where we separated—my husband going back to Gmunden while I made my way to Holland. The journey was gruesome, for the revolt had spread westwards and I thought I would never see my husband and children again. However, the thought of my seriously ill mother drove me on.

The joy of reunion with my parents was indescribable, but I was upset to see how old my father had grown and how my mother's illness had changed her imposing appearance. The suffering of my parents hurt me dreadfully.

Already, one and a half years had passed since they had come to Amerongen, and the Bentinck family had done everything to make life easier for them. They showed an extraordinary measure of tact and readiness to help. The old axiom that it is hard not to have an occupation or daily duties to perform was never truer. My father sawed and split logs, learned Dutch and disposed of correspondence, while my mother's sole occupation was her correspondence. 'Perhaps I would get some strength back if I had something to do in my own home,' she said. 'Here, I always have melancholy thoughts and, at the most, letters to write.'

H.R.H. Princess Viktoria Luise, 1913, as painted by Szankowski.

The Imperial visit to London, May, 1911. As we entered Buckingham Palace, following the **three** Royal Guards: the Kaiser (left) and King George V salute, as the Kaiserin and Queen Mary, **Duke** Edward and Princess Victoria, and the Duchess of Brunswick and the Duke of Connaught follow.

Our wedding banquet, which was held in the White Hall of the Imperial Palace in Berlin. From bottom, seated on the left side of the table: Crown Princess Cecilie (next to the butler pouring), the Duke of Cumberland, Queen Mary of Great Britain, the Kaiser, Duchess Thyra of Cumberland (hidden), the Crown Prince of Prussia, and the Grand Duchess of Hesse. On the opposite side of the table, from right to left: Princess Eitel-Friedrich, King George V of Great Britain, the Kaiserin, the Duke and the new Duchess of Brunswick, Czar Nicholas II, the Grand Duchess Luise of Baden, and Prince Waldemar of Denmark.

To our wedding in Berlin came Czar Nicholas II and King George V of Great Britain, both photographed here in the uniforms of their Prussian regiments.

The day of our arrival at the Palace of Brunswick. 'I can't express how happy we are here in beautiful, beautiful Brunswick! Everyone is bestowing so much love on us!'

On 13 November 1913 the Duke and Duchess of Brunswick watched the wedding parade of the Hussars before Brunswick Palace.

The Kaiser and Kaiserin, 1917.

The Imperial Princes of Prussia, during the First World War. Above from left: Crown Prince Wilhelm, Eitel-Friedrich, and Adalbert. Below, from left: August Wilhelm, Oskar, and Joachim.

The Kaiser, in Doorn, Netherlands, September 1933.

The purchase of a house concerned my parents. After they had rejected several proposals, they were able to acquire the mansion at Doorn, not far from Amerongen, which belonged to the old Baroness Heemstra. Now they had much to plan and think over, and were able to banish some of the sadness from their lives.

We never discussed politics: it was extraordinary how my father got round the subject, an observation also made by others who talked to him. We talked about what was happening to members of the family or friends and even for that the day had scarcely sufficient hours. Still, I was overjoyed to see what good it did my parents to have their daughter with them. After my departure, Countess Keller noted in her diary: 'The good effects of Duchess Viktoria Luise's visit were more than we had thought possible.'

I went to Doorn quite often after that. Three months later, accompanied by my husband, I went to see my parents again. On arrival I was given a report on my mother's state of health by her personal physician, Dr. Hähner:

'. . . The day before yesterday Her Majesty suffered a heart spasm which, thanks to treatment, was alleviated. On this account, Her Majesty must keep to her bed and will, therefore, have to greet Your Royal Highness from her bed,' the doctor said. 'The consequences of this attack have not yet been completely overcome, though the strength of the heart itself has improved, but there is nevertheless an increased breathlessness . . . I hope that if no unforeseen troubles arise, good progress will be made.'

That was on 15 July 1920. Three days later our family was dealt a heavy blow by the sudden death of my brother, Joachim. He had shot himself. We had for some time been apprehensive about the difficulties which had beset him, particularly regarding his unhappy marriage to the 17-year-old Princess Marie Auguste of Anhalt, and remarked upon a growing agitation within him, but we were quite unprepared for the fact that he would take his own life. We feared for my mother and decided to tell her his death had been due to an accident. My father, severely affected himself by his son's death, but

F

caring a great deal for his wife's state of health, undertook the sad task of telling her himself. She took the news calmly and with the usual composure she exhibited when fate dealt her severe blows, but there was no doubt of the pain the news had caused her.

She never got over the death of her son. Her health deteriorated visibly, and in the middle of November we received news in Austria which made us fear the worst. My husband and I hurried to my mother's bedside and found her in a pitiable state. Her apathy and weakness particularly tore my heart to shreds, as I could do nothing to help. The nights with her were dreadful; she was always restless, spoke in her sleep and chattered with her absent children, very often with the eldest, but for the most part with the dead Joachim. What she said was often surprising, almost clairvoyant. One night, when my brother August Wilhelm was keeping vigil, she bade us children goodbye in her sleep. Shattered, Auwi told us later what he had heard.

I stayed a month with my mother before going back to my husband —who had returned earlier—and children. August Wilhelm stayed until Wilhelm arrived, when Adalbert and Oskar relieved him. After them came Eitell-Fritz, so all of us took turns at watching over Mother. I returned to Doorn in January 1921 and stayed five long weeks. They seemed long, not because of the time spent caring for my mother, but because I needed my husband and children and they needed me. Our son Christian had been born in September 1919, and we now had four children all demanding me.

In April, I began the journey back to Doorn. I had to stop over in Nuremberg and there I happened to glance at an advertising pillar where a crowd of passersby was gathered. Instinctively, my gaze fastened on the posters and I was startled to see an 'extra' which proclaimed the news of the death of the Kaiserin. My mother had died early in the morning of that day, 11 April.

In Doorn, Wilhelm, who had arrived first, greeted me. Then I saw my father and Adalbert who had both been able to be with my mother at the time of her death. They told me she had died quietly and gently and without pain. My father's face was painfully blank. He seemed timid and embarrassed, and I believe he did not wish the world to see the dreadful despair which had overcome him. He was now alone, quite alone. He had suffered the loss of his country and his crown and all that had remained to him had been his life's faithful partner, his lifelong friend of more than forty years. She had sustained him through good days and bad. Now, he had lost her, too.

It was my mother's wish not to be buried away from our country. 'I will sleep in my own homeland,' she had once said. That, for my father, was very hard to bear: it meant he would never be able to stand at his wife's grave. Still, he followed her wishes and negotiations with Berlin were begun. Though the government agreed, they demanded that the special train which was to take her remains to the capital should travel only by night, and that no announcement of any kind was to be made concerning the arrangements. For her interment, the Temple of Antiquity was chosen. It had been built by Frederick the Great as his own intended resting-place and was in the neighbourhood of the New Palace.

Now it was time to bid my mother farewell and we all gathered together at her coffin, covered with the Standard of the Prussian Queens, to say our prayers. Very few mourners had been invited, among them Count Bentinck, Count Goltz from Arnhem, the Governor of Utrecht and the Mayors of Amerongen, Doorn and Leersum. Night had already set in as the procession moved off to the station at Maarn where the train was waiting. A reverent silence lay over the route as the inhabitants waited for the coffin to pass and only the sound of horses' hooves could be heard.

In the train we stayed for a little while with my mother, then the Kaiser, the Crown Prince, my husband and I returned to Doorn while Adalbert and Oskar remained to accompany her on her last journey. I would have liked to have accompanied her, but my brothers had asked me to remain with my father in Doorn. So I didn't go to Potsdam and stayed to comfort my father as much as I could.

Three dark-green coaches of the former Court comprised the train, and as it passed through the Dutch stations the flags were at half-mast. Thousands of Dutch people lined the railway tracks to pay their last respects. As the train crossed into Germany the population turned out all along the 600-kilometre route in one long, single line. No one had ordered them to do so, no one had called them, but they were there unbidden. 'The Kaiserin is coming!' echoed all down the line.

The black, white and red flags of happier times were brought out and covered with black crêpe. From Emmerich to Potsdam the sombre chimes of church bells greeted the homecoming of the dead Kaiserin, and from the frontier to her last resting-place, thousands upon thousands lined the railway tracks, which were leading their revered Princess home. Wherever the train stopped, there were hundreds and thousands, in their mourning clothes, waiting to say farewell. Church choirs sang, and bands played the music of hymns. And along the countryside, waiting by the railway embankments, farmers' wives sank to their knees and prayed.

A whole people were mourning their beloved Empress.

In the dim light of day, the train drew up at Wildpark Station. Members of our family, including my brothers Eitell-Fritz and August Wilhelm, and all those who were near to my mother, had assembled there. One after the other they came up to the coffin. Dryander, the Court Chaplain, uttered a prayer as he had done in Doorn before accompanying the cortege back to Potsdam. Then officers of the Kaiserin's two regiments, the Pasewalker Cuirassiers and the 86th Schleswig-Holstein Infantry, took over the vigil for the night. Next morning came the burial ceremony, and the cortege wound its way from the Wildpark to the Temple of Antiquity.

The crowd was immense, more than 200,000 appeared, perhaps a quarter of a million, at the funeral, reverently quiet. No one spoke aloud, there was no noise of any kind, no pushing and shoving. A veritable sea of flowers and wreaths had been laid all round the circular, ivy-covered edifice of the Temple of Antiquity. After the coffin had been placed in front of the altar in the mausoleum, my brothers took over the vigil, their swords drawn, while Pastor Dryander gave the funeral oration, finishing with the words, 'They that sow in tears shall reap joy.'

Many weeks had gone by, and together with my brother Wilhelm and my husband, I had steadfastly stood by our father. Finally, I was permitted to go to my mother's tomb, and hardly had the day awoken one Monday morning than I went to the Temple of Antiquity, accompanied by my brother Oskar and his wife.

My mother had, I knew, prepared herself for the end. In a letter to us she had written:

'In case Papa and I, by God's Will, never see you again, this letter brings you our final greetings and our blessings . . . I know, my dear children, that you will, with God's help, be brave. It is bitterly hard to say goodbye, but our warm love for you transcends the grave. And now, God protect you until we meet again with God.'

Here, in the Temple of Antiquity, I was able at last to have a final communion with my dear mother.

13   *A Matter of Honour*

The Kaiserin's death had left a large void in my father's life. 'I miss her dreadfully,' he wrote. 'Nothing can replace her. I often sit quietly by her bed and talk to her in spirit. Perhaps she is there? Her pictures simply emphasise the severity of her loss.'

Doorn had truly become a lonely place. The little circle which had surrounded the Kaiserin drifted away, and only General von Gontard and young Captain von Ilsemann remained with the Kaiser. In every respect now he realised the complete loneliness of exile. Neither the love of his children and grandchildren, nor the numerous demonstrations of loyalty and constancy, which were amply demonstrated in his daily mail, could shut away the bitter recognition that German public opinion was increasingly vociferating the view that he, the Kaiser, had left his army in the lurch. The untrue assertion that the Kaiser had fled ignominiously was certainly the most infamous and insidious of the accusations laid against my father, and they wounded his honour deeply. Anxiously, he waited for the man who had advised him to lay down his Crown and to leave his army to come forward and say so publicly, but he waited in vain. Not a word was said about it even in Field Marshal von Hindenburg's war memoirs, which could effectively have brought about a change in public opinion.

There were others, too, besides my father, who were involved in the events at Spa, who waited for the Field Marshal's correction of the prevailing misinterpretation of the facts and that he would explain his individual part in the affair to the German public. When the confessions failed to materialise, General Baron von Marschall,

Colonel-General von Plessen and General Count von der Schulenburg, took the initiative to clarify matters. They managed to obtain
the support of a high judge of the Chief Administration Court of
Prussia and a long-serving member of the Reichstag, Kuno, Count von
Westarp. Westarp got to work to produce an actual record of the
events which had taken place in Spa on 9 November 1918. He soon
realised it was not an easy undertaking. He remarked:

> 'The critical point concerns the question as to whether and in
> what form Hindenburg expressly advised the Kaiser to abdicate
> and go to Holland.'

The Generals' assertion that Hindenburg had given the Kaiser such
advice was strongly denied by the Field Marshal. Hindenburg made
his own report, in which he did not mention any indication that such
advice was either given or pressure used to make the Kaiser abdicate.

A lively discussion developed between Hindenburg and Westarp.
The latter maintained that the Field Marshal had indisputably told
the Kaiser in Spa that he could no longer guarantee his safety, while
Hindenburg reiterated in a memorandum dated April 1919 that
it was not true and could not possibly be. He argued: 'I have never
said that I could not guarantee his safety for another night, for the
responsibility for the security of the All-Highest Person lay not in
my hands but in those of the two Commandants at General Headquarters.' For the other participants in the argument, this was taken
to mean that the final responsibility for the safety of the Supreme
Commander-in-Chief was held to have been not that of the Field
Marshal but of officers of the rank of Major, and Hindenburg,
therefore, could not have given such advice.

In a letter to Westarp in May 1919, Hindenburg quite categorically
denied that 'either he or General Groener had proposed that the
Kaiser go to Holland'.

The Generals were indignant at this assertion and on 1 June
Schulenburg wrote to Westarp:

> 'I am of the opinion that the Field Marshal really must admit
> publicly that it was he who advised His Majesty to go to Holland
> immediately. . . . His Majesty still holds the view today that

the way out proposed on 9 November 1918, was the correct one and he is particularly deeply grieved that Hindenburg now denies having given him the advice to take this way out and that the truth of the events of 9 November is still not known.'

Schulenburg was even more emphatic in a letter to Colonel-General von Plessen:

'His Majesty has again and again urgently requested Your Excellency and me to make public the truth concerning the events of 9 November. Our dear Sovereign's request is to us sacred. Your Excellency, Marschall and I are no longer in any doubt whatever concerning the events of that darkest day in Prusso-German history and we know that His Majesty will be very well served by the publication of the facts confirmed by the knowledge of various witnesses to the known facts. I am of the opinion that we should now finish our report insofar as we can be sure of our ground. We have sent it to the Field Marshal in complete loyalty and taken both his wishes and amendments fully into consideration. But this loyalty cannot go so far as for us to remain silent regarding a truth which is so important to His Majesty, neither can we attenuate it. I also wish that all conceivable respect be bestowed upon the Field Marshal, but this respect cannot go so far as to allow the High Command to dictate what we sign our names to. Our stand in these instances should only be taken as a representation of the bare facts, and should not become a defence and a justification of the High Command.'

One can understand how the Field Marshal's attitude rendered Westarp's task 'so painful and difficult'. In his conversations with the Generals, Westarp remarked how 'there was an undertone of distrust of Hindenburg's credibility and readiness to intercede on the Kaiser's behalf and to take over his actual responsibility'. Once more, he turned to Hindenburg. In a personally handwritten reply, the Field Marshal told him that ever since the turn of the year 1918/19, he had wondered whether it would be appropriate to make an announcement through the Press concerning the events at Spa, but had come to the conclusion that 'it would be inadvisable to stir the matter up again'. Hindenburg then demanded that Westarp should investigate if 'His Majesty's closest entourage were agreed on the circumstances of his journey to Holland on the evening of 9 November'. That was a question of secondary importance, for Hindenburg's advice had already been taken. What Hindenburg meant was to be found in the closing lines of his letter: 'If this is confirmed, then I am ready and willing personally to accept part of the responsibility for the way His Majesty acted.'

Every effort by Count von Westarp and the Generals failed to stir Hindenburg into admitting his actual part in the decision that had been made in Spa. The only palpable outcome was a public declaration he made in August 1920, in which he said:

> 'His Majesty the Kaiser and King never deserted the colours. It is a slander I indignantly reject! The Kaiser went away from us because his people had deserted him. A hero's death at the head of his army was impossible because an armistice had already been concluded. Had His Majesty stayed, then there would have been an outbreak of civil war and the recommencement of foreign hostilities against us. The unfortunate Sovereign wanted to spare our Fatherland from both. It is easy to kick a dead lion.'
> —von Hindenburg
> General Field Marshal.

They were certainly vigorous words, but once again they failed to make the necessary reparations and once again, no word of the part played by Hindenburg.

The Kaiser's bitterness grew. I shared my father's feelings and views, and felt deeply for him. It was awful to see how the insult of a so-called flight had not only hurt his self-esteem, but that he was literally being dragged through the mud while the man who had brought about the sorely criticised affair, and who bore the main responsibility, remained silent.

Two more years were to pass before the Field Marshal was to write to his former Supreme Commander, but the poison of lies had already been deeply ingrained in the minds of the people for Hindenburg's letter to have any effect. This is what he wrote on 28 July 1922:

'I bear the responsibility for the unanimous proposal made by all the competent advisers whose ready decision was that Your Majesty should go abroad on that unlucky 9th of November.

'As I have already established, the serious danger threatened that Your Majesty would sooner or later be seized by mutineers, and delivered either to our internal or external enemies. Our Fatherland had in all circumstances to be spared from such an outrage and infamy! It is on these grounds that I, on behalf of all of us, recommended the transfer to Holland that afternoon of 9 November, a step I considered at that time to be transitory and extreme. Today, I am still of the opinion that it was the correct decision.

'At the close of this explanation, Your Majesty, may I respectfully reassure you that all my life I have always shown boundless loyalty to my Kaiser, King and Sovereign, that I will always do so, and that I am determined to bear overall responsibility for the decision of 9 November.'

My father's reply to Hindenburg mirrored his disappointment over the Field Marshal's long silence. The motive behind his departure, my father wrote, had *finally* been explained. He had suffered severely from the mistrust and abuse heaped upon him, but had nevertheless kept silent 'in the hope that the time was not far off when the participants would spontaneously decide to reveal to the world that the decision to leave was taken against my inner convictions and was forced upon me by my responsible military and political advisers'.

The disappointment over Hindenburg's attitude had also led to an alienation between him and authoritative national circles, although criticism in public had generally been repressed. It was considered that as long as Hindenburg remained at the head of the army, which was holding down the Spartacists, it would be irresponsible to undermine his military and national authority. But even after his departure in July 1919, the name of Commander-in-Chief von Hindenburg was still esteemed as a national property against whom criticism of any sort had to be avoided as far as possible.

Today, as I write my memoirs, these former considerations have been overtaken by time. Apart from that, I believe I owe it to my father to say what really happened. To those who deplore my revelations concerning the Field Marshal, I ask for understanding. His immortal services as Army Commander cannot be darkened by the entanglements of 9 November 1918. That was what my father wrote to the Field Marshal in a final acknowledgement, and that is what I think, too.

In the loneliness of his exile, my father took quite an understandable step. He decided to marry again. Considered from a personal point of view, it was nothing out of the ordinary that a lonely man in exile should need someone he could have permanently by his side. But for me it was very hard to contemplate another woman taking the place of our mother.

In Germany the question of my father's re-marriage was vigorously discussed, and there was some criticism here and there. It seemed incredible that their revered sovereign Princess should have a successor, but for my father there was no such problem. His love for his faithful wife and life-partner was unchanging, and no one could replace her, no one could put his memories of her away. He had once compared her life and her tragic fate to that of Queen Luise after the collapse of Prussia in 1807, and now that comparison was close to him personally. He remembered, too, that Friedrich Wilhelm III had married again after the death of his beloved and revered Queen.

My father had fallen ill and he wrote to me:

> 'Lying alone and miserable in bed, a frugal pleasure which doubles the severity of loneliness, in that one lacks the true devotions of a woman who can help and make things much easier. In my despair I telegraphed old Fräulein Heym, who was near by, to come here. She sat quietly by my bed and read aloud or knitted, and we spoke of dear old Potsdam, of Friedrich Wilhelm IV, Queen Elizabeth, great uncles Karl and Albrecht, Fritz Carl, aunts Luise and Anna, etc., with all of whom she had had dealings!'

Quicker and more decisively than we children and associates had expected, my father decided he would have to have a change in his circumstances. He must have known that to exist in such tormented loneliness would soon cut him off from this life. I believe he had also felt it instinctively. Despite our love for our mother, we thought, when we discussed his future, that my father should marry again, but that it would perhaps occur in the distant future. I was abruptly informed of his intention to marry again when I arrived on a visit to Doorn in July 1922. My brother Oskar had been told already, but he was not quite as unprepared as I was. The news had already leaked out in Potsdam. Now we learned that Princess Hermine von Schoenaich-Carolath had arrived in Doorn a few days before us, and that the Kaiser had become engaged to her. Oskar and I were utterly dismayed. August Wilhelm, as I heard, had reacted impulsively and begged my father not to marry. Oskar and I were of the same opinion, and it stemmed from the feeling that our mother's place could only be taken by someone who was particularly worthy. We were so upset that we wrote our views in a letter to Father signed by myself and Oskar.

He replied:

> 'My dear children,
> Many thanks for yours and Sissy's frankness of views. . . . I understand and respect your feelings, because I share them, and you are, and remain, my much beloved children. I do not take them amiss, for I love you too much and am so happy to have you here with me. It would be yet another pain for me if you were to turn your back on your lonely father, so there can be no question of your departure or even of shaking the dust of Doorn from your feet. I am happy at your presence here.
> Your sincere Papa W.'

It was only in the following months that I learned how this quick engagement had come about. Princess Hermine had been widowed for two years and had five children aged between fifteen and three years. My father had hardly known the Princess, and had only met her on a few occasions in peace time. When he was wondering whom to marry, he hardly knew in which way he could even meet his future bride. He was tied down in exile, but who really would come to Doorn? Princess Hermine was the first to come. One of her sons had written the Kaiser a nice, childish letter, and straight away came an invitation for him and his mother to come on a visit.

Before she went to Holland, Princess Hermine went to see the Crown Princess, my sister-in-law Cecilie, who asked her outright with what intentions she was going to the Kaiser. Princess Hermine and the Crown Princess were agreed during this conversation that Hermine was hardly the wife for the Kaiser, as she had so many children and so many different interests. 'However,' she wrote later, 'we suit each other. I have decided to take this step because I never do things by halves and, besides, we are mentally compatible and I know I shall do my best to ease his severe loss. . . . I shall do my utmost to see that the Kaiser never regrets the course we are taking.'

I openly admit that these words, which were relayed to me by Cecilie, did not convince me at all; they seemed to flow just that bit too facilely. However. . . .

In October 1922, the Court Marshal, Admiral von Rebeur-Pachwitz, sent me an invitation to the engagement celebrations—just a small party, a dinner in Doorn, then breakfast next day, followed by the Register Office ceremonies conducted by the Mayor, Baron Schimmelpenninck van der Oye, and the chaplain, Dr Vogel. I could not bring myself to attend, but I wrote to Father giving these reasons:

'. . . God willing, we are expecting a baby next spring and the journey would be difficult, so I would prefer not to undertake such a long trip. But I would, dear Papa, not be telling you the truth if I were to tell you these were the sole reasons, for it is not possible for me to let a lie come between us.

'I send you my warm wishes in your new life, and I beseech God that the step you are about to take will bring you what you want. But it is not possible for me to come to Doorn and take part in the wedding celebrations in the same house where Mother suffered so dreadfully, and from where she departed from us. I could have no joy in a celebration such as is demanded of me.

'I beg you with my whole heart not to take offence at

my candid words, and that you should understand my feelings fully.'

At the wedding, which took place at the beginning of November in Doorn, the Crown Princess, my brothers August-Wilhelm and Oskar—besides myself—were conspicuous by our absence.

My father's second wife differed in all respects from my mother, even outwardly. She was relatively small, dark, with an unprepossessing figure. She lacked my mother's goodness and her quiet ways. She was lively and industrious, liked to argue, and was ambitious. Princess Hermine switched to a new existence in the life of an exile, and the quiet which had been that of the house at Doorn evaporated. Steadily and energetically the Kaiser then began to write in vindication of his policies and to counteract the propaganda picture which had been painted of him. Two volumes of memoirs appeared, then a work about his ancestors, and scholarly treatises which received considerable recognition, such as *Royalty in Ancient Mesopotamia* and *Memories of Corfu*. At least we saw now that Father was busy, that he had a great deal of respect for his new wife and, as time went on, we, too, managed a better relationship with her. However, I always avoided broaching delicate family affairs with her, but always in such cases she endeavoured to explain certain aspects to me. She would then tell the others after we had, just the two of us, been on a walk together: 'As usual, Sissy was again completely uninformed.'

My brother Crown Prince Wilhelm, too, was in exile on the small Dutch island of Wieringen, and I finally managed to visit him during the third winter of his stay there. The island was bare, hardly a tree or a shrub—only wind. Very depressing! I felt for my brother's suffering very deeply, and wondered what his life there had been like. Certainly he was on very good terms with the islanders and they had helped him, loved him, and were very proud to have him in their midst. I was not in the least astonished to find him working with the village blacksmith, and he told me that an American journalist had offered the blacksmith twenty-five guilders for a horseshoe wrought by the Crown Prince. 'The world must wonder whether people like us have swollen heads,' my brother said to me. 'At one time they used to pick up cigarette butts I had thrown away, now a snob buys a bit of iron that I've hit with a hammer—and at what a price!' That was typical of my brother Wilhelm. He had not lost his sense of humour despite the fact that the future for him was dark and he did not know what Fate had in store.

Despite his seclusion he was able to gauge the state of German affairs quite realistically and had no illusions. He used his enforced leisure to ponder the realities and possibilities of his personal existence from the ground up. I believe one of the results of this contemplation was the decision to lead his future life more independently of his father, just as he had done in the past. 'It is frequently the case,' he wrote me, 'that father and son are completely different in character, temperament and nature, and it seems to me—as far as I know the Kaiser and I know myself—that we are really different, too.'

That was so. And actually, on important questions the views of the Crown Prince and his father the Kaiser differed greatly. Significantly, I found these observations of Wilhelm's in a letter he wrote me from Wieringen:

> 'Who can say whether the days of the Monarchy will return? But as long as one can live in one's own country and work for the Fatherland, one can be happy. A crown is not the only worthwhile aspiration. To be one's own master on one's own soil also means a great deal. We must not allow ourselves to be robbed of one's belief in a better future for our Fatherland, for we Germans are still a capable, intelligent and hard-working people through and through.'

In October 1923, I received a surprising piece of news from Wieringen: 'Certainly hope that my exile will soon come to an end.' Fourteen days later my brother returned home after five years of exile. I betray no secrets when I say we had Stresemann to thank for his release. In the autumn of 1921 he had visited my brother in Wieringen, and since that time had worked hard to find ways and means of ending the exile. After Stresemann had become Reich Chancellor in August 1923, his intentions had swiftly turned into reality, and in October the Cabinet agreed on the Crown Prince's return, a decision which also found favour with President Ebert. My brother had sent him a request that he be allowed to return home through his Adjutant, Ludwig Müldner von Mülheim, and Ebert had replied: 'I have no objection to his return.'

My brother's homecoming started a controversy between him and my father. The Crown Prince had made all his preparations under conditions of the strictest secrecy, for he feared the Dutch Government might refuse and raise political objections, certainly where the Kaiser was concerned. When the Kaiser received his son's farewell letter and learned that he had already departed from Wieringen, his consternation was great. The feelings of both father and son were reflected in their letters to me. My father wrote:

'. . . That Wilhelm is now with his wife and children makes me happy for him, but he chose the wrong moment. That is generally acknowledged. However, the fact that he left me completely in the dark regarding his plans has wounded me deeply.'

He added a few observations about Stresemann, whose plans the Kaiser distrusted. His aversion to the Chancellor dated from the time when he had voted for Bülow as Bethmann Hollweg's successor.

Wilhelm wrote me:

'It is a long time now since I heard anything further from Doorn. He (the Kaiser) is still very upset that I returned home. What he thinks about it is not obvious, but I had no intention of ending the evening of my life there.'

My brother's return home and my father's remarriage marked the end of the immediate post-war period for my family. The deaths of the older generation of the Houses of Hohenzollern and Hanover reminded us of the end of this era, too. The matriarch of our House, my great-aunt Luise, died. She was the last representative of the great old days, the daughter of the then Prince Wilhelm of Prussia, and was born during the reign of my great-great-grandfather Friedrich Wilhelm III. Dead, too, was the old Duke of Cumberland, who had for decades been the focal point of the Guelph family.

But for me and my family this particular period was one of the happiest of our lives. Gmunden, Austria, was a veritable oasis and, as time passed, much of our royal style of living disappeared. We lived as private people, and the country around the Traunsee became my second home. Certainly there were financial problems which had to be overcome and only through great sacrifices, like the sale of Crown jewels and the world famous Guelph treasures, allowed us to get by.

Gmunden was a paradise for our children and we were overjoyed that they could grow up amid the magnificent alpine scenery and no longer had to suffer the pangs of hunger of previous years when they had not known chocolate or oranges, even. We wandered all over the place, rucksacks on our backs. On Sundays and holidays we went to the castle with the children, the boys dressed in white or blue sailor suits and Friederike in her Sunday dress. I cannot really say which season I enjoyed the most. I loved them all. For me, the mountains were a wonderful experience. We went on long ski tours and my husband learned mountaineering. Often we went hunting, as he was a passionate hunter.

Our two eldest boys were sent to the Gymnasium (grammar or secondary school) at Hamelin where they lived with their teacher, Dr Oppermann. At first our plans to send Ernst August and Georg Wilhelm to local schools seemed unusual, but it was at Dr Oppermann's suggestion that this way they would learn so much more about their own country. It was a wonderful opportunity and we took it. Both boys went with Dr Oppermann on long expeditions into the Hanover countryside.

It was hard for me to have to part from the boys, and it took me a long time to get used to it. Ernst August took the parting better than Georg Wilhelm, who was still very young, but that was not all. It pained him to leave his younger sister, Friederike. I can still see the two of them going out together when they were younger with our daughter tediously pushing her doll's pram. She didn't really make much fuss over dolls, and as soon as he felt he wasn't being watched by the others, Georg Wilhelm would take the pram from her and push it himself. He felt it would be much better for the dolls, as Friederike didn't know how to care for them properly.

Our two eldest sons remained some years in Hamelin before going to Salem where Prince Max of Baden had established a boarding school also attended by his son, Berthold. Salem had once been a Cistercian monastery, but had been secularised at the beginning of last century.

Max, who lived in Salem, had, after the signing of the Treaty of Versailles, decided to set up a school there together with Kurt Hahn, an educational theorist. The education at Salem was not only highly intellectual and physical but emphasised character training. Fair play was its maxim, too. Many important personalities attended Salem later, including Prince Philip, Queen Elizabeth II of England's husband. Her son Charles, the Prince of Wales, attended Gordonstoun, Salem's British equivalent.

I became closer to Prince Max. Ever since the events of November 1918, he had been calumnied and hated. I knew how misjudged he had been and realised the wrongs that had been done him. Both my husband and I felt deeply for him and, in fact, suffered with him. What was particularly distressing for me was that my father was still continuing to reproach Max severely and he categorically refused to listen to any arguments in the Prince's favour. My father had always resented the fact that Max had, without his express orders, announced his abdication. He also sharply condemned Max's action, not only in publicising his abdication as German Kaiser but also as King of Prussia in addition. During those dreadful hours in Spa when my father tried to avoid having to be forced to leave the army, *his* army, he adopted Count von Schulenburg's recommendation that he abdicate only as Kaiser, but not as King of Prussia. That appeared to my father to be the only way out of his fearful mental struggles. He had immediately accepted Schulenburg's recommendation and declared: 'I am and remain King of Prussia and as such I remain to my troops!' In this respect my father felt that the Reich Chancellor's declaration had been a *fait accompli* and he considered himself betrayed.

In Prince Max's favour I must say that in the forenoon of 9 November, when the news of the Kaiser's intended abdication reached him, the idea of a renunciation, which should not concern the Prussian throne, was not under consideration. The question had actually come up for discussion only early that afternoon. According to German constitutional law, the King of Prussia was the German Kaiser and a severance of the Reich Crown from that of the Prussian would have been necessary. Count von Westarp commented: 'There would have to be an amendment to the Reich Constitution with the agreement not only of the Federal Council and the Reichstag, but that of the Prussian State Ministry as well.' As it was, there was neither the opportunity nor the time for this in view of the rising tide of revolution which was sweeping the country. Even if someone in Berlin had thought of such an amendment it would merely have been an academic exercise.

My father saw things in a different light. For him the fact remained that it was a Prussian General, moreover someone of his own class, who, unauthorised, had proclaimed the abdication of his own King and Kaiser. In his mind, as he told me, there was room for no other interpretation.

I tried to show him how Max had always been devoted to him, but he didn't believe it. My father very distinctly let me know early in the 1920s how very much he disapproved of my good relationship with Max. He wrote:

> '. . . To my astonishment I have heard from several quarters that you have been with Max in Salem. The people in Baden as well as those in our homeland are very disturbed and cannot understand your attitude. As my daughter you must surely possess sufficient tact not to consort with him further. I am therefore asking you to discontinue your association. It could, considering the assumption that I approve of it, put me in a false light.'

My father's attitude hurt me deeply, though I understood him completely, as I did Max. Nevertheless, despite my father's injunction, I did not sever relations with Max. I felt entitled as I was convinced that after due process of time History would render him justice.

My brother Wilhelm, too, behaved harshly towards Max and I tried to intercede—in vain. Antipathy towards Max spread to the Officer Corps, and an open breach all round was revealed at my great-aunt Luise's funeral in Karlsruhe, when it was generally considered that Max should be shunned altogether. The sensation at the funeral, however, came when Colonel-General von Plessen refused to shake his hand and then ostentatiously turned his back on him. The incident was widely spread abroad and everywhere people could be heard remarking: 'Yes, Plessen was wonderful. He handled the situation quite marvellously.'

During my stay in Salem I saw Max's book, *Recollections and Documents*, which he was writing in conjunction with Kurt Hahn, taking shape. In it he defended his honour and described his anguish at the events in which he had had to play such a part. Then, his strength going, his health failing rapidly, he died in 1929, aged sixty-two. In the truest meaning of the word, his fate was tragic. He had taken over the task of Reich Chancellor knowing that he would personally be sacrificed. There was no doubt that, in the end, Max of Baden made the supreme sacrifice for his Fatherland.

14   *National Socialism*

Symbolically, it seemed, the death of the last Chancellor of the German Empire in 1929 signalled the beginning of the end of the young German Republic. At the end of that year, the Wall Street crash with its world-wide ramifications naturally dragged Germany into the whirlpool, and the tormented country, already suffering from the heavy burdens imposed by the Versailles Treaty and reparations, underwent a more severe economic crisis than the rest of the world. Industrial production fell, and incomes with it, while the number of unemployed rose until several million were jobless. Many millions of Germans went hungry. The Treasury had to help and, obviously, this state of affairs could not last long before ruin stared the country in the face. The reparation demands of the Allies completed the economic catastrophe. The struggle of millions for their daily bread led to the hitherto unknown radicalisation of the masses, and political strife even spread to the streets. Parliament—the Reichstag—was powerless. The middle class which formed the basis of the Weimar Republic lost all control as it split up into innumerable splinter groups in the wake of the crisis.

My father wrote me: 'Political idiocy is celebrating a veritable orgy in our poor Fatherland. To have to witness all this chaos from abroad is frightful.' The events in Germany occupied him incessantly, though not to the extent of actually intervening personally. Such thoughts had been banished from his mind forever, although the notion remained that he would interfere only if it were legitimate to do so.

I went down to Doorn every year, mostly in January, on his birthday, and noted with what great interest he was following the events in Germany, news of which he assiduously accumulated from visitors, letters from home, but mostly from the newspapers. Every evening the Kaiser would read all the newspapers for the benefit of his entourage. Then, after dinner, they would all gather unconventionally in the smoking-room, where the Kaiser would lay out clippings not only from German but foreign newspapers which he had cut out himself. There were also summaries of the news which he had written out in his own hand. All the serious problems of the day were then discussed quite freely. While he would listen carefully to all the arguments, he also took notice of other opinions. Unresolved arguments of the night before which had been contrary to his own opinions he would resume immediately on the following morning, admitting in the meantime that he had changed his mind.

As the crisis in Germany mounted, my father was meticulously put into the picture by his second wife, Princess Hermine, who spent long periods in Berlin where she lived in the Kaiser Wilhelm Palace and where she received her various contacts, personalities high in the political and economic fields. It has been said that my father at that time suggested there should be a dictatorship in Germany. Certainly he was of the opinion that Germany was now ripe for a strong man, for only such a man could rescue the country. It was an opinion widely shared throughout. Generally, since March 1930, the governing Presidential Cabinets were considered somewhat dictatorial although without an individual strong man.

The exigencies of the time called for my brothers. Eitell-Fritz, August Wilhelm and Oskar, as well as my brother Wilhelm's eldest son, had joined the *Stahlhelm,* an organisation of front-line soldiers whose members maintained that order and discipline should be their way of life, and which increasingly interfered in political affairs. My brothers joined as ordinary *Stahlhelm* men and marched with the rank and file. Eitell-Fritz was even under the command, for a time, of his erstwhile section leader of the 1st Guards Regiment. My brother Wilhelm, too, finally joined the *Stahlhelm* after holding back for a while. As Crown Prince he had promised Reich Chancellor Gustav Stresemann that he would not involve himself in politics, but following Stresemann's death no longer considered himself bound by that promise.

We regarded the rise of National Socialism—which was soon to become the largest political party—more or less in the same light as millions of others in all strata of our society. After all the dreadful things which have happened since then, I must say a few words here as to how the National Socialist movement seemed to us at that time. Perhaps they would be better said in the words of Theodor Heuss [later President of the Federal Republic of Germany after the Second World War; Ed.], an honest Liberal who was then a Democratic Party representative in the Reichstag and a lecturer in politics:

> 'Hitler,' he wrote, 'was a volunteer in 1914 and he served bravely, indefatigably and faithfully in the field. He was very impressive. No one could deny the perseverance of the man who, just released from prison, was so painstakingly and persistently aware, and who understood how to fit the broken fragments of his party together again. . . . He is proud of what he has done, and he has cause. One is conscious, perhaps, when he talks about the historical development of the people and the State, that he is trying to clarify a pedagogic theory.'

Heuss meant, 'For all I care, this or that may be false, perhaps even nonsense, but here is a will that will conquer come what may.'

In later years, when Theodor Heuss was reproached for saying what he did, he dismissed his critics with the retort that he had been so well brought up at home that he had never considered that the criminal abuses which the National Socialist State had later perpetrated could possibly have come about. What Heuss felt then was also felt by many others, including the many men eventually involved in the 20th-of-July assassination plot (1944) against Hitler. They, too, had once seen the National Socialist movement in a favourable light, and when the time came, they judged accordingly and gave their lives to save their Fatherland when they attempted to depose the Führer.

It was none other than Colonel-General Ludwig Beck [later Hitler's Army Chief of Staff; and one of the leaders of the plot against Hitler; Ed.] who enthusiastically celebrated the election victory of the N.S.D.A.P. on 14 September 1930 at his own headquarters during manoeuvres which were then in progress. Major-General Henning von Tresckow, too, later admitted that when he was a Lieutenant in the 9th Potsdam Infantry Regiment he had vigorously pledged himself to support the National Socialist programme. When three Lieutenants—Scheringer, Ludin and Wendt—were arraigned before the Reich Supreme Court in 1930 for belonging to the Nazi Party, their commander, Major-General Helmut Stieff, wrote: 'Unfortunately, one could only subscribe to their views.' He had hoped for the 'genuine national movement which could not be stopped', and remarked: 'Of course, since these events, the bitterness today is tremendously deep.'

Even Colonel Count Stauffenberg [who planted the bomb in Hitler's bunker on July 20, 1944 and was later executed for his part; Ed.], when he was in Bamberg at the time, referred to National Socialism as 'a genuine seizure of power by the people', which he compared to the wars of liberation against Napoleon. Enthusiastically and in uniform he had marched at the head of a procession celebrating the seizure of power in Bamberg by the Nazis in 1933.

In order to show another example of how National Socialism was regarded in those days, the statement of Vice-Admiral Hellmuth Heye, later military deputy of the Federal Parliament and son of Colonel-General Wilhelm Heye, will give some idea. In a letter to General von Schleicher [the last Chancellor of the Weimar Republic, who was in office for only fifty-seven days; Ed.] he wrote:

'I am far from expecting that the Nazi State will be the real blessing for the country, but I believe that the inclination of young officers who still have greater ideals than a mere struggle for bread and who, though they are not inclined towards the Nazis' programme, nevertheless feel they can find an active means of preventing the downfall of their country.'

Our people's misery and the failure of government were the reasons why my family could not stand aloof from politics, but had to take part in them. Certainly we took up a special position although, as in every other family, we all had differing points of view, but we were neither a partisan nor a patriarchal clan.

It was my brother Wilhelm who had the first contact with Hitler in

1926. Hitler sought him out in the Cecilienhof, and my brother was not in the least surprised to hear from him that his national political goal was the restoration of the Monarchy. Wilhelm remembered that during the November 1923 *putsch* in Munich, Hitler had proclaimed himself an ardent monarchist. But the Crown Prince had given him the cold shoulder. He told Hitler:

> 'I agree that I would once have been Kaiser, but now I'm a private citizen and have duties only towards my family. As you can see, I'm wearing a tweed jacket and knickerbockers.'

Hitler also tried to make contact with my father and sent Hermann Goering to Doorn. As a famous Luftwaffe pilot of the First World War and decorated with Germany's highest military honour, *Pour le mérite,* Hitler considered him a suitable spokesman. He was quickly disillusioned. The Kaiser received Goering coldly and somewhat angrily, since the man's crude and outspoken manner clashed brusquely with the more staid customs of the Court.

During the first year of the great crisis, 1930, my brother Oskar wrote to me: 'One cannot really describe the Nazis in a few words; they are important, but their manifesto does really need to be altered. . . .' That was more or less the opinion of all my brothers, but as the Nazi Party's manifesto did not change and in practice grew progressively more radical, my brothers' reserve towards it increased. However, they welcomed the movement's arousal of the nation, even though they did not become National Socialists themselves, with one exception.

August Wilhelm was the *bel esprit* of the family. An outstanding aesthete, he loved art, music and science, and consorted with numerous professors. He included many Jewish families among his close friends, and always had a fascinating circle of important personalities around him at his home in Berlin-Wannsee. It was August Wilhelm who introduced Max Reinhardt, the avant-garde producer of the German Theatre, into Society. We knew 'Auwi' as someone who longed for and loved beauty, so it came as a tremendous surprise to us that he, the only true civilian among my brothers, should turn to politics. His was not the nature to find enjoyment in marching, yet he turned to politics, involving himself in them in an enthusiastic idealism which we had never seen in him before, and found a new element in the comradeship of the combat units. The poetry he now wrote had political overtones.

When I recently read Heuss's book, *Hitler's Way*, which shows, true to life, the National Socialist movement in the early thirties, and learned how that incorruptible politician described the illustration of the S.A. [*Sturm Abteilung*, the Brownshirts; Ed.] as 'clean young men marching in fine harmony'—I felt I was hearing once more the words with which Auwi once described his comrades to me.

The reports which August Wilhelm sent me contained passages such as the following, when he still belonged to the *Stahlhelm*:

> 'Those days in the *Stahlhelm* were wonderful, so exalting! Had superb billets, fifteen men. Coffee morning and evening. Were on the march for two hours, nine stationary on the way on Sunday. Alexander (my brother's son) stood for four hours in the stadium during a splendid tattoo, 2200 flags, about 100,000 spectators, and for seven hours on Sunday without food! The population, too, were greatly enthusiastic. Charlie, too, stayed for seven hours.'

Charlie was Carl Eduard, Duke of Saxe-Coburg and Gotha, the son of the Duke of Albany, Queen Victoria's youngest son.

Fascinated by the thoughts of national fellowship, August Wilhelm joined the National Socialist movement. He made innumerable speeches, gave lectures, travelled constantly from meeting to meeting, put up with severe police beatings, and sacrificed his means. The sort of life he led can be summed up in a letter I received from him in 1932:

> 'I had to neglect your birthday because I suddenly had to go to Hamburg on Saturday and then on Sunday to Königsberg. Forgive me! My belated heartfelt wishes—when had they been more needed than now! My petty offering enclosed—I need every pfennig for our movement's needy poor: their army swells daily!'

August Wilhelm's political involvement naturally led to conflict within the family. I, myself, for instance, thought in several aspects differently from him. Apropos the controversy, he wrote me in Gmunden:

'You know that I have always considered resentments and grudges quite absurd, and after our agreement of years ago, have never quarrelled with you over politics, though by airing our different interpretations, we would only continue to wrangle about what I now consider and have always held to be right in order to hold the family together. We want to remain brothers and sisters at a time when a thousand forces are at work erecting barriers. And I will not join in this at any price!'

What tensions there were in our family were demonstrated in a report sent me by August Wilhelm in April 1932, which gave me the background to the Reich Presidential elections of the time. It read:

'The circumstances were thus: Phase 1, Wilhelm wanted to have himself nominated, encouraged by his *Reichswehr* (Army) friends. Hitler was to be Reich Chancellor, Brüning [a famous representative of the Roman Catholic Centre Party, later persecuted by Hitler, emigrated and became a professor in America; Ed.] Foreign Minister, and Hugenberg [Leader of the Conservative Party; Ed.] Economics. It was quite an impossible plan and collapsed after a week. Then there were suggestions from Hugenberg and the *Stahlhelm* that it should be Oskar, but Hitler, who, from a "rational" point of view, was against any Royal candidate, rejected. Finally, despite the fact that he had not even spoken to me, he said he knew I would turn the post down even though I was the only one who could really be considered for it. In any case, he thought I would thereby lose the movement a lot of votes which would never be replaced by "Hindenburg's customary votes". There were great cries from Hugenberg and Seldte [Leader of the *Stahlhelm*; Ed.] that I would be unsuitable since I was a Nazi. Flop! That was the end of the pro-monarchists and the whole thing was buried, especially when we found out that the Old Man (Hindenburg) was to put himself up as a candidate even though a whole company of Prussian Princes were to march up!! Then a couple of adventurous men, among them a certain Herr von Ostau, a former stage-manager and now quite an unimportant little Nazi *Ortsgruppenleiter* [district leader; Ed.], proposed Wilhelm at the last minute, without asking Hitler or Hugenberg, nor even the *Stahlhelm*. Two days before the close of nominations, Wilhelm was to enter the list while they went off to Doorn carrying a letter from him. You can imagine what joy that aroused!'

It is known that my father disapproved of the plan to have the Crown Prince as a candidate for the post of Reich President, but somehow Wilhelm did not incur his displeasure, though August Wilhlem did. Wilhelm wrote me from Rome in 1932:

'Up to now, I haven't been thrown out on my neck. They threatened to stop all my activities for the movement or to force me out of it, if I continue my activities. They wanted to send me to the Canary Islands for six months, but I came here instead. I'll be back soon, quite indifferent to whether it's "convenient" or not.'

Soon after, August Wilhelm went to see his father in Doorn and wrote of the outcome:

'He treated me as if I did not exist! Unfortunately I lifted my arm a little, quite unintentionally, out of custom, and was snapped at terribly.'

Regarding the 30 January 1933 events [the day Hitler assumed the Reich Chancellorship; Ed.], August Wilhelm sent me some interesting details, writing in English. His first sentence explained his personal feelings about the National Socialists:

[*sic*] 'You warned me so often I should be disappointed; I knew I would not.' He then continued: 'I can't risk writing all that has happened. The night of 29/30 Jan. was terrible because Mr Kreeper [General Kurt von Schleicher, then Chancellor; Ed.] tried to frighten A. H. [Adolf Hitler; Ed.] out of his wits and pretended he would prevent the takeover of power by the troops from Potsdam (they never got the order!) and he had planned to march off the Old Man [Hindenburg; Ed.] to East

Prussia (as a sort of prisoner) and to grab the position for himself. I warned them—also P. [Crown Prince Wilhelm; Ed.] —since 1½ years—he very nearly succeeded. We had to get hold of his successor, Bl . . . berg [General Werner von Blomberg as Reichswehr Minister; Ed.] who was to be imprisoned and the Old Man's son took him quickly to his father's home [the Reich Presidential Palace; Ed.] where the oath was taken and all arranged in half an hour. . . . You can't imagine what a difficult position A. H. has with Hugi [Hugenberg; Ed.] etc., but he has good nerves and is very pleased with all we could—till now—change.'

My father would have nothing to do with the National Socialists. When the pogroms against the Jews started and the synagogues were attacked, he was shocked. 'It's a scandal what's happening at home,' he told me. 'It's high time the army intervened. They've allowed too much to happen and in no circumstances must they have anything to do with it. All the old officers and upstanding Germans should have protested, but they witnessed murder and arson, and no one lifted a finger.'

In 1933, the same year Hitler assumed the Chancellorship, the Kaiser issued the following orders which would come into force in the event of his death:

'Should God decree that I should be recalled from this world at a time when there is still no restoration of the Monarchy in Germany, it is my firm resolve that if I should go to my eternal rest while in exile in Doorn, then I am provisionally to be buried in Doorn. My coffin shall be placed at a spot opposite the house where my bust is erected in front of the rhododendrons and where my approved tomb, designed and built by Betzner the architect, will be situated. It will be protected against the weather by a canopy. Flowerbeds of cinerarias and salvias shall surround the tomb. The solemnities shall be simple, quiet, and dignified. *No* deputations from Germany, *no* swastika flags, no wreaths. That will apply if H.M. dies in Doorn. If I die in Potsdam, then my bones shall be laid in the mausoleum of the

New Palace in between those of the two Empresses. Military funeral, *no* swastika flags, no funeral orations, hymns nor prayers.'

No swastika flags, and again no swastika flags, whether in Doorn or Potsdam. There was no room for doubt where my father's feelings lay as far as the Nazi movement was concerned. But the order also showed that he always lived in hope of a restoration of the Monarchy. As representative of the dynasty which had led Prussia and Germany to its historical greatness, he could think of nothing else. But today we know that the restoration of the Monarchy would have probably spared Germany from a great deal of harm.

The differences in their political views following the assumption of power by the Nazis was a sore trial for my other brothers, and they quarrelled angrily with August Wilhelm. He wrote me: 'I don't take the slightest notice of all their opinions, but just march on.' He did. He became a representative in the *Landtag*, a member of the new Reichstag, and was elected to the recently established Prussian State Council. He worked enthusiastically, praised the 'superb tempo', as he called it, of the rebuilding of Germany, and worried constantly whether the Reich Chancellor was physically able to stick it out. Auwi wrote: 'At last poor Hitler has taken a short holiday in south Germany, as he couldn't stand it any longer. People were continually running after him.'

Whatever Auwi's enthusiasms, there were already signs to show the precariousness of his position with the N.S.D.A.P. [Nazis; Ed.]. One reason was his background. Back in 1932 Theodor Heuss had remarked that 'the inclusion of some Princes in the Nazi Party was in no way desired by all active members'. Other reasons were the extreme conservatism of Auwi's brothers, the brusque rejection of Hitler by the Kaiser, and the Crown Prince's rebellious remarks that the Führer was 'a demagogue and a little philistine'. There were also the antagonistic public statements of my nephews, Wilhelm, and Louis Ferdinand, the Crown Prince's eldest and second sons. Very early on Auwi accused them of 'making my position very shaky within the movement and creating only bad blood against the family— just what I wanted to avoid. I've warned them often enough, but they still want to play "1914".'

There were further reasons, too, for Auwi's tenuous position. He did not agree with the Party's racial policies and he had many Jewish friends—which conflicted with the Party line. He tried to help them whenever he could, and enabled many to go abroad.

During the Roehm revolt [Ernest Roehm, Chief of the Brown Shirts, *Sturm Abteilung*, the Storm Troops, who was murdered on Hitler's orders on 30 June 1934 by the S.S. for opposing the Führer; Ed.] he had been put on the Nazis' death list, but Goering prevented his arrest, saying: 'Hands off!' From now on August Wilhelm was to be merely an outward symbol for Hitler. He was always invited to be present during royal State visits or when foreign statesmen came officially to Germany. Hitler did not think of any other rôle for him. It was difficult for August Wilhelm to confess his disappointment at the turn of the political developments, but he kept, as his letters to me show, full confidence in me. Yet after he had actually survived this blow, he only remained closed in discussing his idealism. He must have used a great deal of self-restraint before he could bring himself eventually to tell me: 'There has been so much suffering, and so much fighting, that one has to be very brave never to show signs of dejection.'

I first met Hitler in 1933, when he invited my husband and me for talks in Berlin. The fact that it was Joachim von Ribbentrop, at that time Hitler's foreign affairs adviser, who had issued the invitation, showed on what basis the talks would be held. We were to discuss Anglo-German relations. Hitler appeared extraordinarily polite, was very correct, and spoke in friendly fashion. My husband explained his point of view in a long discourse, the quintessence of it being that he considered that an understanding with England should be the foundation of German foreign policy, and that an Anglo-German *rapprochement* needed careful and prudent preparation. England herself, he said, had to be convinced that it was in her own interests to go along with the Reich, and a settlement with England was, after all, a question of psychology. The English, my husband went on, were clear-headed calculators and realists who looked after their own interests, and ideological sentiments were not sufficient to convince them. Only facts and facts alone.

In this connection my husband warned against the chauvinism which was being very loudly expressed in Germany, and offered some typical examples. Then he took the opportunity of giving Hitler his opinion of Nazi plans for the reorganisation of the Reich. He said he had never been in favour of the small-states system and on the other hand was a definite opponent of centralisation. He was convinced, however, that Germany had to build again on its own foundations. Although my husband had offered Hitler these general views, he did not fail to offer special advice regarding the questions affecting Hanover and Brunswick, in which he had, naturally, a vested interest.

The Reich Chancellor showed himself to be an attentive listener and then gave us his own observations on the problems under discussion. When he had finished we felt he had hardly been precise, having just given us a general, overall picture which seemed to have been directed at people who were not at all acquainted with the subject. Finally he asked my husband to explore all possibilities for reaching an understanding with England. As we left Hitler, I thought perhaps he had accepted this or that supposition of ours, but my husband, who was always a sceptic in such matters, remarked drily: 'Maybe.'

I met Hitler a few more times in the following years, and he made contact with us many times through von Ribbentrop, but an extensive discussion such as had taken place in 1933 was never resumed. However, my husband and I worked extensively for *rapprochement* between England and Germany. My husband occupied himself in pursuing the point that if a real understanding between the two countries could not be achieved, then a new war would eventually be inevitable.

We were both in England during the time the Naval Treaty was under discussion, staying as King George V's guests, and had wide-ranging talks with the King, the Prince of Wales, and Prime Minister Ramsay Macdonald. Prince Edward was very forthright. I had the impression that he took great pains in getting himself extensively informed, particularly regarding Germany, and in obtaining unbiased reports of exactly what was happening there. Prince Axel of Denmark, who like King George was my husband's cousin, accompanied us to see the Prince of Wales.

Our talk with Ramsay Macdonald took place at Chequers, the Prime Minister's country house. Macdonald was a self-made man and came from a small Scottish farming and fishing village—'from a fisherman's hut' as he called it. I thought, as I sat opposite him, that he looked just like a professor, but not at all dry. On the contrary, he was quite vivacious and not lacking in *bons mots*. His manner of speaking, often asking only brief questions or making sharp observations in a very few words during our talks, impressed me. I had the feeling that there sat a man who was not only thoroughly well versed, but who knew exactly where the nub of the matter lay. The Prime Minister told us he was absolutely prepared to come to an understanding with Germany. He said he considered it vital not only to have an Anglo-German agreement, but to have a general arms limitation as well. He was also very much inclined, he added, to prepare the way for actual friendship between our two countries.

At Chequers we also met the then Air Minister, Lord Londonderry. He was a tall, lean, typical English aristocrat, candid, yet discreet. On the question of Germany, however, he was very reserved. We asked him to come over on a visit, but he refused courteously, saying he had his department to look after. Two years had barely gone by when we saw Lord Londonderry again, this time in Germany, together with his family. In the meantime, though, he had left the Cabinet and had become an enthusiastic supporter of Anglo-German friendship and occupied himself with learning about the problems of the German people.

In the naval agreement with England, Germany was to reduce her warships relative to England in the proportion of thirty-five of ours to one hundred English. The treaty, from the German side, appeared to introduce a policy for reconciliation brought about by the so-called facts my husband had mentioned to Hitler at the time. I wouldn't like to say that this came about as a result of our efforts, though we believed this then. After all, with the knowledge we have today, we cannot say with any certainty whether Hitler was in earnest about any understanding with England. In no way had he cared nor prepared the means for friendly relations. On the contrary, he showed that he had neither gauged nor correctly estimated the English mentality, nor saw where that country's interests lay. He had instead imposed

G

stresses and strains which could only have led to a rupture of relations between the two countries.

As far as von Ribbentrop is concerned, I believe that I can say this for him, that Anglo-German reconciliation at that time became not a question of tactics, but one of persuasion.

15 *Greek Tragedies*

Our meetings with the ruling faction of the Third Reich from now on happened predominantly by chance, usually on social occasions. I got to know Dr Goebbels as a *Homo novus* who took the greatest care to appear cultivated and well-mannered, and my impressions of him were fully confirmed when I encountered him at von Ribbentrop's. Accidentally meeting him in Heiligendamm one day, he spent the time giving me a detailed account of some of the current topics of the day, and it was very interesting to hear what he had to say. He spoke with such intensity that we could have thought that our own education on that subject was the closest thing to his heart. Later, when he ironically announced that kings and princes in Germany were only to be found in fairy tales and operettas, we had to ask ourselves whether or not this really was the same person who was standing there talking to us.

But already there were other things, too, which made us shake our heads in amazement! His wife was quite his opposite. For a time I had been seeing Frau Goebbels quite frequently, when she stayed at the same sanatorium as my husband, and we often ate together. I found her really sympathetic and her children were delightful, but their births, which had quickly followed one another, had left their mark on her health.

My meeting with Himmler was really quite accidental. Had I not known that it was the Chief of the S.S. who was sitting next to me, if he had not been wearing his black uniform with the silver piping, I would have taken him for a schoolmaster of olden days. The pince-nez high on his nose and the knowledgeable way he lectured on a particular theme heightened the impression. He spoke to me about ancient farm folklore and had, as I heard, an astonishing wealth of detail on the subject. I took the opportunity of asking him about the fate of the farmers of Lower Saxony who had been forced to leave their several-hundred-year-old farms and homes in order to enlarge the armed forces' training grounds, but he declined to answer, saying military affairs took precedence and the farms would have to be abandoned. My husband had campaigned on behalf of these smallholdings, whose owners were the guardians of their ancient farming traditions, and I thought it significant that Himmler, who was officially charged with their well-being and the rights of their heirs, was quite unconcerned.

I got to know Goering in Gmunden, when he suddenly arrived unannounced. He told us a great deal, much of it new, and it was he who monopolised the conversation. His visit certainly surprised us, and we asked ourselves what purpose it was supposed to serve. The next time I met him was at the British Embassy in Berlin during a reception. The evening began most embarrassingly, for Goering arrived extremely late. The British Ambassador, Sir Eric Phipps, waited and waited, but there was no sight or sign of Goering. I could see the Ambassador getting more and more angry as time went by. Finally, unable to wait for his distinguished guest any longer, he got us into dinner. Two hours later Goering appeared. He calmly told us that he had been on the telephone to Hitler, who was in Venice meeting Mussolini.

I had a long conversation with Goering that evening, mainly about the altercation concerning the Lutheran Church. The Bishop of Hanover, Dr. Marahrens, whom I esteemed greatly, had told me of the difficulties confronting the Church. Goering was an attentive listener, very open and, as I heard from Bishop Marahrens later, had taken up some of the points I had made and helped. I had taken up a great deal of Goering's time that evening, so I thought it only right and proper that I should apologise to my host for being with Goering so long. The Ambassador was still somewhat piqued at his guest's late appearance, but nevertheless showed some understanding over the length of my talk. He spoke as if he knew the way the conversation had gone, that for such discussions it was obviously more suitable to hold them on the neutral ground of an embassy.

Some time later the Bishop approached me again and told me of further aggravations against his Church. He asked me to speak to Goering again, which I did immediately, and this time we were able to speak together alone. Goering was again very understanding, but somewhat reserved. I resolved to clarify the situation, but that proved unsuccessful. He turned to one side and began to meditate aloud: 'What is God, what is the Church, what's this and what's that?' Obviously my efforts were proving unavailing. It was only later that I learned what it was all about. Goering had had increasing difficulties concerning his original intercession on behalf of the Lutheran Church and now obtained as little support from the hierarchy as he had ever received previously.

I next spoke to Goering again on the occasion of the Olympic Games in August 1936, when he gave a garden party. He behaved like a schoolboy and obviously enjoyed having so many prominent international personalities there in attendance. Frau Goering was charming, amiable and always extraordinarily friendly when we met, and the Goering family generally exhibited a remarkable degree of independence. Goering's brother Albert, for instance, was an outspoken anti-Nazi. One significant incident concerned his sister Olga Goering, when she met my sister-in-law, Crown Princess Cecilie, at the State Opera one evening. She curtsied then kissed Cecilie's hand. When she was asked why she had done that, she retorted: 'Why should I be embarrassed in doing in public what I do in private?' On the following day Hitler took Goering to task for his sister's unseemly behaviour, but Goering told his Führer: 'My sister can do what she pleases.'

That evening, 'Putzi' Hanfstaengl, Hitler's Foreign Press Chief, who was a friend of my brother August Wilhelm, was sitting next to me. It was the last time I was to see him before he fled abroad. Having actively supported Hitler during his earliest campaigns, Hanfstaengl, the son of a well-known Munich art publisher, had managed to open many doors for his leader both at home and abroad. That night, however, he seemed very sceptical of everything and yet was very apprehensive of everything. Others present criticised the

National Socialist government so loudly and unhesitatingly that on several occasions I feared for all of them.

The 1936 Olympic Games, the grandeur of its organisation, and above all its sporting performances, impressed me tremendously. It was fantastic. But what a strain it was to try and see everything—and I must confess I was extremely keen. I was always on my feet. When the German women's team in the 4 × 100-metre relay had the misfortune to drop the baton on the last lap and lost a certain world record, I nearly wept with disappointment. After my agitation had abated somewhat, I realised that I, in common with many of the spectators around me, had fallen on my knees when the calamity occurred.

All the events were utterly spellbinding. Forty years have gone by since then, yet I can still see the athletes and their achievements as I saw them then. There was the American negro, Jesse Owens, who ran like an engine and jumped as if he were on springs; there was the dashing Handrick, victor of the pentathlon, or Tilly Fleischer throwing the javelin, and last, but not least, our horsemen. There was Lieutenant Pollay's superb dressage, then Lieutenant von Wangenheim who broke a collarbone when he was thrown, yet mounted again to win the 'Military' with Captain Stubbendorf and Captain Lippert. Then there was the heroic feat of Polish Cavalry Captain Kawecki who never gave up despite several broken ribs. Not least was the exciting struggle for victory in the great jump-off for the *Prix des Nations* by Kurt Hasse, who won the Gold Medal just ahead of the Rumanian, Lieutenant Rang, and the Hungarian, Captain von Platthy; and the victors in the 'Military' team event, Hasse, Captain Brandt and Captain von Barnekow.

I found the 1936 Winter Olympics in Garmisch-Partenkirchen even better than the Berlin Olympics. If the capital's was on a grand scale, then the winter games had their own special stamp on them. In any case, that's how I found them. The games were not on a pompous note, neither had they been organised on the giant scale they had been in Berlin. In Garmisch-Partenkirchen they were wonderfully natural, and there I experienced the great comradeship which existed between the various sportsmen, foreigners and Germans, participants and spectators, strangers and natives—all made just one whole. They seemed simply to belong together, and that was the feeling that prevailed throughout, whether it was in the field, on the slopes, on the ice, or, in the evening, in the pubs and inns. I was out all day—I didn't want to miss a thing—and I missed only one day there, when we went up the Zugspitze and skied.

During our stay in Garmisch-Partenkirchen there occurred an event which showed us that we were no longer as young as we used to be. We received a letter from Prince Paul of Greece, asking us for our daughter's hand. My husband and I were completely surprised: we realised once and for all that our children had grown up.

All of our children had gone their different ways. The two eldest had taken their school-leaving examinations at Salem, but there they had experienced the Nazis' attempts at politically 'co-ordinating' the school as they called it, and the arrest of Kurt Hahn in March 1933. We were furious! My father wrote from Doorn: 'This affair at your school is lamentable! How could the authorities be so stupid! I'm afraid there are difficult times and sharp struggles ahead.' Their schooldays over, Ernst August began his literary pursuits while Georg Wilhelm joined the *Reichswehr*, as he wanted to become a regular officer. The two youngest, Christian and Welf Heinrich, went to school near Weimar.

Our daughter Friederike stayed with us in Blankenburg until her confirmation. Then, in 1934, we sent her to boarding-school in England, at North Foreland Lodge, near Broadstairs, Kent. While we were in England we visited King George V and his family, and the then Duke of York and his wife and daughters Elizabeth and Margaret, besides other relatives. We had a most interesting visit to Kensington Palace in London, where we met the old generation, 'the old aunts' as they were called, who lived there. It was really walking into history, for we met Princess Victoria, widow of Louis of Battenberg, still unbelievably fresh and lively. There was also Princess Beatrice, whose husband, Heinrich of Battenberg, had died during an expedition on a ship off Sierra Leone in 1896, and whose daughter Victoria Eugenia later became Queen of Spain. There, too, was Beatrice's elder sister, Louise, the Duke of Argyll's widow. She was eighty-six years old, but looked wonderful for her age. Princess Louise seldom received guests, so it was a very special occasion for us. She took us on a tour of Kensington Palace and stopped in one of the rooms. 'Here,' she said, 'here in this room, my mother was entrusted with the Crown of England.' We were back almost a hundred years and in the room where the young Princess Victoria, daughter of the Duchess of Kent, had been awoken and told by the Archbishop of Canterbury and Lord Conyngham that she was now Queen.

It was after this sojourn in England that we received an astounding demand from Hitler, conveyed to us by von Ribbentrop. It was no more nor less than that we should arrange a marriage between Friederike and the Prince of Wales. My husband and I were shattered. Something like this had never entered our minds, not even for a reconciliation with England. Before the First World War it had been suggested that I should marry my cousin, who was two years younger, and it was now being indicated that my daughter should marry him. We told Hitler that in our opinion the great difference in age between the Prince of Wales and Friederike alone precluded such a project, and that we were not prepared to put any such pressure on our daughter. Besides, we told Ribbentrop, we were determined that Friederike should be free to make her own choice, and it was most improbable that it would fall on Edward, Prince of Wales.

The following year we sent Friederike to Florence where she attended the college, mostly attended by American girls, run by Miss Edith May. The headmistress, though, had reservations about her entry and told my husband: 'My school isn't intended for princesses. We practice true democracy here and all the pupils are treated equally. They make their own beds and call each other by their first names. We cannot make any exceptions.' Laughingly, my husband reassured her, for we expected nothing else.

Two of my Greek cousins lived in Florence, daughters of King Constantine and Queen Sophie, my father's sister. The younger daughter, Irene, was at that time still unmarried, though she wed Prince Haimon of Savoy-Aosta in 1939. The other daughter, Helene, had been married to King Carol II of Rumania, but she divorced him on account of his lurid affaire, much publicised at the time, with the red-haired Madame Lupescu. The two sisters inhabited the Villa Sparta in Florence, where they were occasionally visited by their brother Paul, who lived mainly in England where his brother, King

George II, had lived since the declaration of Greece as a republic in 1924.

It was here in the Villa Sparta that Friederike met Paul again. They got to know each other very well though my seventeen-year-old daughter did not yet realise how fond the Prince was of her. He had already kindled the fires of love, however, and, as we got to know later, come to the decision that he would have Friederike at all costs or no one. This was the time when Greece was once again changing her régime and Eleutherios Venizelos, the arch opponent of the Greek Monarchy had to flee the country. In November 1935, the Greek people voted for the restoration of their Monarchy, and King George once more ascended his throne. Since he had no successors, his brother Paul naturally became Crown Prince.

Here I must go back a little in time. The 27th of January 1932 had been the quietest birthday my father had ever experienced. Not only was he ill—he refused to allow his children to come and visit him on that occasion—but his birthday had been overshadowed by the fact that two weeks earlier his second youngest sister, Sophie, had died. I wrote to him saying:

> 'My thoughts are especially with you on your forthcoming birthday, particularly as you have not only suffered endlessly during these past years, but have now had to bear the pain of the death of our beloved Aunt Sophie. My heart is ever closer to you.'

I told him how the funeral had gone in Kronberg-am-Taunus, near Frankfurt, and of our meeting with our Greek relatives and added: 'They have all gone through a great deal.' And so they had, God knows.

When my aunt Sophie had become Crown Prince Constantine's radiant bride in 1889 and had entered Athens, everything seemed to be sweetness and light. Although it was October, wherever one looked there was the blossoming splendour of summer, with roses and oleander everywhere. They seemed to indicate that nature, too, was celebrating this, their day of glory. The Prince and Princess of Wales had come over from England, Prince Nicholas, heir to the

Russian throne, the King and Queen of Denmark were there, as were Sophie's brother, the Kaiser, and his Empress. The royal families of Europe had made a rendezvous here. One of my mother's ladies-in-waiting described the scene of the wedding as 'colossal pomp, the glorious vestments of innumerable ecclesiastics resembling the ancient paintings, the splendid toilette of all the foreign ladies . . . but Crown Princess Sophie the most delightful'.

At the conclusion of the celebrations there was a grand ball for over a thousand people, which seemed more like a folk festival. Everyone from every walk of life wanted to share the good fortune of their rulers. It was said that coachmen and servants, too, were in the company, and as proof the story was told of the German Ambassador's Greek coachman who, when ordered by his master to drive him back to the castle, refused, saying he could not do it because he had been invited to the ball.

King George I had been particularly loved by his people. He had reigned for fifty years, since 1863, when, as Prince Wilhelm of Schleswig-Holstein-Glücksburg, he had been offered the Crown of the Hellenes by the Greek National Assembly. The pistol shots of an insane shoemaker which killed him in March 1913 marked the turning-point in the destiny both of Greece and its ruling house.

When the First World War broke out the following year, King Constantine I, who had succeeded his father, wanted to keep his country out of it, but the Allies tried to entice him in with offers of additional territory. He stood firm. England and France tried to force him out of his neutrality by occupying Salonica and blockading it for many months. They then seized Corfu, landed troops in Piræus, marched on Athens. Both the people and the army raised themselves against the invaders and, against the odds, put them to flight.

After their defeat the Allies launched a new, decisive attack on Greece and once more imposed a blockade. This time they forced the King to disarm his army and interned the troops in the Peloponnese. Once again an Allied squadron penetrated into the Bight of Salamis and they sent an ultimatum demanding the abdication of the King and Crown Prince. They had to leave the country. The Allies and Venizelos had achieved what an earlier murder attempt had failed to do. Only twenty-five kilometres north of Athens they had tried to kill the King, by burning down the royal summer residence at Tatoi with him in it. The deed had been so thoroughly prepared that they destroyed not only the house, which had been built by George I, but the beautiful woods surrounding it. My cousin Paul, the King's third son, managed to raise the alarm, but only the gardener, his family, and the King and Prince Paul were able to win the race against death in the hell of the invading flames.

The Allies' dethronement of the Greek King occurred in June 1917 immediately after the abdication of the Czar, Nicholas II, who was a cousin of King Constantine's. Maria Feodorovna, the Czar's mother, and King George I were brother and sister. Constantine's second son, the twenty-four-year-old Prince Alexander, was then called to the throne. Venizelos, an extreme nationalist who had once dreamt of incorporating Constantinople into the Greek kingdom, formed a new government and immediately broke off relations with Germany and her allies. His policies certainly gained Greece more territory, but no luck at all. In a bloody war provoked by Greece, they were beaten by the Turks led by Mustafa Kemal and the consequences for Greece, including the expulsion of millions of Greeks from Asia Minor, were catastrophic. There was no more peace.

The young Alexander was King in name only. He had neither power nor the authority to make decisions and he died in horrible circumstances from an infection caused by the bite of a Rhesus monkey, only three years after ascending the throne. In his feverish dreams before he died he called incessantly for his mother, but she could not come, as the government refused to let her cross the frontier. My aunt Sophie never got over the anguish of those days nor the fate of her darling son, and only the elderly Queen Olga was allowed to be present at his last rites.

Venizelos was overthrown after my cousin Alexander's death and fled. The Greeks then voted for King Constantine's return to the throne and he came back, even though he was tired and ill. He had never got over the attempt on his life in Tatoi, and never really recovered. Two years after his return, Venizelos once again got the upper hand and the King was deposed once more, to die two months later in exile in Palermo, aged fifty-four. His eldest son, George II, ascended the throne amidst much civil strife. Ministers and Generals were shot as scapegoats, and in hardly more than a year, in December 1923, George II was deposed and Greece became a Republic.

The Royal Family lived abroad, forbidden ever to set foot on Greek soil again. Queen Sophie then went to live in Switzerland and I was able to visit her there, at Kreuzlingen, with her sister Margarethe, my father's youngest sister, after the war. She eventually went to live in Florence, and my husband and I received an invitation to visit her there in the spring of 1931. She died a few months later after a serious illness.

The turn of events in November 1935, with King George once more on the throne of Greece after twelve years of banishment, meant that Prince Paul could now approach us officially, and in January 1936 he asked for Friederike's hand. As I have said, we were completely surprised. Not that we didn't like him: we did. He was tall, dignified, and we appreciated his good judgement and natural courtesy. We had seen him several times when he visited us at Blankenburg with his mother, and we liked his realistic approach to life. During his exile in England, for instance, he had worked in an aircraft engine factory in Coventry. He was about sixteen years older than Friederike and was a near relative of hers on the Danish side. Therefore, the thought even of the possibility of marriage had not entered our heads and, as a rule, we were in no hurry to make a decision to marry her off, and indeed we had taken no steps in this direction.

Paul was my daughter's second cousin, for his mother, Queen Sophie, was Friederike's grandfather's (the Kaiser's) sister. Paul's grandfather, George I, was the brother of Sophie's Hanoverian grandmother, Thyra, Duchess of Cumberland. Paul's great grandmother on his father's side was Princess Alexandra of Russia— Friederike's great-grandmother's sister on her father's side, Queen Marie of Hanover. What it all boiled down to was this: of Friederike's and Paul's sixteen great-grandparents, twelve were mutual and direct ancestors or brothers and sisters.

When Paul came to the Olympic Games in Berlin, 1936, as Greece's representative, he and Friederike met again. He visited us in Blankenburg and we immediately perceived that the affair had become much more serious, but engagement was still in the air as it were. Friederike herself could not decide when we asked her about it and wanted time to think it over, so she went to stay with my aunt Margarethe where she could discuss it and come to a decision without having to be influenced by her own parents. Margarethe later told us she was convinced that both young people liked each other very much, and it was obviously a love match.

Paul then came to visit us in Gmunden, and he and Friederike went for car rides and long walks together. One day, when they came back, they had become engaged. Paul described the moment it happened very delightfully and with some humour: 'We were going along a charming valley which suddenly came to an end,' he said, 'and we were faced with a rock cliff which barred our way. Had the valley been longer, we'd have gone on and on and on, and who knows . . .?'

That was in the spring of 1937. The wedding itself took place in January the next year in Athens. Permission, of course, had to be obtained from the King of England and the following notice appeared in the Court Circular: 'Assent to marriage of German Princess: The King held a Privy Council at Sandringham on Sunday night. It is understood that he gave his formal assent to the marriage of Princess Frederika [sic] of Hanover to Crown Prince Paul of Greece. Present at the Privy Council were the Dukes of Gloucester and Kent, the Earl of Athlone and Sir Eric Melville.'

Our journey to Athens was far from pleasant, and we thought we would freeze in the train when the heating failed. Just as icy, however, was the political wind blowing from Berlin. Hitler demanded not only that the German national anthem but the Nazi 'Horst Wessel' song as well should be played during the marriage ceremonies, and that swastika flags should be flown. My husband refused, saying we had no right since we were no longer the ruling house.

King George of Greece was in full agreement with his brother's choice of bride. Peculiarly enough, while George was with us in Potsdam years before, and serving with the 1st Guards Regiment, it was being whispered that he would be marrying me. Now, by a strange twist of fate, his brother was marrying my daughter. George was an outstanding character and was very much loved by his comrades in Potsdam. It was not easy for him in those days, as he had very little money from home and had to tighten his belt considerably.

Still, he came to see us often at the New Palace and we all liked to have him there. His destiny, too, was troubled; his grandfather was murdered, his father and himself forced to abdicate, his brother King Alexander I died young, his father succeeded to the throne once more, only to abdicate two years later. Then he ascended the throne once more, just for a year this time, before having to flee to exile until 1935, when he was recalled. From a fresh young Guards Lieutenant he had become a very embittered man, as we could see during the intervening years in England. When we met again in 1938 he told me: 'It's lamentable that we should learn so much from life, and learn to trust no one.'

The wedding aroused a great deal of enthusiasm in Greece. Friederike herself travelled there in the Simplon Orient Express. Wherever the train stopped—in Prague, Budapest or Belgrade, she was tumultuously greeted by Greeks, and when she reached the border town of Eidomeni she was ceremoniously met by a delegation headed by Prime Minister Metaxas, while a huge crowd chanted 'Kalos orissati!'—welcome! Then the Crown Prince got into the train with her to Athens. There, the thunder of cannon announced the arrival of the bridal pair. Thousands of people were gathered at the station and along the freezing streets. There was no balcony, no window in the city empty—the place was black with people.

The King, Princes, Princesses, the Archbishop, the Ministers of State, the High Officials of the Crown, and all the foreign diplomats were there at the station. The Mayor of Athens, Kostas Kotzias, came forward and bid the bride a hearty welcome. 'From this historic moment on,' he said, 'every single Greek will vie with the other for love of you.'

On the wedding day the whole of Athens was woken by the noise of cannon shot, and they all gathered, like a swarm of bees, to watch the procession. Then followed a 21-gun salute to indicate that the wedding party was leaving the royal castle for the cathedral. My husband accompanied our daughter in her splendidly equipped coach, while I travelled with my cousin George. Friederike wore a superb diadem which had once belonged to my aunt Sophie, and an attractive little crown always worn by Hanoverian Princesses at their weddings.

The Archbishop of Athens, attended by thirty bishops, met the bridal procession and conducted the ceremony according to Greek Orthodox rites. One of the witnesses was sixteen-year-old Prince Philip, son of Prince Andreas of Greece and Princess Alice of Battenberg, who looked no less charming to me then than he did when he later married Princess Elizabeth of England.

The Greek Orthodox ceremony was very long, but most impressive, as was the sight of so many ecclesiastics and row upon row of dignitaries in their silk, gold-braided vestments. My thoughts wandered back to my own wedding and to those delightful and happy times in Berlin. There was just one thought which did not enter my head. At my wedding in 1913, the world stood but one year away from war. Now, in 1938, at my daughter's marriage, there was coincidentally but a year to go before another.

I returned to Greece in November when Friederike brought her child, Sophia [the present Queen of Spain; Ed.], into the world. Now I was a grandmother. Great-grandfather telegraphed me from Doorn:

> 'Heartfelt thanks for dear detailed letter and photos. Thank God everything went well and will continue to do so. Charming picture of Friederike and baby. Happy to have it. Give her my thanks for touching words. Good luck and blessings to gorgeous baby—your fortunate and proud great-grandfather.'

The fact that the Kaiser was now a great-grandfather reminded me of the time when Friederike, after she had become Queen of Greece, met Winston Churchill for the first time in England. Churchill asked her almost reproachfully: 'Wasn't the Kaiser your grandfather?'

My daughter retorted: 'That's as you see it. Certainly the Kaiser was my grandfather, but Queen Victoria was my great-great-grandmother. If you had the Salic Law in England, my father would be your King today.'

My father's eightieth birthday on 27 January 1939 was the next occasion for a family celebration. He was supremely happy to have such a huge gathering about him to pay him honour, especially when so many friends of his had already died, and many of the Generals who had so close to him had been recalled to that great Army in the beyond. The events in Germany had done more than enough to turn attention in directions other than Doorn, and he was not unaware of this fact, but he did not complain. But now and then he would let slip a word or two which indicated how he felt. In a telegram I received from him he said:

> 'Just had a very pleasant and interesting visit from the King of Spain whose sincerity and fidelity was in the old tradition—so seldom known these days—and so heart-warming.'

Among the guests at Doorn were Crown Prince Rupprecht of Bavaria, Grand Duke Friedrich Franz of Mecklenburg, the Margrave of Meissen, Grand Duke Vladimir of Russia, and Crown Prince Paul of Greece. Naturally, his children and grandchildren were there, too, as was Prince Bernhard of the Netherlands, who brought him the Queen of Holland's good wishes. Field Marshal von Mackensen, the Kaiser's faithful old friend, was there. It was ten years since I had seen him last, and it was very pleasant to see him and the Kaiser sitting together, and, like all old veterans, talking of the past.

What pleased my father particularly was the fact that he had been remembered by the King and Queen of England. Throughout King George V's reign, the English Court had, since 1914, completely ignored the Kaiser's very existence. Now, twenty-five years after the outbreak of the First World War, the King's son, George VI, who had succeeded his brother, Edward VIII, had sent his heartiest congratulations.

It was altogether a magnificent occasion, which reminded me of the grand Court festivities of the past. My father wore his ceremonial Life Guards Hussars uniform, the same one he wore in Georg Schöbel's painting *Court Ball in the Royal Castle*.

But, sadly as it turned out, this was to be the last time there would be a fnll gathering of the Kaiser's family. That same year the Second World War broke out, and at its conclusion the picture of our family had been changed beyond all recognition.

16   *Death at Doorn*

It was with some consternation that we watched the light-hearted manner in which any chance of reconciliation and friendship with England was literally being thrown away by the dictatorship of the Third Reich. My husband tried to warn them they were heading for a calamity, but no one listened. He pointed out that they had not only failed in their assessment of the British mentality, but had wrongly estimated their strength as well. The British policy of appeasement, he told the Government, was not to be taken to mean a lack of toughness or determination.

In a final effort, my husband once more offered his services to Hitler as mediator between Germany and Great Britain. It was quite a spontaneous gesture on his part; he had not been advised to do so. On the other hand, no one wanted to take his advice, either, nor his offer to mediate. His pleas fell on deaf ears. There was not even the hint of a reply from Hitler.

The Führer had no experience whatever of foreign affairs. He had never even trodden on foreign soil if one discounts his time on the Western Front during the First World War, and that we considered a severe handicap for a Head of State. One cannot learn about foreign countries in the classroom. Hitler, it appeared, was self-taught, and though he had distinguished himself in so doing, his education in foreign affairs and policies still remained incomplete. And there is nothing more dangerous than imperfect knowledge.

Certainly Hitler had visited Italy before the outbreak of the Second World War to see his ally, Mussolini, and it revealed his weaknesses. His first appearance in Venice, for instance, showed him up as an excited, cramped and insecure Reich Chancellor, who simply threw the painstakingly prepared briefs of diplomats like Konstantin, Baron von Neurath, and Ulrich von Hassell overboard. He simply failed to come up to expectations. Mussolini made this comment: 'Instead of talking to me about current problems, he kept quoting from that dreary old book of his, *Mein Kampf*, which I've never been able to read beyond the first couple of pages.'

Some years later, when he was in Rome, Hitler unwarrantably insulted the King, Victor Emmanuel—whom he called 'King Nut-cracker'—in such a way that it was bound to come out in public, even though they had talked behind closed doors. Hitler came to Italy with the conviction, as a Fascist diplomat said ironically, 'that Mussolini's role *vis-à-vis* the King was that of nursemaid to a seven-year-old boy who had to be played with then put to bed early. During the day, however, he had to be benevolently yet firmly handled.' When Hitler found out how wrong he was, he became very angry. In later years, when the King had the Duce arrested, at least he got his own back.

I would like to mention here that Hitler forbade the ladies of the Embassy in Italy ever to curtsy to the King and Queen, and that 'a suitable bow' was all that was necessary. One of my cousins, the wife of a Counsellor at the Embassy, never obeyed the order. She told me: 'I was brought up differently and behave accordingly.' Her husband was immediately recalled.

All in all Hitler formed his own opinion of foreign countries and his dilettante handling of affairs in this area led to catastrophe especially when the occupational disease of all dictators, megalo-mania, overtook him.

In 1935 Churchill wrote: 'We cannot tell whether Hitler will be the man who will once again let loose upon the world another war in which civilisation will irretrievably succumb, or whether he will go down in history as the man who restored honour and peace of mind to the great Germanic nation and brought it back serene, helpful and strong, to the forefront of the European family circle. It is on this mystery of the future that history will pronounce. It is enough to say that both possibilities are open at the present moment.' But Hitler had already switched the points. He was obsessed with power.

There are two examples to illustrate his obsession. Just before he assumed the Chancellorship, his Press chief, Dr Otto Dietrich, recorded the following incident:

> 'It was late at night and Hitler was sitting with a few of his close colleagues. He was tired and during a pause in the conversation fell into a slumber. A few minutes later, startled out of a dream, he said quite unexpectedly but in great earnestness to Goebbels, "I insist that you must not make me Kaiser or King!" Goebbels stammered a few words of agreement and from then on studiously avoided the subject.'

How could such thoughts have entered Hitler's head? How could he even contemplate being called to the Throne? The example surely sheds some light on his innermost thoughts.

On another occasion in Dresden, after his seizure of power, Hitler, in evening dress, attended the opera there. One of his intimates, his official photographer Heinrich Hoffmann, related:

> 'As an attendant opened the door of the loge, Hitler noticed a golden crown above the door. "What does this crown mean?" he asked.
>
> '"My Führer, that is King Friedrich August of Saxony's box," one of the local Party leaders replied, not without pride.
>
> '"And you expect me to sit in the box of an abdicated King? Never! Those of you gentlemen who wish to stay, stay!"
>
> 'And with these words Hitler stalked angrily out of the theatre, and together we went back to our hotel.'

After three or four years of success, Hitler must have felt that he had been chosen by Providence to lead the German people to their position as a world power and to ensure it for hundreds of years to come, and that he had to seize this opportunity given him by Destiny before his strength gave out. At the beginning of November 1937, he summoned the Commander-in-Chief of the Wehrmacht and the Foreign Minister, Baron von Neurath, and revealed his future military plans. According to the minutes taken by his adjutant, Colonel Hossbach, Hitler said: 'The solution of the German question lies in the use of force.' As his first goals he named Austria and Czechoslovakia.

A few days later, Lord Halifax, representing the British Government, met Hitler at Obersalzburg and assured him: 'The view in England is that the present misunderstandings between us can be removed, and we fully recognise the great services which the Führer has rendered in the reconstruction of Germany.'

On Armistice Day that year, Churchill said in a speech: 'One can abhor Hitler's system and still admire his patriotic achievements. If our country were to be conquered, I hope that we would find such an admirable champion to give us back our courage and lead us to our proper place among the community of nations.'

The next year Prime Minister Neville Chamberlain came to Berchtesgarten, but in the meantime Hitler had annexed Austria and was aiming at Czechoslovakia. On his return the British Premier told his Cabinet colleagues:

> 'It is impossible not to be impressed by the power of this man. His aims and intentions have been firmly limited. He assured me that he would be content as soon as the Sudeten Germans have been incorporated into the Reich. I believe that Herr Hitler is telling the truth.'

With the signing of the Munich Pact in 1938 the threat of war seemed to recede and my father wrote to Queen Mary, King George V's widow, expressing his joy at the British Prime Minister's determination to keep peace. She understood how my father felt and remarked: 'Poor Wilhelm, he must have been horrified at the thought there could yet be another war between our two countries.'

We were no longer so optimistic. In July 1938, August Wilhelm told me, 'Things don't look very quiet for the future!' In the summer of 1939, my husband and I went to Florence to attend the wedding of my cousin, Irene of Greece and Haimon, the Duke of Spoleto. Once more, the European royal families had made a rendezvous here on this wonderful summer evening, one which I shall never forget. But the feeling crept upon me that there was so little time left before catastrophe would overwhelm us, and I could already hear the steady ticking of the time-bomb.

The overriding theme of our conversations concerned the danger of a German-Polish conflict and its world-wide political ramifications. King Victor Emmanuel was very worried. On the following day I spoke with my aunt Margarethe, while we were standing on one of the balconies of the Villa Sparta, the house of my cousin Helene, the former Queen of Rumania. I told her of my anxieties for the future, about the war which I feared would shortly break out, but she did not think, in fact considered it was impossible, that Hitler would provoke a war. My aunt could not bring herself to believe that a statesman who had done so much for his people could risk such a gamble. It was an opinion I had encountered for a long time everywhere.

On the journey back, I decided to take certain precautions. It was abundantly clear to me that in the event of war my three eldest sons would immediately be mobilised, and before that happened I wanted to see them all again. Georg Wilhelm and Christian were already on active service, and I came to an understanding with them that if their units were given their marching orders they would immediately send me the coded message 'The parcel has arrived.' Then, in Blankenburg I set up a small petrol store, obtained some cannisters, and made sure that any trip to see my sons would not be frustrated by a shortage of gasoline.

Some weeks later my husband and I were at the theatre in the little town of Harzburg, where they put on unpretentious shows which nevertheless gratified the public. During the show a door banged. Some thought it was sheer clumsiness on someone's part, some thought it was just thoughtlessness. Then another door banged, and again and again some door was opened and was letting in light into the darkness of the theatre, while people groped about and whispered. And always, there was the door banging. I have never been able to forget these doors and the noise they made. It was uncanny and boded only ill.

After the show, just as I entered the castle courtyard, someone shouted for me to rush to the telephone as Prince Christian was calling. I hurried into the house, picked up the receiver, and heard my son's voice saying, 'The parcel has arrived.' Then he put the phone down. An hour later there was another call. This time it was Georg Wilhelm and he repeated the same coded message. I quickly had the car made ready and went to Lüneburg. In a little inn there I took leave

of my sons, Ernst August and Christian, then went back to Blankenburg where I stayed briefly before going on to Torgau to see Georg
Wilhelm. Unfortunately, he had very little time for his mother: this
troops were all ready to move off.

It was war, once more. For the second time we were to experience
the holocaust. I wrote to my father in Doorn:

> '. . . How one has hoped and prayed in these last weeks that this
> terror would pass us by. The last dreadful war is still too close to
> us, but the Lord God has decreed otherwise.'

My sons and their Prussian cousins were in the field, serving with
the infantry, cavalry, armoured units and the air force, all doing their
duty for the Fatherland. My father wrote me: 'God be with us and
our House and all our loved ones, whether at home or in the field, and
may He protect all our dear boys. God be praised that Mama never
lived to bear such anxieties for her children and grandchildren!'

The House of Hohenzollern's first victim was Prince Oskar, my
brother Oskar's eldest son. He was killed at the beginning of
September 1939, in Poland while serving as a Lieutenant with
51 Infantry Regiment. My brother sent me the news from the West
where, as a Colonel and Commander of an infantry regiment he had
been since the outbreak of war. Young Oskar's divisional commander
had written: 'Prince Oskar, a very brave Prussian officer, fell while
at the head of his platoon, leading them in an attack against an enemy
position. He was a shining example to all his comrades.' My brother,
in telling me the news, added: 'I don't need to tell you what I'm going
through. The dear, good, faithful boy. Now he is gone from me. It's
too dreadful—and for what!!'

Next to die was my brother Crown Prince Wilhelm's eldest son,
Wilhelm. He had been very severely wounded during an attack
against a French-Senegalese position in Northern France in May 1940
and died two days later. His body was brought back and buried next
to my mother in the Temple of Antiquity in Potsdam. Thousands
attended his funeral.

The campaign in the West brought my father directly in contact
with the war and his position was made extremely difficult. There
were all sorts of rumours and conjectures going around about his

attitude and General von Dommes, my father's long-standing adjutant, had to issue this statement on 21 May 1940:

> 'Should there be an entry into Holland by the Germans in the course of the war, His Majesty has laid down the following guidelines:
>
> 1. He will desist from what could malevolently be represented as flight.
> 2. He does not wish to claim the hospitality of any enemy of Germany.
>
> The swift commencement of a state of hostilities does not make it possible for the Kaiser to join the German troops. Doorn, as is known, lies between the two Dutch defence lines, and the Dutch Government has advised His Majesty on many occasions that in the event of war he should seek a place not directly in the battle zones. The Kaiser, nevertheless, has decided to remain in Doorn. On the outbreak of hostilities His Majesty, together with Her Majesty, Princess Henriette and their closest entourage, as well as some of their personnel, were interned in Doorn. The greater part of their personnel have been transferred to an internment camp in Northern Holland. As all radio sets had to be surrendered immediately, House Doorn was completely cut off from the world. The only news which reaches Doorn tells of the failure of German attacks in Northern France and Belgium and the successful resistance to the Germans in Holland. In Doorn one experiences air raids and alarms. At midday on Whit-sunday Baron Nagell, the Mayor of Doorn, appeared before His Majesty with an offer from the British Government. In view of the old family relationships and the Kaiser's dangerous situation in the war zone, the British Government offered him asylum in England. His Majesty, understandably, refused.'

The General's record of the events in Doorn at that time continued:

> 'On Monday, 13 May, the Grebbeberg, east of Rhenon, was captured by German troops after a tough battle, and with it

ended the resistance of the southern sector of the Grebbe line. Dutch troops holding the line withdrew through Amerongen and Doorn in the direction of Utrecht and pursuing German troops advanced through Doorn during the course of the morning. The General Staff officer in charge of this Division, Lieutenant-Colonel von Zitzewitz, reported to His Majesty, and informed him on behalf of the Führer that he was from now on under the protection of the German Reich and that the Wehrmacht, and later the Field Security Police, would take over the watch on the Kaiser.

'German troops pressed on to take Utrecht and a demand was made for the surrender of the city through an intermediary. When the Commandant refused, the Germans opened fire, but in the meantime came the news that the Dutch Army had laid down its arms and hostilities were at an end. The German troops were thereupon ordered to bypass Utrecht and head towards Amsterdam. But a small unit (one officer and eighteen men) remained in Doorn for guard duties and to keep order. During Wednesday and Thursday, members of the household who had been interned returned to Doorn and life resumed its normal tempo. During the church service on 19 May, the unit on guard came and took part. His Majesty said a prayer both at the beginning and end of the service, which he addressed to all the young soldiers present. These prayers thoroughly warmed their hearts.'

In his reply to Queen Wilhelmina's offer that he should choose a safer place than Doorn, my father answered: 'I am deeply grateful for your offer, but I shall not be able to take advantage of it as I am looking forward to meeting my destiny here where I am living.'

Now that Doorn was under German domination, my father was given to understand by the Nazi leader that no hindrance would be put in the way of his return to Germany. The Kaiser refused this offer also and remained where he was.

As far as the Kaiser was concerned, life changed only insofar as he was now surrounded by German soldiers. A description of what went on was given me by one of his entourage:

'Outside, endless columns of German soldiers marched past and all inquired after the Kaiser. Every officer undertook the duty of reporting personally to him—not just the old front line men, but the young ones, too. They all pressed into the Kaiser's private quarters and would not rest until their Emperor had smilingly shaken each one by the hand.'

It is not difficult to understand my father's feelings when he learned the news of the cessation of hostilities with France, and heard that the armistice had been signed in the same railway coach and in the same wood at Compiègne where, in 1918, the German negotiators had had to yield to the terms imposed by the enemy. The rôles of victor and vanquished had truly been reversed now, and the Kaiser, already over eighty, just stood there, tears streaming from his eyes. The former German Supreme Commander-in-Chief of the First World War was practically speechless with gratified emotion. The tables had been turned at last. It was with some difficulty that he was able to turn to his entourage and venture to say: 'I can only quote my grandfather's telegram to his wife—"what a change, wrought by God's grace. Now thank we all our God." '

That was a glance into the past, but despite his great age my father had not for a single moment lost sight of the problems of the present. The war against England distressed him, but his real concern lay in the East. That same year he had written to an American friend of his youth, Poultney Bigelow, to whose attention he had brought his own conviction 'of the necessity for every State in Europe to unite and fight together against Soviet Russia because she will soon threaten not only Europe but the whole world'.

In spring 1941 a new German campaign was launched, this time in the Balkans, directed against Greece and Jugoslavia. The reasons given were the *coup d'état* against the Belgrade Government which was friendly to the Germans, and the defeat of the Italians on the Greek front where, in 1940, they had penetrated through Albania. The Italians had wanted their Blitzkrieg, too, and they had intended to subjugate Greece in three weeks. But, apart from their initial successes, the Italians could make no further headway and their German allies had to rush to their rescue.

On 6 April 1941, German units from Bulgaria stormed into Greece and the Greek Army, which had fought so bravely against the Italians, were beaten and the admirable unity with which they had hitherto campaigned broke apart. The military support they had received from a British expeditionary force proved quite insufficient. King George II, however, was determined not to lay down his arms and while the Jugoslav Army surrendered, my cousin declared: 'The honour of Greece and the destiny of the Greek people preclude any thoughts of capitulation, for her moral catastrophe would be greater than any other misfortune.' Hardly were the words uttered than they were betrayed. One of the Ministers called on the troops to surrender. In deep despair Prime Minister Korytzis put a bullet through his head.

For three days the King sought unsuccessfully for a new Prime Minister. No one had the courage to link his name to the most tragic chapter in Greek history. That is the advantage a politician has over a King: he can take the responsibility of saying no and still try to retain his good name. A monarch cannot. He may not put a half-full jug to one side but must drink it to the last bitter drop.

The burden of decision rested on King George's shoulders. I have a record of the time, in which it was written:

> 'He is King, Premier, Foreign Minister and War Minister, all in one. Every vestige of colour has drained from the Monarch's face. His hands shake as he holds cup and saucer. George has not slept for days, yet he summons up the moral courage not only to deny the Germans' demand to cease fighting but uses every opportunity to cover the British retreat. Even in this distressing situation, the Greeks' centuries-old custom of hospitality is sacred to him. Once more, in the name of his country, he calls for an honourable decision.'

Finally, on 21 April, Tsouderos declared himself ready to take over the Premiership. Throughout his political life he had never concealed his anti-monarchist feelings, yet he wrote in his diary: 'Now there is only one among all the others, who are but mere shadows about me, who remains true, consistent, deeply sincere and determined to do his duty to the very end: the King.'

Thermopylæ fell, the British troops retreated and were shipped out, and very soon after the flags with the swastikas on them fluttered over the Acropolis. We waited, full of anxiety, for news of our daughter, Friederike—in vain. We heard nothing. What had happened to her? What had happened to our son-in-law and our grand-children—Sophia and Constantine, the latter not even one year old? We were completely in the dark regarding their fate.

While we were worrying about our daughter and her family, I received an alarming report from General von Dommes in Doorn that my father's health was giving rise to the greatest anxiety. I therefore decided to go there at once. Fortunately I was able to get a travel permit from the German authorities and travelled there by rail accompanied by Louise Holzheuer, my lady's maid. The journey was beset by difficulties as the lines were full of troop transports and we could only go very slowly. I was also informed that all trains stopped at night and this proved to be the case: we halted at Hengelo, so I telephoned Doorn, but again had a long wait as the doctor took his time to get to the telephone. However, he reassured me and said that a car would be sent to fetch me.

After more hours of waiting, the car arrived and eventually we reached Amerongen. All the time I sat there thinking—would this be the last time I would come to see my father? I asked the gentlemen of his entourage whether I had arrived in time and was told that he was a little better but very weak and was at that moment sleeping. While I waited for the call, I wandered with heavy heart through the park and over the bridge which spanned the canal and watched the wild ducks swimming on the water, which my father used to feed every day. Back in the house my step-mother greeted me, looking composed but very depressed.

Then I went into my father's room. He was lying very still. His first question to me was: 'Have you any news of Friederike?' Her picture stood next to his bed, for he loved her dearly. He looked at me most imploringly, as if he had waited only for my arrival to tell him some-thing about his fate. But I knew nothing, either, though I could not bring myself to tell him so. Instead, I said: 'Yes, she is well.' He looked as if he had been relieved of a heavy burden and lay back. 'Thank God,' I heard him say. The tension eased from him and he closed his eyes, breathing easily. I sat there motionless while my father slept.

The small improvement in his condition was sustained and the doctors there said they thought there would be weeks yet before he succumbed. My husband, who had joined me in the meantime with August Wilhelm, went back home, as did the others. Besides, board and lodgings were scarce and the food supply was very short. Only my nephew Prince Louis Ferdinand and I remained, for he was a great consolation to his grandfather.

When my father spoke to me again, he discussed world affairs and wanted news of this or that, but his thoughts invariably switched to England. He asked me: 'Are we still going to attack England?' Very seriously he added: 'Should that really happen—and should we win—we must immediately stretch out our hand to England and go together. Without England we cannot endure.' His eyes seemed fixed in the far distance and seemed to be asking, what will become of our Germany?

The improvement in my father's condition gave me little hope that his hitherto strong constitution would help him. One day I was suddenly called into the house. As I went into my father's room I could see that the shadow of death had already begun to lengthen. I sat on his right side and took his dear hand. He opened his eyes, but he could no longer speak. I knew, however, that he had recognised me.

Hour after hour I sat by my father's bedside with Princess Hermine and Louis Ferdinand. Over the bed hung that wonderful picture of my mother by Lenbach and I knew that my parents would soon be reunited. The night went by. Late next morning the Kaiser, my father, died. It was the 4th of June 1941.

Outside, the garden he had tended was blooming, seeming to send him their last greetings. Louis Ferdinand and I stood by my father's bed and bade him farewell. We held hands and were grateful to have been able to be there during those final hours. I took the first vigil that night so that I could be alone with my father once more. Memories flooded back, stayed, then ebbed away again, many of them distinct, others like a haze. My father was far removed from them all; his features were inexpressibly peaceful. As in life, so in death, he had yielded to God's Will. A truly fulfilled life had gone home to God.

While I was keeping watch, the door of the room opened quietly. One of the servants entered cautiously, careful to avoid any noise. Then he stood to attention as he had once done in the ranks of the 1st Guards Regiment when his Kaiser had stood at their head. He was taking leave of his master. Louis Ferdinand took over the vigil for the next half of the night. As he relieved me he put his arms sympathetically around me. He knew what these last hours had meant to me.

One would have thought that no one would wish to disturb the dead, but Hitler did. He insisted that the Kaiser be given a State funeral in Potsdam. He wanted to claim the dead Kaiser for himself despite the fact that my father had expressly wished to be buried in Doorn as laid down in the codicil to his Will. 'He wants to use this opportunity to walk behind the German Kaiser's coffin in front of the whole German people and the world, to show them he is the legitimate successor,' declared Louis Ferdinand, not without justification. Doubtless Hitler had been influenced by Prince Wilhelm's burial at my mother's side in the Temple of Antiquity after he had been killed in action. Tens of thousands had been at the funeral, not only because Prince Wilhelm had been loved but because of the people's affinity and devotion to the House of Hohenzollern.

It was far from easy for the Crown Prince to negotiate with the Reich Chancellery and get them to respect the Kaiser's last wishes, but he eventually convinced them. When Hitler realised he could not prevail he ordered that the funeral, if it had to take place in Doorn, 'would coolly observe the minimum proprieties only'. Goebbels informed the Press that they were to report the funeral purely as a minor event, and in his own newspaper, *Das Reich*, he recalled the Kaiser as 'one who only floated on the highest crest of a surging surf. He was only a floating particle, a distinguished particle, to be sure, but nothing more.' The whole article was one of scorn for the man who, even in death, had resisted Hitler.

My father was buried on a radiantly sunny day, and the park through which the funeral procession passed was a blaze of lilac and rhododendrons. A guard of honour comprising three companies from the army, navy and air force under the command of Colonel von Gersdorff was drawn up. Field Marshal von Mackensen, General

Reinhard, and numerous high-ranking officers from neutral or countries allied to Germany were there, as was the Nazi Governor of Holland, Dr Seyss-Inquart, who represented Hitler. The Wehrmacht itself was represented by Colonel-General Haase, Air Force General Christiansen, Admiral Densch, and Admiral Canaris as representative of the Commander-in-Chief. Only two of my sons, Ernst August and Welf-Heinrich could come as Georg Wilhelm and Christian were with their units in Poland and could not be reached.

The procession wound its way from the house to the chapel in the same park where my father had decreed his tomb should be erected. At its head marched General Karl Count Goltz with the Kaiser's Marshal's baton, then Colonel Count von Moltke bearing the cushion with the Kaiser's orders and decorations, and lastly the Court chaplain, Dr. Doehring. Finally, with a roll of drums and the sound of the tattoo, the coffin was laid to rest and the Battalion of Honour marched away to the tune of Beethoven's 'Yorck's Marsch'.

There could be a great deal more to say about the day Germany's last Kaiser was taken to his honourable rest, but I will confine myself only to what remains in my memory. I shall never forget the extremely touching sermon preached by Doehring who had for decades been my father's faithful friend and confidant. His every word accentuated the pain of my father's death. Nor shall I ever forget the sight of the ancient Field Marshall von Mackensen slowly raising his baton in a final salute to his Commander-in-Chief then dropping on his knees beside the coffin in the chapel and brushing aside all efforts to help him up. He did it alone, unaided, using his sword as a lever, raising himself laboriously until he was upright again.

Nor can I close without thinking of the part played by the Dutch. They were suffering under the occupation of an enemy power and they could have had no kind feelings towards us Germans. Yet they came, nevertheless, with wreaths in their hands to bid farewell to the German Emperor who had lived for so long amongst them. I saw their tears, tears for a stranger whom they had learned to love and honour. Whenever I went into Doorn in the next few days, the Dutch people came up to me, hands outstretched and full of sympathy. They were simple people, but they knew what they—and I—had lost.

Two and a half weeks after my father's death, Hitler invaded Russia.

17   *Purge of Princes*

Hitler's invasion of Russia in the very early hours of 22 June 1941 signalled the beginning of the worst catastrophe ever to befall our people. The decision to take this momentous step was due to the Führer's complete misunderstanding and total lack of comprehension both of international and military affairs. But my main personal worries concerned my three eldest sons, all cavalry officers who now took part in the invasion of Russia. As in 1914 when I had waited anxiously for news of my husband, so now I awaited word from my sons. We received only brief field postcards at first, but at length we were able to read a fairly detailed account of what had happened from Christian:

'. . . At last the time came for us to attack. You'll hardly believe what a fabulous feeling it is to be waiting with the unit in readiness for the attack and looking at our watches—still ten minutes to go—five—three—and then away. First we attacked the woods, then headed south to St Bishop on the other side of the Dnieper. There was fierce fighting in the woods against marksmen hidden in the trees and positions so well camouflaged that we only recognised what they were when we got near. Then we came back to the same positions we had assaulted the previous day and took prisoners who told us that we had created confusion everywhere. Then we went on to find the Russians entrenched and offering tenacious resistance. They were continually counter-attacking and smothering us with artillery fire.

'We should have been relieved after the first attacks, but the infantry failed to advance and we were stuck there for a further five days. Truly, the utmost was demanded of us—daily attacks which were six kilometres in breadth, first in extreme heat, then in rain, and at night we had to lie outside in the filth and wet, always on the lookout for renewed counter-attacks.

'Rations didn't arrive very often. I didn't think it possible the men could endure so much. Unfortunately, we also suffered losses. In the last attacks our regiment alone lost four hundred men and eleven officers, as did Georg Wilhelm's squadron. At last we are now being relieved by two Infantry Regiments and will have eight days rest. I have thought about you both, a lot, these last days and often thought I would never come out of this witches' cauldron alive. I had a glancing shot from a bullet on my steel helmet, one through my gas mask belt and twice I had my rifle shot out of my hand. . . .'

.Georg Wilhelm was a General Staff Officer with No. 2 Panzer Group under the command of General Guderian and fought at Smolensk, Kiev, and Orel, while my eldest son, Ernst August, served with another Panzer Group under General Erich Hoepner.

Then came that dreadful winter of 1941/2 and our armies' advance got stuck in the Russian mire. Snow and frost later froze them there. The catastrophe made Hitler look for scapegoats on whom to lay the blame and Georg Wilhelm's commander, General Heinz Guderian, among others, was relieved of his command. We esteemed him greatly and my son would have gone through fire for him. When we heard that Guderian had been dismissed, my husband said: 'Let's go to him.' And we did. We felt deeply for him, particularly as this distinguished soldier, who had proved himself so gloriously, now had to sit at home just because he had told Hitler the truth about the military situation.

What Guderian had to tell us was scarcely encouraging. He told us how he had spent hours at Hitler's headquarters describing the exact state of affairs at the front to the Führer and what he considered would have to be done, believing that Hitler would concur with the opinions of his experienced front-line General or at least discuss the matter in detail. Guderian recommended that the German forces should be withdrawn to suitable winter quarters, but Hitler hectored him and commanded: 'They must dig in and defend every square metre!'

The General rejoined that this decision would mean going over to static war in unsuitable countryside and that would lead to large losses in human life without any military advantage being gained. He told Hitler: 'We will be sacrificing the blood of our officers and non-commissioned officers quite needlessly and those losses will be irretrievable.'

'I know you have pledged yourself and have been with your men a great deal,' Hitler retorted. 'I recognise that. But you are standing too close to events and you are letting yourself be influenced by the troops' sufferings. You should stand farther back. Believe me, you'll see things far more clearly from a distance.'

The General refused to give in. 'Of course it is my duty to ameliorate the suffering of my soldiers as best I can,' he told the Führer. 'But it is extremely difficult to do so when my men still have no winter uniforms and the greater part of the infantry is still running around in summer khaki drill trousers. They're either completely lacking boots, underwear, gloves and woollen helmets or find themselves in generally distressing conditions.' 'Hitler', Guderian continued, 'was enraged, like a man stung by a tarantula, and screamed at me—"It's NOT true!"'

On 26 December 1941, six days after his showdown with the Führer, Guderian was transferred to the reserves. Just after he had left that day, he heard Hitler tell Field Marshal Keitel, 'I just have not been able to convince that man.'

Guderian has been blamed for later placing himself once more at Hitler's disposal, but he was a soldier through and through and did it because he thought it was his natural duty to serve as a soldier for his Fatherland. Later, he told us: 'Once, at a difficult time, a Prince of my Royal House sent me a small portrait of Frederick the Great, on which he had written the words that the great King, in danger of defeat, had once communicated to his friend, the Marquis d'Argens—"Nothing will change my innermost soul and I will go on in my own

H

way and do what I consider useful and honourable.'' That little portrait has been lost, but these royal words remain in my memory and serve as a model for my actions.'

Hitler's attitude to old Germany and to those who, in his eyes, still represented her, became more and more obvious. It was hate, unfathomable hate. Even at the very beginning of his career, after the November 1923 *putsch* in Munich, he had told the Bavarian State Commissar, Gustav von Kahr, who had asked him where he stood as far as the Monarchy was concerned: 'For me this day is the start of a settlement to make good the crimes of five years ago. Above all, I will repair the injustice which, five years ago, a horde of common criminals perpetrated on His Majesty the King's late father.' Yet, the way this same man thought after he had reached the height of his success is related by Dr Henry Picker in his notes on Hitler's table talk at the Führer Headquarters. On 5 July 1942, Hitler remarked: 'Hardly anyone is as boundlessly stupid as a King.'

Hitler had already considered German Princes as being the root cause of unrest and division throughout German history and in another conversation remarked: 'The fact that our Social Democrats have done away with this ferment . . . means that we should now rid ourselves of the influence exercised by the Hohenzollern brood—for example as officers in the Wehrmacht.'

We had not known of Hitler's hate-filled outburst at the time, neither had we known of his order for the dismissal of all members of the former ruling houses from the armed forces, including my brothers and sons. His command was accompanied by the words: 'The Third Reich can do without Royal defenders of the Fatherland.' The first signs of Hitler's designs were when my brother Oskar took over No. 230 Infantry Regiment at the beginning of 1940, and was shortly afterwards promoted to Major-General and transferred to the Reserves. The Army Commander, who informed him of this order, did not tell him, however, what had transpired two weeks earlier during a military briefing with Hitler. 'The Führer was highly indignant to hear Prince Oskar was in command of a Regiment,' Colonel-General Jodl, the Chief of the General Staff, noted in his diary. Hitler ordered the Prince to be removed.

In 1942, my brother Eitel-Fritz died in Potsdam. Hitler decreed that this brave soldier's burial should take place without any military honours. It was shameful. My brother's faithful friends in the Wehrmacht, who included two well-known Generals of the Second World War, had to attend the funeral in civilian clothes.

The first of my sons to be dismissed on Hitler's orders was Welf Heinrich who had joined the Luftwaffe as an officer cadet in 1941. Just before he was supposed to go to war training school in October that year, he was called to his Commanding Officer and told that despite his good qualifications he could not become an officer. Welf Heinrich at least begged him to let him join as aircrew, but that, too, was denied. A few days later a telex message arrived with the order that he be released, and he returned home very disappointed and unable to grasp why he should have to sit at home while everybody else was at the front fighting.

We told our other sons of Welf Heinrich's misfortune and Christian had his own to relate. He had been recommended for the Knight's Cross of the Iron Cross by his commander but that had been turned down. We felt it was because the bravery of a Prince of our House could not publicly be recognised by the régime.

My husband and I tried to get an explanation of these Royal dismissals and wrote to Hitler asking for enlightenment. No answer. I wrote to Goering in the same vein. Again, no reply. I also wrote to Frau von Ribbentrop among others, but she answered saying that she could give me no exact information. Shortly afterwards, however, I received a report concerning a talk my cousin Philipp, the Landgrave of Hesse, had with Hitler. Philipp was married to Princess Mafalda, a daughter of King Victor Emmanuel II and had been entrusted by Hitler with diplomatic missions either to his father-in-law or Mussolini. Prince Philipp wrote:

'On 21 February I had an audience with Hitler at Headquarters and had an opportunity at the end to speak to him alone. I told him quite frankly that I'd heard there was a decree in existence which stipulated that Princes were no longer to be allowed to join the army and this gave me great cause for anxiety concerning my sons. He answered: ''A decree in such a form does not exist and your sons can naturally become officers at any time. I must, however, refuse entry into the army of the sons of Royal Houses who have either verbally or by their actions opposed the National Socialist State or me." '

At the beginning of 1943, Christian was dismissed from the army. In December it was the turn of Ernst August, and in January 1944, Georg Wilhelm's. Now I had my sons back home with me, and whenever I looked at them all, either at table or in the castle courtyard, I had to shake my head: I had with me one General, one Major, two Cavalry Captains and one ensign—retired. And in the middle of a war, too!

I had heard practically no news of my daughter Friederike, but finally received some via Crown Princess, later Queen, Luise of Sweden, and learned of Friederike's adventurous flight through Crete to Egypt with her husband and two children. From Egypt they had taken refuge in South Africa at General Smuts's invitation. But it was to be some weeks before we were to hear from Friederike herself, again through Stockholm. Now at last we were content. She described her life in South Africa and added:

'The feeling of having no home is terrible, particularly when one has children and when one has become as unhappy as we are. The only virtue of this war is that it has taught us not to hang on to material things, as one can lose them from one day to the next.'

After describing the climate, she added:

'I wouldn't like to live anywhere but in Greece, and Palo, too. I believe no one has such a passion for Greece as we have. However it goes, we must all find the courage to start again, find all our old friends again—on whatever side they were—for our personal friends never change and they are the only bridges we have, not only to overcome the bitterness and hate, but to bring all the countries nearer to one another again.'

When Egypt was chosen as the base for the Greek Government in exile, my daughter had frequently to be separated from her husband. To be a stranger in a foreign land was not easy and Friederike wrote us:

'Parting from Palo was terrible, as you will fully understand. I absolutely wanted to go but, both Palo and Georgy resisted, saying that as the children naturally couldn't go, I had to stay. Besides, they are still so small. It is cruel, when one thinks of all that we have been through together, we must still be separated. Who knows when we shall see each other again. They were four weeks on the way and I have had no idea whether they still exist or not.'

In the autumn of 1944 the Wehrmacht had to retreat from Greece, step by step, as the Russian advance rolled on towards the Balkans, and on 12 October Athens was cleared. The Greek Government in exile returned home. The King, the Crown Prince and all members of the Royal House, however, were not allowed to return by the British Government. They wanted to come to terms with the Communist partisans without hurting their anti-monarchist feelings. When British and Greek ships took to sea from Alexandria, Crown Prince Paul and Friederike were left standing on the pier. Hitler had ejected them, and now Churchill was preventing them from returning to their home.

We were now in the sixth year of the war, and death had reaped a dreadful harvest, not only on the fronts, not only among those who had rejected Hitler and his policies, but among the population of the cities and villages which had been pulverised by the inhuman air raids. Germany sank in a heap of dust and rubble. To me it seemed as if the powers of this Earth had sworn to exterminate the world in which I had grown up and lived. Brunswick was destroyed. In Königsberg, the Royal castle and the old city fell victims to the fury of the war.

My brother Oskar wrote from Potsdam:

'In a heavy daylight air raid on Berlin yesterday, they hit our beloved castle. So now, even this piece of our beloved homeland has been laid waste, and nearly all of our abodes in Berlin have either been demolished or severely damaged; those with which our childhood or youthful memories are particularly associated —the castle, the old Kaiser Palace, the Crown Prince's Palace,

Monbijou, Bellevue. Shattered, I wandered along over the castle bridge, between the Spree and the former Kommandantur (opposite the armoury) to the Gendarmen Markt, the Mauerstrasse, Kaiserhof, Wilhelmsplatz, Leipziger Strasse, Potsdamer Platz—all ruins. The streets have changed to such an extent that I can hardly find my way about.'

During the last winter of the war, the Gestapo arrested my eldest son. Police officials suddenly arrived at Blankenburg Castle with a warrant for Ernst August. We were shocked, especially when we asked the reason why and received no answer. I helped my son pack, but the whole time he remained silent though very agitated. Then the men took him away but we knew not where. We did everything to find out what had happened but made little headway. Some said he had been taken to Brunswick, others that he had gone to Berlin and was in some hotel.

As soon as we heard that he could be in Berlin, I set out with Georg Wilhelm as my husband could not accompany me. He had undergone a stomach operation and was still feeling very ill. In Berlin I went from office to office to try and get some more information about Ernst August. We had a shock in one of the offices when an official noticed Georg Wilhelm's briefcase. 'Put that case away,' he ordered. To me, the command sounded like 'Hands up!' but Georg Wilhelm answered him calmly. 'I gave my weapon up downstairs,' he said. Naturally, I also looked up my brother, August Wilhelm, and asked him to try and help us and our son.

Our efforts brought a measure of success when at last Ernst August was allowed to write. It was a remarkable letter, censored by the Gestapo, and many sentences had been excised, but at least we learned that he could be found at the Gestapo office at No. 10 Meineckestrasse, room 70.

Finally I received permission to speak to him, and I went along to the Gestapo office, my heart thumping. When I reached the entrance, where I had to show my pass, I looked at the Gestapo men: they gave me the shudders. But I was astounded when one of them, who was checking my papers, suddenly said softly, 'Your mother was a good woman.' I thought I was dreaming; it sounded so unreal. Had he really said that to me, or was my agitated imagination playing tricks? But when I slowly raised my head and looked at him I knew that, despite his unchanged attitude and his aloofness, I had not misheard. However, the officials I had to deal with were smooth, smarmy, foppish, but loathsome characters, and I knew there was nothing I could do with them which would free my son. My meeting with him was brief. He looked very weak and we couldn't say much as we were being supervised and besides, they had allowed us so very little time. Then they led Ernst August away again. As a mother, I need hardly describe my feelings on that occasion.

It was a dreadful period, especially as we did not know why he had been arrested, but we kept trying. On one of my trips to Berlin I was caught in an air raid on the Autobahn, and I thought my last hour had come. Bombs detonated all around me and the flames from burning cars lit the highway like flaming torches right up to the capital. . . . Once in the city, I went from office to office again—without success.

My brother Auwi was in the meantime doing all he could, and we finally succeeded in having Ernst August released. He arrived home in Blankenburg a few days before Christmas. It turned out that he had been arrested for being critical of Hitler's policies in some conversation he had had, and was denounced.

There were other worries beside Ernst August's arrest. My cousin Prince Philipp and his wife Mafalda seemed to have disappeared from the face of the earth. Philipp had not returned from a trip to the Führer Headquarters, where had had been summoned in September 1943, and had simply vanished. Mafalda's tracks had ended in Rome. Nobody knew where either was.

The Hesse family had endured great hardships already: seldom could a woman like the old Landgravin Margarethe of Hesse, my father's sister, have undergone such tribulations. Both her two elder sons had been killed in the First World War and her son Christopher, a Luftwaffe officer, had been killed in the Second World War over the Apennines. He left a wife and five children and when he died, his wife, Princess Sophia of Greece, one of the Duke of Edinburgh's sisters, was awaiting another child. In an air raid on Frankfurt in 1944, Margarethe lost her daughter-in-law, Marie Alexandra, her son Wolfgang's wife. She was the daughter of Prince Max of Baden.

It was not until very much later that we learned what had happened. At the end of August 1943 Princess Mafalda had gone to Sofia to attend the funeral of her brother-in-law, King Boris of Bulgaria. Queen Joanna was her sister. Owing to the Italian constitutional crisis— Mussolini had been overthrown and arrested and King Victor Emmanuel had appointed Marshal Badoglio to lead the government— Mafalda went back to Rome to pick up her children. Immediately on her arrival she was lured to the telephone by the Security Service of the S.S. and during the conversation was made to believe her husband was waiting for her in Germany. She hurried to the German frontier and was immediately arrested, and her unhappy children had to be left behind. The Vatican looked after them until their grandmother, the Landgravin Margarethe, took them under her wing.

Princess Mafalda was sent to Buchenwald concentration camp and registered there under a false name so that no one would know she was there.

Prince Philipp had been ordered to Hitler's Headquarters, the 'Wolf's Lair', in East Prussia. The next he knew was that Hitler was holding him there, though still as a guest, which he later found out was a pretext. Then one evening, while talking as he usually did with Hitler, though still being chatted to amiably, he was arrested and sent to a concentration camp at Flossenbürg after being held for a while in the Gestapo prison in the Prince Albrecht Strasse in Berlin.

Princess Mafalda, a charming but delicate woman, had to endure dreadful things in Buchenwald, but bore them all like a heroine. On 26 August 1944, Allied aircraft bombed Buchenwald and Mafalda, crouching in a slit trench, was severely wounded and buried in debris. She had to have an arm amputated but on the following day succumbed to her wounds. Italian prisoners, who had recognised her as their King's daughter, marked her grave and when they were released later, put up a simple wooden cross with her name carved on it. That was how the family eventually found out how her sufferings had ended.

Prince Philipp was put into solitary confinement for twenty months, and in April 1945 he was transferred to Dachau where the Gestapo had assembled many prominent personalities including the former Austrian Chancellor, Dr Schuschnigg, Colonel-General Halder, General von Falkenhausen, Hjalmar Schacht, the former

French Prime Minister, Léon Blum, Suffragan Bishop Neuhäusler and Prince Friedrich Leopold of Prussia. As the Americans advanced the Nazis wanted to transfer some of them, 136 in all, to the Alps, but a unit of the Wehrmacht managed to free them from the S.S., but Philipp of Hesse did not obtain freedom. He had been President of Hesse-Nassau Province, which was reason enough for the Americans later on to seize him. He was interned in twenty different prisons and internment camps and was not freed until New Year's Day, 1948.

At the beginning of April 1945, the Americans stood before Blankenburg and the Harz district was declared a Wehrmacht stronghold to be defended by the 11th Army. The American troops took up positions on the northern range of the mountains and between the Harz and the Thüringen Forest in the direction of Magdeburg and the Elbe. They formed a pocket and we were completely surrounded as the battle raged around us. The Potsdam Division was then brought in to reinforce our troops and our soldiers fought with exemplary courage.

The town of Blankenburg came under artillery fire and the once peaceful little Harz village was bombarded from the air. A hospital was hit and we took the wounded into our care. It was a sad procession which slowly wound its way to the castle. Those who could barely crawl had to make their own way as there was no transport available. Our forces even brought us their wounded from the battle fronts and I helped those severely hurt down from the transports.

The castle, which stood high above the town, resembled an anthill with all the people climbing towards it. Apart from the refugees we had nearly a hundred families from the surrounding district who had sought shelter with us. Even French prisoners of war who had worked in the area—and for us—came. They had heard rumours that with the advance of the approaching enemy armies they would be carried off and killed, but my husband reassured them and said if it should come to pass they could find refuge with us. When the first preparations for their evacuation became known they hurried to us in the castle and we hid them in the cellars.

During the air raids the Frenchmen helped the old, the sick, and the children into those cellars. They were always ready to help.

As we had so many wounded, my husband wanted to hoist the Red Cross flag over the castle but a fanatical army doctor forbade it, saying: 'I will not tolerate it. It looks as if you want to protect your castle!'

There were irreplaceable works of art in the castle vaults, brought there by Dr Kurt Seeleke, the Brunswick curator, who had rescued them from the Brunswick churches and the Duke Ulrich Museum when the bombing started. There were Van Dycks, Ruisdaels, Rubens, Steens, Rembrandts, Holbeins, and included Vermeer's *Girl with the Wineglass*. Seeleke was in despair. The art treasures he had so painstakingly rescued were now again in danger of destruction. He asked the fighting commanders to evacuate Blankenburg town on account of its hospital and the art treasures, even though he knew he was risking his neck in making such a proposal. The awareness of the gallows in the market place was telling him enough. To say the least an excited confrontation with the military commanders took place. Seeleke believed everything was lost. However, a little later, the General came to see us at the castle, and the upshot of his brief visit to us was that the castle would not be included in the battle lines and would not be defended, either.

As the enemy assault on the town and castle intensified, and artillery and aerial bombardments reached their climax, we decided to lay out a makeshift Red Cross flag, made out of sheets, in the castle courtyard, ignoring altogether the ban which had been imposed upon us. There was nothing more to answer for.

In between two air raids I ran to a neighbouring establishment to fetch food. Suddenly, I was aware of a terrible noise, the like of which I had never heard before. I stood perfectly still behind some trees then, after a little while, parted some branches to see what it was all about. There was a long column of Russians, prisoners, trailing along painfully. They were being driven through the woods by S.S. guards. Suddenly, there was a shot, then another, and a whole fusillade of them. I saw the prisoners falling. It was truly horrifying. Inexpressible disgust overcame me.

American troops were now drawing nearer and our pocket of resistance shrank more and more until, on 20 April, the entire headquarters staff of the 11th Army were taken prisoner and

Blankenburg itself fell. Shooting wildly and indiscriminately the Americans surged up to the castle itself, behaving generally just like Texas cowboys. However, that was just one aspect of them. Their commanders behaved absolutely correctly and the men themselves were scarcely inferior.

The occupation forces' most pressing and urgent questions concerned the whereabouts both of scattered and single S.S. men and Hitler Youth who, either alone or in groups, were waging their own war of resistance against the Americans. The Harz mountains, thickly wooded and scattered with many gorges and ravines, offered ideal operational conditions for the remaining resisters, and on that account American officers kept haranguing my husband. They told him of the continued dangers a partisan war would impose, for the resisters would have to depend on the villages and hamlets for their sustenance and that in turn would lead to compulsory retaliatory measures by the Americans against the innocent inhabitants.

My husband told them he was ready to do everything in his power to help avert this danger, and asked if the insurgents could not be treated as regular soldiers if they could be persuaded to lay down their arms. He also suggested that they could then be sent to ordinary prisoner of war camps and be neither shot nor punished. The Americans agreed then raised the drastic ban, generally imposed, which restricted all movement, just for this purpose, and my husband went to work. He sought out all our foresters and asked them to help him in this somewhat risky task. Then they all began searching everywhere for the hidden stragglers and fighters who were, crazily enough, calling themselves Werewolves. Day after day my husband and our sons scoured the area with only one end in view: they wanted peace and quiet to return as speedily as possible and wished only that in our district at least no further victims should be added to an already large list.

But there were plenty of victims elsewhere. I heard from my brother Oskar in Berlin: '. . . Here, nearly all districts have either been destroyed or severely damaged. How glad I am that dear Papa did not live to see the destruction of all he held so dearly. I don't know how or when I shall get out of here. . . .'

He finally managed to leave Potsdam, a rucksack on his back

containing all he had left of his possessions, and one day just appeared before me in Blankenburg. He had somehow managed to get through the well-guarded American lines, through woods and fields, had gone from hiding-place to hiding-place, always in fear of being caught.

Now he was here with me and the Americans had taken over the whole area. Hardly had they marched in, however, than the British, too, arrived.

18   The Whip Hand

The arrival of the British troops, commanded by a General, immediately caused no little consternation at the castle. Their interest lay primarily in a number of crates which had been deposited in the cellars on orders from the German Foreign Office. We were given to understand they contained files, and the boxes had been dispersed in several other castles also. More than that we did not know, and we were completely ignorant of the exact contents of the boxes. The British, however, seemed to know precisely what was in them, much to our astonishment. The General informed us that they contained copies of files whose originals had been distributed elsewhere, and that he was not only requisitioning them but that he would be taking them away.

On one of the following days—my husband was away searching for the so-called Resistance Fighters—my servant reported the presence of two Americans. I told the servant to tell the Americans that both my husband and sons were away, but he came back to say the soldiers still insisted on seeing me. I went to meet them. Both were different in appearance: the first tall and solemn, the other small and of few advantages. It was he who turned to me and said: 'We know that you have documents in your cellar.'

I replied: 'Your allies, the British, have been here and have already established that. They've confiscated everything and are going to take them away.'

'It's quite immaterial to us what the British have done,' he rejoined. 'We're Americans and we're going to take possession of the stuff. We're taking it all away, right now.'

The key of the cellar in which the boxes were was held by an elderly man in town and the two Americans told me to accompany them there in their jeep. I informed them: 'You'll have to excuse me, but I won't do that. If you mean that I have to accompany you, then we'll walk.' So we walked. On the way, the taller man remarked: 'I was there when your brother August Wilhelm was arrested.' I was somewhat surprised to hear this and listened to him tell me how August Wilhelm had been held near Frankfurt. When he had finished, he added to my astonishment: 'I also know your eldest brother and played golf with him.'

'How's that?' I asked. 'Perhaps in England?'

'No,' he replied. 'In Berlin-Wannsee. I come from Glienicke. I was born there and was confirmed by Pastor Bassange.'

'Well then,' I answered, 'if you grew up there, perhaps we can speak in German.' So we conversed in our German mother tongue, and he told me he had once lived directly behind the Cecilienhof. Naturally, I knew the district very well for the Mendelssohn family and others all had their beautiful villas there, which extended right to that of the old Prince Alexander of Prussia.

As we approached the castle again, my husband and my son Georg Wilhelm arrived and I told them of the object of the Americans' visit. Georg Wilhelm turned to me and told me in low tones that he just had to speak to me alone. We went to one side and he asked me who the big American was and I told him that he had given me no name but that he had said he came from Potsdam, and from his allusions was obviously of Jewish origin. My son felt the American bore a remarkable resemblance to a friend of his and was probably his twin brother, so he asked the American if he were related to that friend, Baron von Thüngen. The American replied: 'Yes, my mother was a Thüngen, but my parents emigrated and I went with them, though I didn't really have to.'

Both Americans then sent for trucks and the crates were loaded on one by one. There were negroes among the truck drivers and I had never seen a negro in a steel helmet before. They made a remarkable first impression upon me, for they were friendly and good natured. They went around saying to the people: 'We're slaves, now you're slaves.'

A few days later the British came back to take away the boxes of files but my husband could only show them the empty cellars and tell them their allies had already cleared the place. There were some long faces among them then.

According to my recollections of the time, the U.S. forces undertook other tasks, one of which had been set them by my daughter, Friederike. She had asked for news of our whereabouts from United States Headquarters, so various soldiers were dispatched to find us and one by one they appeared at the castle. We got the impression that in a typically American fashion they seemed to be taking part in a race or some sort of motor rally. When they first caught sight of us they would storm in with a great deal of noise and we didn't know what was happening—it seemed like an invasion. Then they would thrust a note into my hand and say: 'Now read that right through, your daughter's inquiring after you.' Then we would give them news of how we were faring and they would jump back into their jeeps and roar away. A couple of hours later others came storming in. Again the same procedure, the same question. But they were disappointed when they were told they were not the first to arrive on the same quest.

I must say the United States Occupation Forces behaved in an exemplary manner. Their commanders showed a great deal of understanding towards the people, transporting the sick to hospital, putting food at their disposal, and protecting them against raids by plundering foreign workers. They always helped whenever and wherever possible.

With the British who relieved them, however, it was a different story. They were the reverse, particularly the Colonel who was in charge of the Blankenburg area. He behaved extremely badly. He imposed himself as lord and master and tormented the population whenever he could. He came to us at the castle, riding-crop in hand, and ordered my husband and me to appear at his office. When we got there he left us standing in front of his desk while he lolled loutishly in his chair, before addressing my husband angrily: 'I can have you shot at once! You've got weapons hidden!' It was far beyond my comprehension that a British Army Colonel should simply be allowed to shoot a Prince of Great Britain and Ireland. I can shake my head and smile at that today, but at that time I was in low spirits. My husband tried to explain that he had done only what the Americans had told him to do, that we had had to deliver up all our weapons and that the Americans had locked them all up in one of the rooms of the castle. Churlishly, the Colonel kept on interrupting him and when the interrogation was finished, he indicated that all was not yet over. Nevertheless, we never heard any more about it. He must certainly have known from the beginning that we were in the right and he had no hold over us.

There was no comparison between the behaviour of the Colonel and the Regional Military Government in Hanover who had relations with us. Their officers were correct and friendly even though they refused to shake hands. Their instructions were not to fraternise. My husband, whose chivalry maintained that one should not refuse even the handshake of one's enemy, was, like the rest of us, taken aback at the order.

A few years later two Englishmen came to visit us in Hanover. As they stood before me, I knew I had seen them once before—in Blankenburg. They said they had come to apologise, because when they had come to the castle with their commander they had seen how he had refused to shake hands with us. This, they thought, was incomprehensible, but had, nevertheless, also obeyed the order though they were ashamed to do so. However, they had been constrained to obey.

One day we got the hint that it would be advisable to leave Blankenburg, though no one actually said the Russians were coming. At the Potsdam Conference the Allies had ceded large tracts of the territories they had conquered to Stalin, including the eastern part of the Harz region, though no public announcement was made. But there were rumours that the range of the Soviet Occupation Zone was going to be extended farther west. The advice we had been given was enough: the threatening danger was going to turn into a certainty.

My husband acquainted our neighbours of what we had heard and went to Rossla, too, where Princess Hermine, my father's second wife, was staying. After my father's death she had first returned to her own home in Saabor, Silesia, earlier having fled together with a huge stream of refugees, until she reached her sister Ida's house. However,

Princess Hermine refused to believe the reports my husband brought her of the forthcoming Russian incursion, as the Americans were already in occupation of her region which at that time included Halle and Leipzig and stretched to the Elbe. My husband told her: 'You must not stay here, for it's all been decided. You must get away.'

She answered: 'The Russians will not come. It won't happen. In any case, the Americans would tell us if there were to be any changes.'

My husband continued to urge her to leave. 'You must consider who you are,' he told her. 'You dare not fall into Russian hands.'

She replied simply: 'I have nothing to reproach myself for. I'm staying here.'

The Russians came, and the Americans warned no one of their coming. Princess Hermine was arrested by Soviet military police, and a long time afterwards she suddenly reappeared in Frankfurt on the Oder where she lived in a house on the outskirts of town. She died in August 1947. 'A sudden heart attack released her from her uncertainties and spiritual sorrows,' said her son, Prince Ferdinand of Schoenaich-Carolath. 'But her heartfelt desire to see her beloved homeland and to be with her own children was not fulfilled.'

Like Princess Hermine, many others suffered delusions regarding the attitude of the Western Allies towards the Russians. No one would have believed it possible that the British and United States governments would have surrendered the territories they had conquered to the Russians, not even Stalin himself. Only recently published documents concerning the Potsdam Conference revealed this hitherto strongly guarded secret. Even in Blankenburg no one believed the city would be delivered to the Russians, yet some set off and many others would have gone and taken their possessions with them had it not been for the vexatious difficulties put in their way by the district commander.

We packed our things, not an easy task, as there were many valuables from Herrenhausen Castle which my husband had brought here to protect from the bombings, and all the packing and transport could not all be accomplished at once. Our transports had to make several journeys, carrying irreplaceable *objets d'art* and that was one reason why, on this occasion, the British Occupation Authorities gave them the protection of so-called Scouts.

Our goal was Marienburg castle, and by going hither and thither our trucks eventually reached the main road on the northern end of the Harz range. But one day we noticed Russian signboards. The Russians were here! So we now had to travel via the Oberharz range from Tanne in order to each Blankenburg. In the miserable state of the roads and the pitiable condition of the trucks, that was quite an adventure. We often got stuck fast, and vehicles frequently had to be pushed up steep inclines. At length we learned that the Russians were already in Thale, hardly ten kilometres from Blankenburg, then, that they had occupied the town. There was nothing more we could do. We had long known we could not save everything, now we had to give up what was left. Finish.

My husband had been quite firm about leaving Blankenburg, but I knew how bitterly hard it was for him to part from the forests he had cared for so lovingly and which were now bearing the fruits of his labour. But he always said how much better off we were compared to millions of other refugees, since we had always had our own homes and that we still had our children with us. Despite the grievous loss of our beloved Blankenburg, he considered that a benevolent providence had at least allowed us to return to the land of his fathers.

Our removal to Marienburg meant we had once more to make the place we had chosen habitable. We had had to do it before, of course, in Rathenow, at Brunswick Castle, and the Villa Weinberg in Gmunden. My husband and I had previously visited Marienburg for a couple of days one summer, and we had had two rooms prepared for us in Marienburg Castle which had been built in Gothic style last century. It had been started in 1857 but never completely finished and had been Queen Marie of Hanover's summer recreation retreat.

The two rooms were all we had and we now had to make the castle presentable as a permanent dwelling—which was difficult as materials were extremely hard to come by in the immediate post-war years. As always, my husband planned the adaptation. The tiny kitchen was set to rights and we cooked everything in a diminutive fireplace. It has always been a source of wonder to me how we managed to prepare meals for the whole family, guests, and refugees who came to us, on a miniature fire like that. But we managed.

There were no lights in most of the rooms, apart from candles, as the electricity had not yet been reconnected, but we took it all very cheerfully. After all, we had not fallen into Soviet hands and that was the main thing. The majority of the rooms in the building were occupied by refugees, and the whole place resembled an army barracks, especially as we were subjected to raids by bands of former Polish slave labourers. But the peasants and farmers from the surrounding districts came to our aid, providing the bare necessities of life. We have these faithful helpers to thank for the fact that we did not fall by the wayside during these terribly difficult times.

As time went by the refugees left the fort and returned either to Hanover or to their own villages, and we were able to rearrange the rooms one by one. Eventually my husband managed to sort out our belongings and once more our pictures, porcelain and Gobelins were put on view. We could now feel that Marienburg was our home.

Life slowly returned to normal and the paralysis which had seized our people during the inferno of defeat began to disappear step by step. The first signs of the new order were manifest and posed some unexpected problems for my husband. There was talk of making him President of Hanover Province, but it came to nothing. In any case, one of his basic principles was not to get involved in Party politics in any way. Besides, the unity of the House of Hanover with its people had grown out of a long historical process which bound all classes and parties together and my husband wished to serve them all and would not be bound to any one social or political group. When Heinrich Wilhelm Kopf was named as President of Hanover Province, the British Regional Commander, Brigadier Lingham, told him: 'The demands that I will have to make upon you will probably be somewhat distasteful, but I expect my orders to be carried out.' That meant there would be no office for my husband.

Kopf, however, a Social Democrat, soon established a confidential association with my husband, just as the authoritative personalities of the other political groups had done—apart from the Communists who had once been considered by the Occupation Powers as being worthy of governing. Heinrich Hellwege and Dr Hans Christoph

Seebohm were two of the men who had constant contact with my husband. It was Kopf who proposed the plan that the States of Brunswick, Lippe-Detmold, Oldenburg and Schaumburg-Lippe should be combined to form a completely new one, but my husband was against it. He simply did not want these States to lose their independence of hundreds of years nor to be bound within a new one created by a foreign military government. The State of Hanover had already lost its identity once under the hand of a conqueror, and he did not want that to happen again.

Though we stood aside from party politics, we did devote ourselves to social affairs: we considered it our duty and we regained our sense of purpose. Our most pressing concerns were the streams of refugees and the paying of reparations which entailed even the dismantling of factories. There seemed no end to either.

Just about that time my husband heard a lecture by Professor Ernst Wagemann, the former President of the Reich Statistics Office. This nationally known economist propounded a theory, which many considered absurd, that the growth of our population through the influx of millions from Central and East Germany could effectively be used in the future and that West Germany's most favourable population density could be achieved in this manner. This theory, which in later years was to be proved correct in the shape of the economic miracle, was repeatedly discussed. We thought that theoretically at least, it could come true, but we wondered what would happen as the dismantling of German industrial factories, which created the loss of thousand upon thousand of jobs, continued and the simultaneous movement of refugees from the East went on. Was this misery not leading us straight into the hands of the Communists?

My husband used every effort to counteract the dismantling and tried to save the former Reich Smelting Works at Salzgitter among other firms. Between 1947–50 he repeatedly petitioned the British High Commissioner and his staff to preserve the works in order to ameliorate distress in the Salzgitter area, but without success. Early in the summer of 1950 we succeeded in stopping the delivery of the Salzgitter blast furnaces to Greece, but following lengthy negotiations the High Commission agreed with the Greek Government that other goods could be exchanged as compensation in lieu of the blast furnaces. Still further negotiations were needed, however, as the blast furnaces were in Hamburg all ready for shipment and they had to be repurchased.

Now came the great debates concerning the rebuilding of the Salzgitter Works. In this connection, the well-known American authoress, Freda Utley, came to visit us in Marienburg. Two of the books she had had published were still being discussed throughout the world. The first, *The China Story*, outlined the catastrophic East Asian policies of the U.S.A., which General MacArthur previously had described as: '. . . the greatest mistake in a hundred years of Pacific policy to allow the Communists to come to power in China. Now we will have a hundred years in which to pay for it.' His was a prophetic statement, as we know today. In the United States Senate, the significance of Freda Utley's *China Story* was compared to Emile Zola's *J'Accuse!* Her profound knowledge stemmed not least from the years she had spent in China as correspondent of the London *News Chronicle*.

In 1948–49, Freda Utley was sent to Germany by the *Reader's Digest* and the Foundation for Foreign Affairs, and the verdict on her findings appeared in her book, *The High Cost of Vengeance*. She wanted, as she said, 'to explain to the American people what had been done in their name and mostly without their knowledge, to a vanquished nation.'

It was with justifiable pride that Freda Utley pointed out to us that since her last visit there had been a radical change in the United States' attitude towards Germany. With regard to the special question of the Salzgitter Smelting Works, she, together with some American friends in Washington, lobbied members of the U.S. Senate to get approval for the rebuilding of the works through the European Economic Council, the O.E.E.C. We were most impressed by the economic and political expertise of this American.

Mrs Utley was an interesting woman. She came from a well-known English Socialist family, her father having been secretary of the Fabian Society and a friend of Bernard Shaw and the Webbs. She was married to a Russian diplomat. When he was purged by Stalin in 1936, she and her son fled Russia.

The indescribable distress in the area of the border between East and West occupied us in many ways, not only in attempting to set up jobs for the unemployed, such as in Salzgitter, but in other industries such as the Blaupunkt Works. I occupied myself, too, in other social work. Having experienced the whole misery myself, I was determined to help. There was no work, no food, wretched mothers and despairing fathers everywhere. The children had to be lifted out of their misery and physically and spiritually restored. With Anneliese Peck, an architect, my husband and I established a children's charity foundation. All of the officials contacted lent a hand, including the Federal Minister, Dr Seebohm. As chairman I travelled thousands of kilometres each year in search of funds and everywhere I found willingness on the part of others to help. It was a wonderful feeling to be able to aid all those needy children. By the time we had finished, the organisation had grown nationwide, the children strong, brown and healthy from the numerous outings and camps set up for them, and, with rucksacks bulging full of good things, they had become unrecognisable from the waifs with whom we had originally started the project. I felt a good job had been done.

During this period our son Ernst August had married Princess Ortrud of Schleswig-Holstein-Sonderburg-Glücksburg and Georg Wilhelm had wed the attractive Sophia of Greece, widow of my cousin Christoph of Hesse who had fallen in the war. Georg Wilhelm, who had been studying in Vienna and Göttingen, was later appointed Principal of Salem School by Kurt Hahn, while Christian had graduated with a degree in forestry from Hann.-Münden. Welf Heinrich, our youngest, had become a lawyer.

Friederike had become Queen of Greece when her husband, Paul, had ascended the throne in April 1947, on the death of his brother. King George had only been able to live for a short time in Greece, for the Allies' mistaken policy of pandering to the Greek Communists had led to civil war. Finally, after a referendum in September 1946, the people voted for the restoration of the Monarchy despite Soviet support of the Communist 'Freedom Front', the E.A.M. That same month the King, Crown Prince Paul and Friederike returned to Athens, but the civil war continued—right until 1949. The ending of the civil war and the healing of Greece's wounds were the new King's constant preoccupation. The energy with which he and Friederike set about their task needs no elaboration from me. It is well known far beyond the frontiers of Greece.

Before we went to see Friederike again we had a visit from the South African Prime Minister, Jan Christian Smuts, who had been her host during her exile in the Union. Smuts had been staying in London and was now making a special diversion to Marienburg on his way back in order to give us news of our daughter and grand-children. The old Boer General had surprised us, not only by his visit, but by the radiant charm so seldom met with in people. He chattered to us as if we had been friends for years and we came to realise how much Friederike had to thank him for during the difficult years of her exile. We, for our part, were happy to be able to express our own gratitude to the Prime Minister. At the end of our talk, Smuts embraced me jovially. 'And that,' he said, 'is a kiss from your daughter.'

At the end of January 1953, the occasion of one of his journeys to England, King Paul once more came to see us at Marienburg. He noticed how ill my husband looked and decided to stay a while longer. A little time before, Ernst August had suffered from a severe eye ailment which had needed an operation. The first was very successful but then he needed another and that was in vain. He lost the sight of one eye. It was a dreadful trial for him, but he withstood it wonderfully and never once lost his sense of humour. However, when we were staying at Almsee, Austria, a little later, he suffered severe inflammation of the lungs and we had to take him to a hospital in Wels. Soon, he began to improve but never completely regained his health.

In the first weeks of 1953, his strength began to fail and he knew the end was near. He asked his faithful doctor how many days he had left. 'I've lived a wonderful life,' he said, 'and I want to go through the remainder courageously.' With indescribable composure, he took great care in explaining his last wishes. One by one, he took leave of the members of our family, then his advisers and all those who had served him, personally thanking every one for the services they had rendered. Finally, he sent telegrams of farewell to all those who had been close to him, including the very old Crown Prince Rupprecht of Bavaria, with whom he had had such a close affinity ever since Rupprecht's grandfather had permitted him to join the German army. Ernst August charged me personally with the responsibility of conveying his thanks to the head of the Bavarian House for allowing him the best years of his service life with the Heavy Cavalry Brigade in Munich. His final greeting closed with the words: 'To my last breath I will remain grateful to the Prince Regent and to the House of Wittelsbach.'

I stayed with my husband throughout his final hours. His last words to me as he lay in my arms were: 'Now I must jump the final hurdle, but God will help me over it.'

As the yellow and white flag flying over the battlements of Marienburg Castle was lowered to half-mast, I knew that my world had been shattered.

The dead Prince of the Guelphs, clad in the black uniform of the Brunswick Hussars, lay in state in the great hall of Marienburg Castle's main tower. Thousands from all walks of life came to pay their last respects, including the eighty-six-year-old Ludwig Alpers, the most faithful of all supporters of the Guelphs. As he passed by his dead Prince, we could all feel that with the Duke of Brunswick's death a piece of German history was being borne to the grave.

The coffin, covered with the Hanoverian flag and bearing Ernst August's sword and Hussar's busby, was then borne to Brunswick Cathedral. A deputation holding burning torches aloft was waiting at the venerable cathedral's doors as the procession arrived. The coffin was carried through and then laid in front of Henry the Lion's vault, where members of the Brunswick nobility were waiting to mount the guard which was to keep the last vigil. I laid a wreath of tea roses and lilacs at the side of the catafalque—my final salute to my departed husband.

The Duke's last journey from Brunswick to the ancient capital of the Kings of Hanover took place among the continued peal of bells and, as darkness fell, the accompanying nobles of Hanover and the supporters of the Guelphs followed the cortège bearing flaming torches—right up to the interior of the candle-lit church, where the coffin was placed before the altar. On the following day thousands of

Hanoverians came to pay their final respects, despite the bitter February wind which blew strongly across the market square to the Market Church itself.

The church walls were draped with Guelph flags, witnesses of a thousand years of German and Lower Saxon history. One foot after the other, the long column of mourners shuffled past the bier surrounded by the yellow and white decorated wreaths of the sorrowing Guelphs. Wreaths there were, too, from the President of the Federal Republic of Germany, the Government, the Prime Minister of Lower Saxony and the State Government.

When the church was finally closed at nine o'clock that evening, more than ten thousand people had filed past the bier.

My husband had wanted to be buried at the Berggarten in Herrenhausen, where, he told me: 'I want to lie in God's beautiful scenery, where children can play around my grave.'

The snow was deep that 6th of February 1953, when the cortège wound its way to Ernst August's last resting-place, accompanied both by riders and marchers wearing the traditional royal red uniform of Hanover. Ahead of the procession was a lone rider wearing a black and gold tricorne—a sight from the past, re-awakened once more just to bid farewell to the last ruling German Prince.

Behind the coffin walked our four sons, King Paul of Greece, the Ambassador of the Queen of England, and many foreign Princes and deputations. I followed with both my daughters-in-law and my husband's sisters, Princess Olga of Hanover and the Grand Duchess of Mecklenburg in carriages, escorted by the foresters of Gmunden in their traditional mountain costumes.

Finally, huntsmen sounded the mort at the graveside: it was goodbye for ever for them. But not for me. For me the comforting certainty remained that I would one day rest again there at my husband's side.

19   *The Concept of Duty*

A new period of my life now began—the final one. After my husband's death I found it necessary to give up my work for the children's charity I had founded. From the tiniest beginnings it had grown into a huge social organisation.

Two years later, it also became necessary for me to leave Marienburg and it was with a heavy heart that I tore myself from the place which held so many memories for me, particularly of the last years of my life with my husband. Now I had to move again, find a new home again and put it in order. This time my husband's careful, orderly direction was missing. Whenever I reflected upon it, my thoughts reverted to him—there were a thousand things which he would have thought out and planned: I was reduced to despair.

My sole consolation was the love I would receive in Brunswick, so I turned there. The castle I had first entered when my husband assumed the reins of government was now just a ruin, so I sought a private house whose owner was only too happy to let me have it. For the first time in my whole existence, if one overlooks the few months I spent in Rathenow, I had to live in a rented house. Its owner leased it to me for life. So, here was I, back in Brunswick, and on my return I was heartily greeted and welcomed. After a few weeks of groping and self-examination I was able to put myself to rights again. I knew that though my circumstances were new, my duties were the same old ones.

Once more I set to work. Although I had had to give up my children's charity, it still gave me pleasure to see how the idea was spreading and bearing fruit. There was also another organisation, bearing my name—'The Duchess Viktoria Luise Association'—which had no political leanings but was concerned solely with the spread of Lower Saxon culture, the care of our growing youth and the alleviation of suffering among the population. It received my full support. Now I could look forward to ensuring that children, orphans, the old, the needy and the deserving would be cared for, that charity would be dispensed either to those in the Soviet Zone or wherever human misery manifested itself.

From the very beginning, from the time the dreadful expulsion of Germans from the East started, I sought to help the pitiful victims. From the time the enormous flood of refugees began to reach our State and I had seen the unspeakable distress affecting these people, the vision of them, denuded of every possession, hungry, insufficiently clad and homeless, gave me no rest. I helped to find them quarters, improvised shelters and obtained food, clothing and medicines for them. We had had so many refugees ourselves in Marienburg that we were full to the roof top. My husband and I drew the attention of the British authorities to these dreadful scenes on the zonal borders and I stood there with them looking into the fearful, pained expressions on the faces of those refugees as they came by. Shots from Red Army soldiers could be heard, as could the sounds of violated women weeping convulsively and children begging imploringly for a piece of bread. My heart stood still at the sight of this misery. My English companions' faces were as white as chalk and they stood there, speechless, unable to grasp the enormity of it all. Here, on the borders of Lower Saxony they must have realised at last how false their conceptions of their Soviet allies had been.

They built a refugee camp at Friedland which was, of necessity, somewhat primitive. Drawn by this misery, innumerable men, women and girls came to help at the camp and I lined up with them. I had no official standing, but knew instinctively that my place was here at this time. At the wooden barrier I met the refugees, went with them through the camp right into the already crammed Nissen huts where I handed them clothing and helped serve them with bread and soup. I asked the men who had returned from Russian prisoner of war camps how I could help them, spoke with the mothers who had been wrenched from their homes and countries, and cheered up the children who had been tossed up like flotsam from the flood of barbarity. The fate of these beaten, hunted and homeless beings affected me deeply, and I shared the sorrows and tribulations of the men and women who were racking their brains trying to find better and more effective means of getting help and transport to take them to new homes. Friends and acquaintances in the country and abroad helped me all they could. Money and clothing from charities flooded in and how happy I was when I was allowed a Swedish house for use as a kindergarten.

In Friedland I got to know the true meaning of the Church through the hell the refugees had experienced. I realised that whatever the great man-made differences in religion it was far more important to have unity of Christian love and belief. I therefore took part in organising the erection of a Catholic church for refugees and obtained money, bricks and cement for it, working together with the prominent Catholic priest Monsignor Krahe. With regard to this, narrow-minded people made me feel that as a Protestant Christian I should not be getting involved. But I told myself: my father had taught me, and my husband had strengthened the concept, that I was there to help everyone, irrespective of their beliefs.

It was in early January 1954, when the great influx of prisoners of war from Russian camps arrived, that I met Chancellor Konrad Adenauer. I had never seen him before nor had I any personal opinion of him though I had heard of the proverbial frigidity of the 'Old Man' as he was called. Certainly he was a politician of soberly cold intellect, otherwise how could one explain his success as a statesman. The modesty with which he met the returning prisoners of war, however, impressed me, as did his dignity and simple demeanour. Even the effusive speeches of thanks of the survivors from the Russian horror camps did nothing to alter his simple diffidence.

Adenauer painted no rosy future for them, though they expected it, neither was there any exaggeration on his part. One had to believe him when he addressed the men as follows: 'I tell you that this day, this hour, is one of the finest I have experienced in the years that I have been charged with the Chancellorship.' Adenauer showed himself generally as being a gentleman of the old school. A few days after our meeting I had a letter from him:

> 'It was a particular pleasure for me to be with you last Saturday to greet the returning transports at Friedland. Owing to the continual conversations I had with the returning men which went on to the very last minute before my train left and which necessitated my hurried departure, it was to my great regret that I was no longer in a position to bid you farewell in peace and quiet. I now wish to make up for it.'

Over two million refugees, prisoners of war, and displaced persons passed through Friedland camp in one great stream and it was not without emotion that I read in a letter from the camp chaplain that it was twenty years to the day that the camp had been kept going. He wrote:

> 'Physically we have often been at the end of our tether. There were always more transports, more new misery, more new suffering. Do you remember the camp leader broke down completely when he greeted one of the additional transports which arrived here? We have become spiritually tired and weary, too. However, we are getting renewed strength and courage from the solicitousness of others, the aid of our friends and the readiness of people from outside to help. What would we have been able to do in Friedland without our friends throughout the country? Our own Duchess stands in the centre of this circle of friendship.'

Very seldom have words filled me with more satisfaction. I knew I had done my duty.

The overwhelming majority of people who fled to the western part of our Fatherland came from Prussia. It had been about 250 years since such an exodus had taken place, though in the opposite direction—from west to east. In December 1700 the Court of the Electorate of Brandenburg and its large entourage had transferred itself from Berlin to Königsberg, going there in four sections accompanied by innumerable carriages and baggage trains which, according to reports of the time, required 30,000 horses. The journey took twelve days, and they reached the old city in the last week of the year. Soon thereafter mounted heralds, clad in brilliant blue and gold embroidered silk tunics and black velvet hats with white feathers, proclaimed the tidings of their Sovereign to the populace:

> 'Now that the Duchy of Prussia has, in God's infinite wisdom, been elevated to that of a kingdom and that its Lord, His Most Serene Highness the Lord Friedrich, has become King, let it be known to all and sundry and publicly proclaimed: Long live Friedrich our most gracious King; Long live Sophie Charlotte our most gracious Queen!'

On 18 January 1701, at a glittering ceremony in the State Hall of Königsberg Castle, the Elector of Brandenburg, Friedrich III had the crown of Prussia placed on his head. He crowned himself as a sign that he owed the Crown only to the Lord God and himself and not to a foreign power. That was two and a half centuries ago, and a mighty empire grew up, an example to other States in its maintenance of law, order, and duty. Prussia gave the newly arisen German Empire its foundation, spread outward atop it, then lastly was buried beneath the ruins of it.

The Allied Control Council decided on the dissolution of the Prussian State, the decree bearing the signatures of General Lucius D. Clay, General Pierre König, General Sir Brian Robertson and Marshal Vassiliy Sokolovsky.

It was a fateful coincidence that the downfall of Prussia also brought down the House of Hohenzollern. Its properties had for the most part been seized or destroyed—Oels, Cadinen, Rominten, the Cecilienhof —lost like the remainder of all the old familiar places, and the members of our House spread far away from their own homes. My nephew Louis Ferdinand had to make his way from Cadinen on a sledge, finally crossing over the Baltic. He was the last to be able to do so. Half an hour after, the Russians closed that escape route, too. Louis Ferdinand's journey reminded him, he told me, of another Hohenzollern's crossing of the Baltic: 'I could only draw a melancholy comparison with the great Elector, who also had to cross the frozen Baltic on a sledge in deepest winter,' he said. 'Only he went over as a victor, not as a refugee.'

The Hohenzollerns reached the West on sledges, on carts, by road, on bicycles or on foot, and a great search began to find out where the others were. One by one we found out from one another where each had been. Only six years had gone by since the last family gathering in Doorn. What a transformation had taken place!

In the autumn of 1948 my brother Adalbert died, having retired and lived for many years in La Tour de Peilz in Switzerland. The following year August Wilhelm died of the ailments he had sustained during his imprisonment in gaol and internment camps, and in 1951 it was my eldest brother's turn. The Crown Prince, like August Wilhelm, had been arrested by the Occupation forces. At the end of 1944 he had become seriously ill and had gone for treatment in the Allgäu district of Bavaria. It was here that he was kept under surveillance by the Gestapo—until the French took over their task. The Crown Prince had never been a Nazi Party member, neither had he held any official post nor a military command under Hitler. Nevertheless, General de Lattre de Tassigny had him arrested and imprisoned in Lindau. On his release, my brother lived in a rented house in Hechingen where I visited him every year.

In 1951, when I was going from Salem to Marienburg, I resisted going to Hechingen as I was pressed for time, but during the trip I had a sudden feeling that I should not travel farther without going to see my brother. I changed my route, but was still not able to see him. He died the same year and I never saw him again. Quietly and in retirement he had lived in his rented house. He had simply resigned. The Crown Prince was no Louis Bonaparte, and had felt himself too closely bound to aesthetic things. He had foresworn the struggle for power. Now he was surrounded by loneliness, and the people who had declared themselves for their darling, vigorous and handsome Crown Prince, had forgotten him entirely. He was buried in the little officers' garden by Michael's Bastion on the Burg Hohenzollern and of his brothers and sisters, only Oskar and I were at the graveside.

On a harsh winter's day in 1958 I again stood at an open grave in the officers' garden on the Hohenzollern. This time it was to bury my brother Oskar. He had died in a Munich clinic on January 27, my father's birthday. Thus, the last of my brothers was gone from me. Of the seven of us, I was now the only one left.

The following year was the centenary of my father's birth, and my nephew Louis Ferdinand, who had become head of the House on the Crown Prince's death, invited the family to a commemoration service in Berlin. It was very moving to see my beloved city again. How often since the end of the war had my thoughts turned to its sorrowful fate. How many times, too, had I made the comparison with the situation created by Bismarck following his victory over Denmark for Schleswig-Holstein, when he wanted to turn the thumbscrews on Vienna's policies: plundered Schleswig-Holstein to become a condominium of Austria and Prussia with two zones of occupation. The distance between the Danube Monarchy and this northern country was very great, whereas Prussia's borders were adjacent and it was always in a position to block direct communications with Vienna. In consequence, this construction brought Bismarck into permanent conflict with the Hofburg, the Imperial Court of Vienna, until it tried to dissociate itself from the claim to Schleswig-Holstein for indemnification. Bismarck did not agree. He considered that the Duchy would one day fall into his lap like a ripe plum. But who learns the lessons of History? Yalta and Potsdam speak for themselves!

In Berlin, the Viktoria Luise Platz, named after me, still remained. Like me it had withstood all the vicissitudes and storms of time. But how the overall picture of the city had changed! It was only with difficulty that I could find my way about in some districts. I stood by the barbed wire which straddled the Brandenburg Gate and at the Glienicke Bridge, looked across and saw the other part of divided Germany. It seemed so sad to see so few of the old trees which had survived the ravages of war standing in the Tiergarten. However, the Berliners were as familiar to me as ever. I could read the joy in the faces of the thousands, old and young, who had gathered to greet me and my family. There were cheers and a great deal of jubilation as we passed through the streets, and it was only with difficulty that the squads of police were able to clear the way for us in the Hansa quarter, so that we could reach the Kaiser Friedrich Memorial Church where a tremendous reception had been prepared for us.

Doorn: the Duchess walking with the Kaiser, *circa* 1935.

The Duke and Duchess of Windsor, visiting Hitler in Obersalzburg, October 1937.

The wedding of our daughter Friederike to Prince Paul of Greece, Athens, 9 January 1938. From left: King Michael of Rumania, Princess Irene of Greece, Duke Ernst August the father of the bride, Princess Friederike, Prince Paul of Greece, the Duchess of Brunswick, King George II of the Hellenes, the Duchess of Kent, and Prince August Wilhelm of Prussia.

At the border crossing-point in Frieland, 1954, with Konrad Adenauer.

With Albert Schweitzer, in Günsbach, Alsace, 1959.

The marriage of our grandson, King Constantine, in Athens, 1964.
Bottom row, from left: King Frederick and Queen Ingrid of Denmark,
King Constantine and his bride Princess Anne-Marie of Denmark,
Queen Friederike, King Gustav of Sweden, and the Duchess of
Brunswick. Second row, from left: King Baudouin of the Belgians,
King Hussein of Jordan, King Bhumibol of Thailand, Queen Juliana
of the Netherlands (hidden), Prince Bernhard of the Netherlands,
King Olaf of Norway, and King Umberto of Italy.

Our eightieth birthday celebration, Brunswick, 1972.

Four generations of royalty. From left: Christina, Infanta of Spain; Sofia, Queen of Spain; Philipp, Prince of the Asturias, heir to the Throne of Spain; the Duchess of Brunswick; Helena, Infanta of Spain; Constantine, King of the Hellenes; Alexia, Princess of Greece; Anne-Marie, Queen of the Hellenes; Paul, Crown Prince of Greece; and Queen Friederike. Brunswick, 1972.

Still, it was not the same sort of rejoicing that we knew in the Kaiser's time. This was the expression of inner joy at a reunion with an old Berlin family, the oldest Berlin family. From early times, since 1451, when the Elector Friedrich II erected a mighty castle between the parishes of Berlin and Cölln and so took the first step towards the foundation of the capital, Berlin had been the seat of the Hohenzollerns. Under its rulers, Berlin had developed from a fishing village into the capital of the German Empire and a city of the first rank.

Louis Ferdinand had taken the greatest care to ensure that the commemoration would not be misinterpreted as being in any way political. My father was to be remembered without pageantry and without any show. Only flowers decorated the newly rebuilt Kaiser Friedrich Memorial Church. After the liturgy our old Court chaplain, the eighty-year-old Professor Doehring asked God's blessing for his Kaiser and he prayed from the heart, for he had honoured my father as a man who, without any hypocrisy, had lived consciously by the Bible. One sentence in particular from Doehring's sermon has remained in my memory: 'He (the Kaiser) knew that a million hearts beat with love for him, yet, at the same time, he knew that he was hated in every dreadful possible way. But neither one nor the other could disturb his composure. He was a child of God.'

The centenary of my father's birth was followed by other jubilees. In 1961 it was the 900th anniversary of the first recorded registration of the House of Hohenzollern, when it was mentioned by the monk Berthold von Reichenau in his *World Chronicles*. A year later it was the 250th anniversary of Frederick the Great's birth which was celebrated on the Burg Hohenzollern and attended by many well-known personalities including Chancellor Kurt Georg Kiesinger and Dr Eugen Gerstenmaier, President of the Federal Parliament. Federal Army officers formed the guard of honour at the great King's tomb.

At these various anniversary celebrations I was made only too well aware that I am the last of the Kaiser's family. In Berlin in 1959, Prince Louis Ferdinand told me: 'That you were here was the main point.' I understood what my nephew meant by that expression—'You have a mission here.'

I

I undertook that mission. I understood it as upholding our traditions. As a great German historian once said: 'A nation that does not honour its past has no future.' The appreciation of historical values, particularly in the military sphere, is a rudiment of life. An army without tradition is no army. Even the great revolutionary armies of recent history, those of the French and Russian revolutions, have not lost sight of this fact.

For my part, I have taken up every challenge to assist in upholding our traditions, not least in our new Bundeswehr (Federal Army) and in the Federal Frontier Force. It is a joy for me to see the fresh faces of young soldiers during an 'Army Day' or when, at traditional gatherings, I meet acquaintances who once served my father. The company of these old soldiers always reawakens memories of the Kaiser's time and the glorious history of brave regiments. I still have close contact with numerous traditional units such as the Association of the 1st Foot Guards Regiment and the *Gardes du Corps*, the 1st Bavarian Heavy Cavalry, the Brunswick Infantry Regiment, the 17th Hussars Regiment, and of course the Life Hussars Brigade.

I always discover how deeply rooted in their hearts their veneration is for my father, their former Commander-in-Chief. In a speech at a meeting of former officers of the King's Infantry Regiment it was said:

'For years His Majesty has rested in ever-lasting sleep in distant Doorn. We, his faithful King's Infantry, still remember with awe to this day and to this hour, our dead Chief who made our Regiment his body guard and who gave us his name. . . . We, who rejoiced with him in good times and remained loyal to him to the last day in war, will retain our loyalty to him, the last King of Prussia, until the grass covers us.'

It was not without emotion that I found how grateful they were that I took part in these commemoration ceremonies for my father, as these words from an old infantryman show: 'You must know, Your Royal Highness, that we also convey the love we have for our Kaiser and King to his only surviving child.'

On a September evening in 1962 a long procession bearing torches, flags and standards formed in Hanover and, accompanied by thousands of Hanoverians, marched to the old Town Hall and the President of the Lower Saxony Rifle Clubs made a speech at the end of which he called for three rousing cheers. It was my seventieth birthday. The Federal President, Heinrich Lübke, sent me a telegram from Bonn:

'People from every walk of life honour Your Royal Highness today. They send their greetings and affection particularly because you have always occupied yourself with the alleviation of misery and helped to restore health. . . . You have shown yourself an example to many. With my best wishes for your birthday I also include my good wishes for your personal well-being.'

I realised that with the recognition and sympathy I had encountered on this day, I had been able to do my duty and how thankful I had to be that destiny had allowed me to do it. I replied to the President:

'Thank you for your good wishes on my seventieth birthday which touched me very deeply. . . . As the daughter of the last Kaiser, I am particularly happy that we can all live and work together as members of the same nation. For you, Mr President, I wish God's blessing in your high and arduous office.'

When one reaches my age one is inclined to allow memories a particularly dear place. I make no exceptions, and my thoughts often wander into the past and I frequently meet people with whom I can exchange reminiscences. One's circle of contemporaries may become smaller and smaller, and one after the other the people pass away. But serious or cheerful things forgotten . . . will live again.

Of the many merry memories which I can bring to mind, there is the story of the Lieutenant and the little Princess, which was recalled to me by Baron von Bothmer, an old King's Infantry officer. It happened at the turn of the century while my father was on a visit to Metz. While he was there, we lived at Urville Castle in Lothringen, and a company of infantry was detailed to guard us.

'Duchess,' said the Baron, 'how often you placed us poor officers of the watch in a deadly dilemma! I remember how you thought it was a tremendous joke to call out the guard, trying to surprise them, leaping out from behind a bush or some other hiding-place. The sentry shouted "Call out the guard! Attention! Present arms! Sound the tattoo!" But we got there too late and our little Princess had scurried off laughing. The officer of the guard then posted extra sentries to watch over the little Princess, but it was in vain because she always outwitted us. Then we planned our revenge. Do you remember, Duchess,' Bothmer went on, 'how Lieutenant Zimmermann, who is now a Lieutenant-General, handed you a big bouquet of lilies of the valley one evening, when we had been invited to dinner by the Kaiser? He had obtained them from a flower shop as there were no lilies of the valley in the woods at all at that time. Delighted, you asked him, "Where did you get these gorgeous lilies of the valley?" Zimmermann answered: "We plucked them in the woods around here for Your Royal Highness." And a few days later you asked Zimmermann: "I've looked all over the woods with my lady-in-waiting and didn't find any lilies of the valley." Zimmermann countered: "Well, Your Royal Highness obviously didn't find the right place." and you, Duchess, searched again and still didn't find anything. However, in the end, the good Zimmermann still was in fear of being ordered to reveal where the lilies of the valley had been obtained.'

Other memories I would like to recall here include those of Professor Otto Hahn, the great physicist, when he met my father at the Kaiser Wilhelm Institute for Chemistry in Berlin-Dahlem. A young physicist then, he was supposed to demonstrate some radioactive experiment to the Kaiser. Hahn, now a Nobel prizewinner, told me what had happened. One of the Kaiser's aides first inspected the room where the experiment was to take place. When he saw it, he was shocked. 'We certainly cannot allow the Kaiser to stay in a completely darkened room!' he expostulated. 'But the Kaiser hadn't the least inhibition,' Hahn told me, 'and everything went according to plan.' It was comforting for me to hear the recognition of my father's great interest in scientific matters from this renowned scientist. 'Without the interest that your father took in the Kaiser

Wilhelm Institute,' Hahn said, 'it would have been impossible to get the money to sustain it and quickly to found other similar institutes. I also know that the Kaiser maintained his interest in scientific institutes to the end of his life.'

I remember, too, just after the First World War when I visited Albert Schweitzer. We had first met in Salem with Max of Baden. My brother-in-law, who was intimately concerned with the work of the Red Cross at the time, consulted Dr Schweitzer about the problems of freed prisoners of war and internees. Together, Dr Schweitzer, my husband and I visited the beautiful old cathedral and my husband requested Dr Schweitzer to play the organ there. It was an unforgettable experience. The art of organ playing was in his blood. Many years were to pass before I saw him again. In the meantime he had become a legend—theologist, doctor and Nobel prize-winner.

I met him in Günzbach in Alsace on the first Sunday in Advent, 1959, and we went for a long walk together in the quiet roads, speaking of our hopes and troubles, and I could see the inexpressible goodness of my companion. His judgement of men and things was very clear and observant.

We spoke about the state of the world, and how it was now torn asunder, and he said: 'Only the spirit can bring about a settlement. The spirit of agreement must be carried from one nation to the other.' We also discussed the division of our Fatherland and he believed we would be reunited. 'Just have patience,' he said. 'You will come together again.' When we spoke of the old days, he said: 'I can still see you with your dear mother sitting at the window of the General Post Office in Strasbourg watching a parade. I was on my way to the university, and naturally had no idea a parade was to take place. So I stayed standing in the street looking up at you both. I had a great reverence for your mother. I admired her quiet help and aid to charities.'

Before we sat down to lunch, Schweitzer went to his harmonium and played us a choral. Then we said a prayer. The day simply flew by and finally it was time to say goodbye. Albert Schweitzer stood in front of his house and waved after us until we disappeared from his view. I often received letters from him from Lambaréné. When he wrote me on my seventieth birthday, he reminded me of our day together at Günzbach and added:

'I can only come to Europe infrequently. My continual work does not permit me to travel as much as I would like. Besides, I am almost afraid of Europe on account of the great claims that are made upon me. I hardly even dare stay in Günzbach, otherwise I have to go about and visit people. I am obliged to so many places and people for their goodness.'

We continued our correspondence and it occurred to me to send him a German fir tree for Christmas, believing it would give him great pleasure to have this greeting from one of his own country's forests. The next year, too, I intended sending him an identical Christmas present, but I learned that my dear friend was now at rest beneath the African earth, next to his wife. A simple wooden cross, made by himself, now marks his grave.

Memories of my happy wedding day came flooding back when, one spring day, I went to Herrenhausen where I was to meet the Queen of England. Fifty-two years had gone by since a British Monarch had visited Germany. Then, in May 1913, my husband and I were the reason for the visit. Visions of the past appeared once again before me—there were King George and Queen Mary, as they rode through the splendour of the Berlin streets to the storms of applause and jubilation; the colourful and gay banquet; the torch dance in the White Room, when I danced with King George and Czar Nicholas, and my father, the brilliant, radiant focal point of these events.

Everything came back to me anew, and with photographic clarity. What had not happened since then! What had not come to pass since I had last seen Queen Elizabeth! At that time, she was just a little girl, and now she stood before me a mature woman of indescribable charm and dignity, a truly regal presence. 'The last time we met, it was with your dear parents and grandparents in London,' I said.

'Yes, it is a long time,' the Queen replied.

Generations had come and gone during those decades.

The invitation to come to Herrenhausen had reached me in Gmunden where I was staying for the birth of a grandchild, my son

Christian's first daughter. Elizabeth spoke to me about my grand-children in Salem, my second son Georg Wilhelm's children, to whom she is related.

'I had such a lovely time in Salem,' she told me. 'It was so restful, and I very much enjoyed seeing your grandchildren.'

Philip, however, recalled Greece to me. 'The last time we met was at the lovely wedding in Athens,' he said. He was referring to the wedding of my grandson Constantine of Greece to the enchanting Anne-Marie of Denmark.

When I said goodbye to the Queen and Prince Philip, in the garden at Herrenhausen, I had a strong feeling of remembrance and hope when I told Elizabeth: 'God bless you.'

The day came when I stepped over the threshold of my ninth decade, in 1972, and I was served notice of it with a vast number of interviews to which I was asked by the Press. I also received journalists of all political hues, and one of them, an extreme left-winger, also known as a very critical author, finished his article with this frank acknowledgement:

> 'I ask myself what sort of horrible type I would have become if my father had been able to make me the gift of a Regiment of Prussian Life Guards Hussars on my confirmation. Reflecting on this, I left number 5 Stresemannstrasse with respect.'

For the reply to this question I can produce a sentence from another pen which wrote about the same occasion:

> 'The history of this Prussian Princess bore the imprint of discipline from her youth onward, the highest virtue of which is self-discipline.'

I take no credit for having learned it: it was thanks to my parents.

The prelude to my birthday was once again marked by the Hanoverian Rifle Clubs, which marched in the evening with their full band, the drums beating, on to the square between the Market Church, so rich in tradition, and to the old Town Hall. The building's venerable old bricks were red and warm and radiant in the light of the torches being carried in the procession. It was a wonder they had survived the heavy wartime bombardments. In my reply to the very

impressive speech of good wishes, I closed with my thanks for the
true loyalty the Rifle Clubs had shown both their sovereign House
and me personally in times good and bad. Then we went into the
banqueting hall and celebrated the rest of the evening with the
delegations I had invited, eating pea soup and bacon, and drinking
beer.

To conclude the celebrations there was, as anticipated, a fête on
the Burg Hohenzollern, given by my nephew Prince Louis Ferdinand.
In the Hall of Peers, as it was called, I listened to a concert given by
Professor Dr Adolf Stauch and the tenor Horst Wilhelm, and on the
evening of the following day I had the wonderful pleasure of attending
a great candle-lit ball organised by the young people of the other
Royal Houses. Finally, there was a programme, beautifully arranged
by my nephew, during which I made a trip, specially for the occasion,
in an ancient museum piece of a steam train, which took me from
Bad Imnau to what had once been known as the Kaiser's Station, at
the foot of the Hohen Zollern. From there I went, as my father used
to do, in an open landau to the top. It was just like old times, with a
great multitude of people coming from far and near to pay me
homage, cheering me all the way, and bringing me flowers.

On my actual birthday, however, I was in Brunswick. Here, too,
there was an extensive task for me to perform. Having received the
first congratulations very early in the morning, looked at my letters
and presents and admired the colourful sea of flowers which was
stacked around the house, I began the day with devotions in the
nearby Riddagshäuser Convent Church. Later, in the heart of the
town, in the historical Draper's Hall, I must have shaken well over
2,000 hands, while police and friendly helpers tried to bring some
sort of order from the throng of Brunswick inhabitants in the old
town market place trying to greet me. Meanwhile the Fire Brigade
Band tried to entertain and contain the masses with rousing marches.

It was very moving for me seeing all these people, friends and
strangers, patiently trying for hours either to have a friendly word
with me or just wanting to shake me by the hand. Late in the afternoon it was my turn to receive all my relatives, friends, and various
dignitaries whom I had invited to my birthday dinner in the Draper's
Hall cellar. When I gazed at the impressive old hall with its historical

I*

murals, its arches, the gaily decorated table, and at the friendly faces
of my guests, it seemed as if it were only a few days ago that I had
gone through the same ritual. But it was just an illusion. It was the
vision of my 75th birthday that I was seeing—five years before. How
time flies when one is old!

The assembled guests waited expectantly for a speech or at least a
toast. My nephew Prince Louis Ferdinand then rose and, speaking
from the heart, recalled what my father had said one unforgettable
day in May 1913, when he had referred to me as the ray of sunshine
which had been brought into his family. Louis Ferdinand added that
now it had been brought into the House of the Guelphs.

It was my son Georg Wilhelm who rose to thank his Prussian
cousin in a reply to that toast, although it had been Ernst August's
duty as the eldest to stand up. However, in spite of the fact that he
was present, he declined to stand to speak either to the guests or even
to address a few words to me. This was due to his extreme reserve.
But I recalled, just as during the dark days of the war when Friederike
had forcibly been separated from us, that my daughter had written:
'We are a family which has always held together, and that is much
more than other people can say.'

With the death of my dear husband, however, the unity of our
family had come to a violent end. All the more reason, then, that I
enjoyed just for these few more hours the close company of my family
on my birthday. I was overjoyed to have my daughter, my sons
Georg Wilhelm and Christian, and my daughter-in-law Sophia about
me. Then there were the grandchildren—Sophia, now Queen of
Spain; King Constantine and his wife Anne-Marie; Friederike, Welf
and Georg, the now magnificently grown up children of Georg
Wilhelm. Also present were my Hesse cousins Philipp and Wolfgang,
to whom I had become closely attached in my old age, and, naturally,
Louis Ferdinand.

Who can blame me when I frankly confess that on this day my heart
had never been so gladdened as by the sight of these happy young
faces all around me. Always, when I glanced round the table which
had been decorated specially for the children, their eyes, bright and
shining, met mine. There were four girls and two boys in the

gathering—Caroline, my second youngest granddaughter; Helena and Christina of Spain and Alexia of Greece, my great-granddaughters; and the two Crown Princes, Nicholaus and Felipe. Each of the children, it seemed to me, were personalities in their own right and I thought what a pity it was that they all lived so far away from me. It might sound theatrical when I say how much I would have liked to keep them all with me, but it is no exaggeration.

During all the chatter at table my thoughts, led it seemed by some unseen hand, wandered into the past to visualise once again long-gone scenes of my family life. I thought I could hear the jubilation of the Brunswick crowds in front of the castle, the noise of which even penetrated into my room, when I gave birth to my first boy, the son and heir to the Throne, so eagerly awaited both by the Royal Family and the country. How different the world had looked when my other children had first glimpsed the light of day. War! Then the first grandchild. It was my father who had reminded me of the speedy passage of time during the period of time waiting for that baby. It was unbelievable how distinctly his words suddenly came into my head: 'How unburdened were the days of your childhood, when you stormed your Mama's table at tea time on your birthday to gaze with astonishment and wonder at your presents! And now you are already standing by to become a grandmama!' As in Brunswick, so too in Athens there had been tremendous enthusiasm at Sophia's birth. Yet how incomprehensibly quickly had the feelings of the people and the country changed since then! What will the future bring these dear little children of whose happy countenances I can hardly see enough?

At that time my daughter and grandson Constantine lived in Rome —in exile—the second time this fate had overtaken them. The first time it had been due to their having been driven out by enemy troops and the second when they were uprooted by internal political upheavals. These vicissitudes, of course, belong to the history of the Hellenic Throne, and were mostly created by powerful foreign forces. England in particular had in the past energetically embroiled herself in Greek affairs, but with the loss of her status as a world power had retired further into the background, to be succeeded in turn by the United States. In the struggle for supremacy in the

Mediterranean, the interests of both the Soviet Union and America intersect at the Greek peninsula.

It is certainly not easy completely to understand the specific aspects of Athens politics, but suffice it to say that a more colourful kaleido-scope of vaster and more changeable groups is scarcely conceivable. Since the resignation of Prime Minister Karamanlis in 1963—he had found himself increasingly and more strongly under attack from the Left and from the Communists—the Greek crisis had heightened and my son-in-law had died, to be succeeded on the throne by my grandson Constantine who was only twenty-three. In Papandreou he found a Prime Minister who wanted to steer the ship of State on to a completely new course, and there was also revealed an officers' conspiracy to overthrow the Monarchy. The Prime Minister himself tried to wrest control of the army from the King. The young King, however, resisted and succeeded in winning the first struggle for power for himself. Papandreou resigned and mobilised the mob, the target of their agitation ultimately being directed at the Queen Mother, accusing her of having propagated Hitler's policies in Greece. Friederike's actual feelings on the matter were completely clarified when she told us in a letter: 'Had we gone over to the Axis, we would have avoided bloodshed, but still lost our country and our honour besides—and that spontaneously. I love these people and this country fanatically.' Friederike's patriotism was one of the reasons why Hitler had dismissed her four brothers from the Armed Services. Still, what is the truth worth to a demagogue?

In a series of cunning chess moves and with the support of the Communists, Papandreou paralysed parliament and rendered the parliamentary system incapable of proper function for a long time. Necessary laws could no longer be passed, strikes were organised which ruined the economy and, in a nutshell, revolution threatened.

It was in this situation that the King went among his people, his very young wife at his side, trying to enlist their sympathies for their country, for law and order, and for his regal office. Wherever he encountered his fellow countrymen, he found sympathy and agree-ment, for they recognised his honesty and intelligence.

It was most useful that Constantine had learned to master Greek and to speak it without an accent—which could not in every case be said for previous Greek kings. He had been carefully coached in his future duties by his parents, and knew from his youth of the responsibility he bore towards the country entrusted to him. He had an outstanding example in his father. On the day he attained his majority his father, in the presence of State representatives, the army, and foreign diplomats, once more brought to his attention the basic principles he had to follow. King Paul said:

> 'I am confident that your love for the Greek people, which is as deep as mine, will give you as much happiness as it has me. While Greece has paid the price of its glorious history and has assimilated the results of its century-old struggle for the defence of mankind until the present, the Greek people have not yet reached and developed their full capabilities or achieved the prosperity which is lawfully theirs. On these grounds it deserves every demonstration of attention and love, and every sacrifice on your part.
>
> 'You must be an upright, benevolent and untiring fighter for the progress and glory of Greece. Dedicate your life to the happiness of your country, for there is no nobler nor more important task. Always reflect on this: rather the King should suffer than that the nation or the country should come to grief. Endeavour to show yourself worthy of the Greek soldiers, whose leader you will eventually be. When the time comes, you will take your place at the head of the Greek Armed Forces, who are the embodiment of a glorious and heroic tradition. Hold them ready to do their duty and be prepared for battle, for they are the guardians of our traditions, and are respected by our friends, feared by our enemies. They are the pride of our nation. Never may they have to fight! Be the protector and guardian of our Holy Church. Take your strength from the love between you and your people. Repay insults with forgiveness, discord with unity, falsehoods with truth, and doubt with belief.'

King Paul had also committed his son to this principle: 'To support untiringly the democratic foundations of our State institutions and the constitutional freedom of our people.' This reminder led Constantine to proclaim new elections, which would enable the people once more to appoint a parliament capable of governing. That was in April 1967. A few days after the publication of this decree, a group of officers seized power and the elections did not take place.

The King was faced with a *fait accompli*. Overnight he found himself as the head of a State governed by a dictatorial junta. He waited patiently for a few months then, supported by his Prime Minister and faithful officers, acted against the new rulers. He expected a broad understanding when he turned to his people in a radio broadcast from Larissa in northern Greece, but his hopes remained unfulfilled. His attempts to restore democracy failed, and he went into exile. The junta finally declared that he had been deposed, and in a popular vote they gained nearly eighty per cent majority approval for their measures.

The new rulers lasted for more than six years before they were abandoned by Washington and removed by an army *putsch*. The question of governmental reform once more became acute. This time, approximately seventy per cent of the voters proclaimed themselves against the Monarchy. In 1946, when my cousin George had been recalled to the Throne for the third time, two-thirds of the population had voted for the restoration of the Monarchy, as they had in 1920 and 1935. My cousins George and Paul were persons of integrity and noblesse like others of their kind, but the young Constantine was never given the chance to show that he was carved from the same block of wood: his democratic qualities were thus treated as negligible.

The vicissitudes of the Greek political system and its connections with the institution of the Monarchy this century certainly resulted from specific situations within this lovely country. Nevertheless, one should not be misled by this, and significant conclusions can be drawn from them. A kingdom today has a different foundation from that of the times I experienced, for modern society is not concerned with the divine right of kings. Where a monarchy exists nowadays, it is due to the fact that people see themselves represented by that institution and by the Monarch himself. Such convictions have their root in tradition, are fed by ethical considerations, and originate in the integral rôle of the Crown, which is above party. It is occasionally the result of a utilitarian calculation. But I believe and feel I can say without being suspected of wanting to criticise, that the Crown and its person has always been presumed to be beyond reproach. However, the moral aspect is only one among many presumptions. When one surveys the landscape of ruined European monarchies, one cannot fail to recognise that the big international conflicts, with their massive and subversive methods of power-extension, have left deep traces behind them, and it would seem to me that we have not yet reached the culmination point in this sphere.

These thoughts occupied me after General Franco's death, when my granddaughter Sophia became Queen of Spain. I have always had a particular fondness for her, and esteemed her modesty, understanding, and goodness coupled with her candid realism touched with a fine sense of humour. There, she is very much like her father. My daughter told me what the little Sophia had once said to her about him: 'You know, Mama, I think we have the nicest Papa in the world.' Childish words, but they convey a great deal.

The education given Sophia by her parents included the characteristic attributes I have already mentioned above. Like her sister Irene, she went to the Kurt Hahn School in Salem where my son Georg Wilhelm had once been principal, and completed her studies there. Then she joined a nurses training school, and after obtaining her diploma spent some time as a nurse so that she could prepare herself in every way for the duties which would fall to her as a Princess of a ruling House. It was in the summer of 1961 when she attended the wedding of the Duke of Kent in England that she met Juan Carlos, and her destiny was decided for her. How pleased and happy I was that it was love and not reasons of State which brought them together.

It was a fairy-tale wedding for them in Athens, under a royal-blue sky, and watched by thousands of rapturous spectators. The Royal pair, however, for whom these frenetic scenes were being enacted, knew they were neither in a fairyland nor expected to go to one. Both were already aware of the dark side of life. Sophia's first childhood impressions were of her flight from Greece, fearfully holding her mother's hand, and in a slimy slit trench in Crete where she had had to shelter from a hail of bombs from attacking aircraft. Then there were the many years spent in exile in South Africa and Egypt.

Juan Carlos, on the other hand, was born in Rome where the Spanish Royal Family were living at the time. The Bourbons, one of the oldest European dynasties, whose ancestry stretches back to Hugh Capet who was created the first King of France in 987, had reigned in Spain for two centuries when King Alfonso XIII lost his throne in 1931. At one time, it was believed that he and I would marry. We had all adored King Alfonso when he had visited Potsdam. He was so charming, so young, and so fresh. But he got engaged to Ena Battenberg who, although she was about the same age as myself, was an aunt of mine. Her mother and my grandmother were the youngest and eldest daughters of Queen Victoria.

The overthrow of the Monarchy brought dreadful trials for Spain. The parliamentary system broke down, and the Republic drowned in chaos. The People's Front terrorised the countryside, plundering and murdering. Even the Rightist leader in the Cortès, Calvo Sotelo, was assassinated by the police. The revolt against the bloody régime resulted in more than two years of bitter civil war, but the deprivations continued, brought about by the Second World War despite the fact that Franco chose to keep his country out of it.

In 1947 the Caudillo saw that the time had come to decide the question of the form of government, and Spain was declared a Monarchy. With the prudence that one seldom encounters in History, he prepared the way for his successor. At a meeting with the Count of Barcelona, the lawful heir to the Throne and son of the deceased King, he came to an understanding with the Count that his two sons would receive their scholastic education in Spain. The schooldays over, another agreement was reached. Having originally met on board a ship in the Bay of Biscay, the Caudillo and the Count now faced each other on Spanish territory. The result was that the now seventeen-year-old Juan Carlos would continue his training in Spain, and would be given the opportunity 'to serve his country in a way appropriate to one of his rank and station'.

The Prince received a military education at the Academy and in all the other branches of the armed forces, and not least in the fields of economics and administration.

The next step followed in 1969. Juan Carlos, who until then had followed the traditions of his House by calling himself Prince of the Asturias, was designated Prince of Spain. Then, in 1971, he was officially appointed as Franco's successor. If the Caudillo was looking for a person of integrity, efficiency and responsibility to lead the State, he could not have chosen better. When I last met Juanito— as he was known in the family—in Germany, his accession to the Throne was merely a matter of time. I was impressed by his regal appearance. I was astonished at his interest and knowledge of economic and technical affairs. When I saw him there before me, tall as a tree, I was convinced that he would have as full a command of the up-to-date problems of State management as he had of the controls of jet aircraft, tanks and ships.

A modern Monarch. High-sounding words came from Juan Carlos' first speech to the nation after he had ascended the Throne. He said:

> 'I am fully aware of the fact that a great people such as ours, who find themselves at the peak of their cultural development and material growth at a time of universal change, demand radical improvements. A free and modern society demands partici- pation in the decisions that are made, in the information media, in education, and in the control of national wealth. It is the aim of the community and of the government to realise this partici- pation to the greatest degree. . . .
>
> 'I would like to be a mediator, a guardian of the Constitution and spokesman of Justice. No one need fear that his cause will be forgotten, no one must expect any advantages or privileges. Together we can achieve everything, if everyone gets a fair chance. I will pay due regard to the laws, and see that they are observed. Justice will be my guide. . . .'

Who can say whether the Spaniards and their King will find the way which is outlined in these words? Does the possibility still exist in the life of the European people to enable them to make their own free decisions, and so tread the path to social, economic and political freedom? The signs of the times are not precisely encouraging. The prophets of materialisation have not brought any nation either success or well-being, and since our continent has lost its former status, the destiny of its people will be directed by the two competing world powers.

When my thoughts stray these days towards Zarzuela Palace in Madrid, I never fail to utter a prayer, a prayer that encompasses all my children and grandchildren. May our Lord God take them in His gracious keeping.

Everything has changed now, radically. For a while, owing to the crises and needs of the time, one was hardly able to notice the tremendous changes which were taking place in the world. The whole geo-political structure of this great continent had in fact altered, as well as the social and economic. Not least, spiritually and ethically, the people, too were different. New generations had grown up, but I have occupied myself in trying to understand them, certainly more intensively than the young people have done to grasp the significance of my times.

There are certain principles and lessons to be learned which outlast political changes, and one of them concerns the young and how they should lead their lives. I bring it to their notice, because it will have to be passed on to succeeding generations. It is something my husband said to one of my sons when he knew that his life was coming to an end: 'If there are two paths which a young man must take, then he must take the more difficult. Only thus can he prove himself.'

I cannot really close this chapter without referring to my beloved mountains. It was not easy for me to find the resolve to go back again to the beautiful mountains around Gmunden, but a great longing to be back in the places where my husband and I had been so happy together overcame me. The mountains called: it seemed they wanted to console me. I went back.

I climbed to the top of the familiar Wallibach, which had been our favourite spot during the hunting season, and looked again at the place from which we used to watch the deer. A boundless sadness crept over me. Did it still have any sort of meaning when my best friend was missing? I wept, but was not ashamed of my tears. Hours went by, then it seemed as if the gentle mountain giants were speaking to me, saying, 'Come to us. Here you will always find new strength to enable you to master life.' I had the feeling they were speaking to me on my husband's behalf.

I made a pact with those beloved mountains, and have never been disappointed since. Slowly, I climbed down and back to Gmunden. From every footing on the way I broke off a fir branch. I wanted them to put round the beautiful area of my husband's last resting-place.

My life has been fulfilled and it has been a richly eventful one. In my parents' house I led an existence which was lovelier than one could wish for. I found a husband whom I loved and honoured above all else, and I was granted the privilege of sharing with our people the destiny of Germany in times both good and bad.

I only pray that God will give me further strength to carry on justly any tasks or additional duties which may befall me.

Appendix

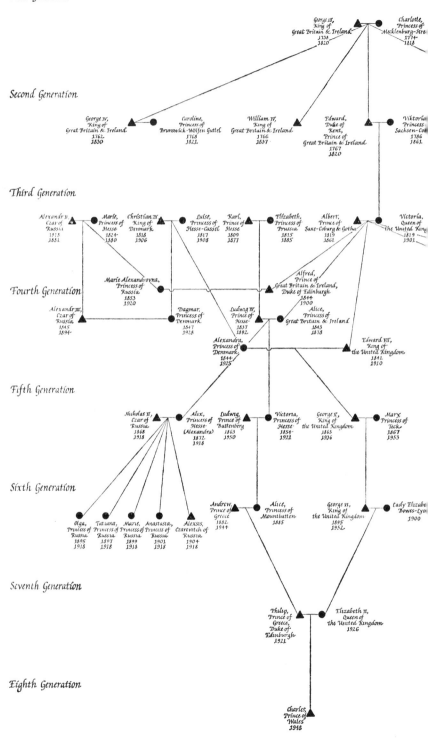

First Generation

Second Generation

Third Generation

Fourth Generation

Fifth Generation

Sixth Generation

Seventh Generation

Eighth Generation

RUSSIA   DENMARK   HESSE   UNITED KINGDOM

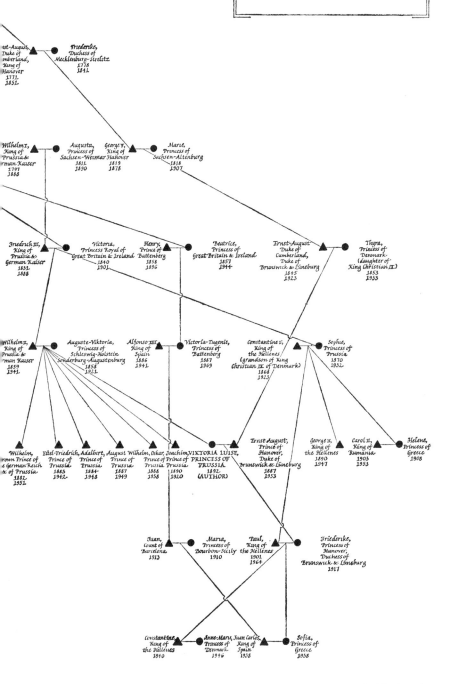

The Relationship of
H.R.H. Viktoria Luise
to the Royal Houses of Europe

Ernst-August,
Duke of
Cumberland,
King of
Hanover
1771
1851

Friederike,
Duchess of
Mecklenburg-Strelitz
1778
1841

Wilhelm I,
King of
Prussia &
German Kaiser
1797
1888

Augusta,
Princess of
Sachsen-Weimar
1811
1890

George V,
King of
Hanover
1819
1878

Marie,
Princess of
Sachsen-Altenburg
1818
1907

Friedrich III,
King of
Prussia &
German Kaiser
1831
1888

Victoria,
Princess Royal of
Great Britain & Ireland
1840
1901

Henry,
Prince of
Battenberg
1858
1896

Beatrice,
Princess of
Great Britain & Ireland
1857
1944

Ernst-August,
Duke of
Cumberland,
Duke of
Brunswick & Lüneburg
1845
1923

Thyra,
Princess of
Denmark
(daughter of
King Christian IX)
1853
1933

Wilhelm II,
King of
Prussia &
German Kaiser
1859
1941

Auguste-Viktoria,
Princess of
Schleswig-Holstein-
Sonderburg-Augustenburg
1858
1921

Alfonso XIII,
King of
Spain
1886
1941

Victoria-Eugenie,
Princess of
Battenberg
1887
1969

Constantine I,
King of
the Hellenes
(grandson of King
Christian IX of Denmark)
1868
1923

Sophie,
Princess of
Prussia
1870
1932

Wilhelm,
Crown Prince of
the German Reich
& of Prussia
1882
1951

Eitel-Friedrich,
Prince of
Prussia
1883
1942

Adalbert,
Prince of
Prussia
1884
1948

August Wilhelm,
Prince of
Prussia
1887
1949

Oskar,
Prince of
Prussia
1888
1958

Joachim,
Prince of
Prussia
1890
1920

VIKTORIA LUISE,
PRINCESS OF
PRUSSIA
1892
(AUTHOR)

Ernst August,
Prince of
Hanover,
Duke of
Brunswick & Lüneburg
1887
1953

George II,
King of
the Hellenes
1890
1947

Carol II,
King of
Rumania
1903
1953

Helene,
Princess of
Greece
1908

Juan,
Count of
Barcelona
1913

Maria,
Princess of
Bourbon-Sicily
1910

Paul,
King of
the Hellenes
1901
1964

Friederike,
Princess of
Hanover,
Duchess of
Brunswick & Lüneburg
1917

Constantine,
King of
the Hellenes
1940

Anne-Marie,
Princess of
Denmark
1946

Juan Carlos,
King of
Spain
1938

Sofia,
Princess of
Greece
1938

Calligraphy by Melanie Marder

PRUSSIA   OTHERS

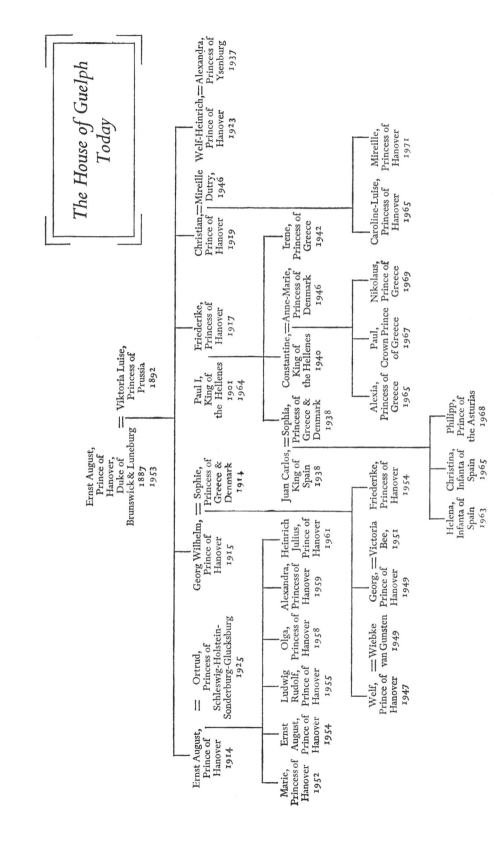

The House of Guelph
Today

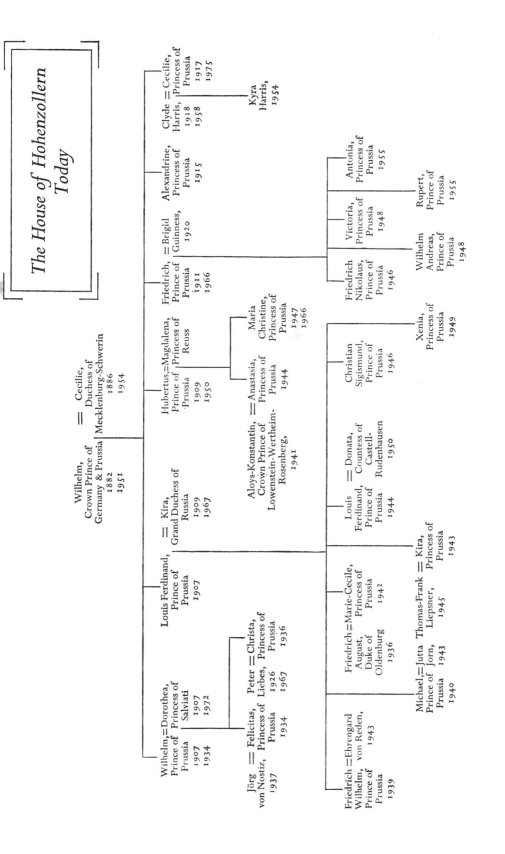

The House of Hohenzollern
Today

Wilhelm, Crown Prince of Germany & Prussia, 1882–1951 = Cecilie, Duchess of Mecklenburg-Schwerin, 1886–1954

Louis Ferdinand, Prince of Prussia, 1907 = Kira, Grand Duchess of Russia, 1909–1967

Wilhelm, Prince of Prussia, 1907–1934 = Dorothea, Princess of Salviati, 1907–1972

Jörg von Nostiz, 1937 = Felicitas, Princess of Prussia, 1934

Peter, 1926–1967 = Christa, Liebes, Princess of Prussia, 1936

Friedrich Wilhelm, Prince of Prussia, 1939 = Ehrengard von Reden, 1943

Michael, Prince of Jorn, Prussia, 1940 = Jutta, von Jorn, 1943

Thomas-Frank Liepsner, 1945 = Kira, Princess of Prussia, 1943

Friedrich, August, Duke of Oldenburg, 1936 = Marie-Cecile, Princess of Prussia, 1942

Louis Ferdinand, Prince of Prussia, 1944 = Donata, Countess of Castell-Rudenhausen, 1950

Christian Sigismund, Prince of Prussia, 1946

Xenia, Princess of Prussia, 1949

Aloys-Konstantin, Crown Prince of Lowenstein-Wertheim-Rosenberg, 1941 = Anastasia, Princess of Prussia, 1944

Hubertus, Prince of Prussia, 1909–1950 = Magdalena, Princess of Reuss

Maria Christine, Princess of Prussia, 1947–1966

Friedrich, Prince of Prussia, 1911–1966 = Brigid Guinness, 1920

Friedrich Nikolaus, Prince of Prussia, 1946

Wilhelm Andreas, Prince of Prussia, 1948

Victoria, Princess of Prussia, 1948

Rupert, Prince of Prussia, 1955

Antonia, Princess of Prussia, 1955

Alexandrine, Princess of Prussia, 1915

Cecilie, Princess of Prussia, 1917–1975 = Clyde Harris, 1918–1958

Kyra Harris, 1954

Index